The Hottest Girl at Burn Camp

KRYSTAL EVANS is an American stand-up comedian based in the UK and is known for her powerful live shows, and also her work with Mitchell & Webb and on Comedy Central. Her stand-up show about the fire, also called 'The Hottest Girl at Burn Camp', won critical acclaim and coverage. She lives in Edinburgh and is the super-responsible mum to two boys. Her favourite food is breakfast burritos, and she has a gigantic photo of Rod Serling in her front room.

The Hottest Girl at Burn Camp

How To Survive A Fire And A Chaotic Upbringing
(Without Losing Your Sense Of Humour)

Krystal Evans

monoray

First published in Great Britain in 2025 by Monoray, an imprint of
Octopus Publishing Group Ltd
Carmelite House
50 Victoria Embankment
London EC4Y 0DZ
www.octopusbooks.co.uk

An Hachette UK Company
www.hachette.co.uk

The authorized representative in the EEA is Hachette Ireland,
8 Castlecourt Centre, Dublin 15, D15 XTP3, Ireland (email: info@hbgi.ie)

Copyright © Krystal Evans 2025

All rights reserved. No part of this work may be reproduced or utilized in any form or by any means, electronic or mechanical, including photocopying, recording or by any information storage and retrieval system, without the prior written permission of the publisher.

Krystal Evans has asserted her right under the Copyright, Designs and Patents Act 1988 to be identified as the author of this work.

Hardback ISBN 978 1 80096 272 9
Trade paperback ISBN 978 1 80096 273 6
eISBN 978 1 80096 275 0

A CIP catalogue record for this book is available from the British Library.

Typeset in 12/16pt Garamond Premier Pro by Six Red Marbles UK, Thetford, Norfolk.

Printed and bound in Great Britain.

13 5 7 9 10 8 6 4 2

This FSC® label means that materials used for the product have been responsibly sourced.

*For my two boys, Sonny and Jesse
(please don't read this till you're older)*

And of course, for Katie

Author's Note

This book is based on my life, experiences, memories and thoughts, and is completely true to the best of my recollections. Some details, names and places have been changed to protect individuals' privacy, in particular the location of our home in Sequim, WA.

Introduction

I've battled within my own heart on the question of whether anyone would even want to hear about the events of my childhood.

My house burned down when I was 14 years old, and my six-year-old sister Katie died in the fire. It was undeniably a total fucking tragedy, and I would not blame you at all if you put this book down right now.

But to tell you the sad details of what happened that night, while they are central to my life, is not the reason I am writing this book.

The question is more this – and I have thought about this more and more, as I've got older – how in hell did I manage to even come close to making my peace with all of the madness of a childhood of which the fire was but one (admittedly major) part? How did I manage to outrun not only the fire, but its aftermath? And more than that – how have I emerged not only sane, but as a person who tells jokes for a living?

Even now as a grown person with a pretty good grasp on what the world and normal society is like, I am still surprised when people express interest in the minutiae of my childhood. This may be because what I've been through has skewed my bar of what's remarkable and what's simply mundane. (For example, is having a pet wolf weird?)

But having locked it up for decades, telling people publicly about my childhood is something that I've now done – and in the end I did it in the form of a stand-up comedy show at the Edinburgh Fringe. The response really surprised me. While it was certainly at times uncomfortable for both me and the audience, the reception was off-the-scale positive.

Along with this, after seeing the show, everyone was seemingly bursting with questions for me. An hour-long performance can't be as detailed and nuanced as reality, so as I played it to more and more people, it slowly began to dawn on me that to really do it justice, I needed to get this story written down fully, and to properly explore what happened.

A book seemed to be the only viable way to do that, and once I started writing, I promise you, I could not stop. And now, here it is. Yes, this book is very sad in parts, but I really hope you'll stick with it and keep reading, because it abounds with light as well. Even though tears streamed down my face at times while I was perched over my keyboard, I also felt a deep joy, and a lot of humour, love and gratitude.

The book's title is a case in point. *The Hottest Girl at Burn Camp* refers to a kids' camp I attended in the summer after the fire, where I arrived and timidly realized that I was one of the least burned kids there. A comedian friend of mine, Heather, listened to me tell this story and immediately shot back, "Krystal.

Are you saying you were . . . the hottest girl at Burn Camp?" Not only was it true, I realized that Heather had given me the perfect way to show the clash of humour and sadness that would define this book.

The Hottest Girl at Burn Camp is a story of trauma and grief; how I shoved it down, ignored it and then figured out what I was meant to be doing with my life, did it and then realized that maybe I wasn't quite as healed as I thought I was. But some things never fully heal, and that's okay. Everything's a process. The main tool I use to deal with my pain is, and always has been, humour. If you can laugh at something, that shows that you have the power and not the thing. And yes, I know not everyone operates this way – because some people are truly humourless cunts.

But, if you're reading this, I'd like to think that means that you do want to hear this story, and I sincerely hope you find it worthy of your time.

Unless, that is, you're feeling like Katie did one night when she was four years old as I was about to read her a third book of the evening.

"Noooo," she implored me, "not another story! I'm tired!"

If that's you, then maybe put the book down right now.

Krystal Evans, Edinburgh, 2024

Prologue

I didn't do the thing. That thing I was supposed to do. What was it? I forgot.

Where are you? Where have you gone? I've forgotten something but I can't remember what it is.

Roaring. Walls being broken. I see the person in the mirror turn and run away, a flash of her oversized white t-shirt the last thing to disappear from the side of the frame.

She's crying.

Or is she? No, no. I'm crying. It's me. But it doesn't sound like me.

Someone screams. A woman.

I'm surrounded by the whitest fire and thick, heavy black smoke.

I fall to the floor, hard. On my hands and knees now, I can barely breathe.

Breathe in.

She's still screaming. No, no. It's me. I'm screaming.

How can I not know if I'm screaming or not? Where is it coming from?

The air is pulled from my lungs as I stand up and my throat feels stuck together with glue. My mouth feels duct-taped shut.

The entire structure rolls around me, flames groaning and rotating like a cursed, haunted carnival fun house, the buttons pushed and levers pulled by an unseen psychopath.

The whole room is burning, my skin so hot and beginning to heat my insides.

Through the fire, I see my face in the mirror again, surrounded by orange and white flames and my face is dripping like wax, but I can't feel it. Only the heat. I touch my face but the person in the mirror just stares at me, hands at her sides, melting to the floor.

My bed, my posters, my CDs, all burn in a pile behind the girl in the mirror. My books. My guitar.

But where is she?

I call for her. I can't find her. Someone's crying.

She's in the woods! She's escaped to the woods by the train tracks! We always play there.

She would have known to run and meet me there. I have to get to her. I have to get out of here to get to her.

Why would this happen? How did this happen?

Who did this?

It was an accident.

The structure of our home lurches and groans like a vast sinking vessel, yawing down to the bottom of the darkest deep. As the ceiling becomes the floor, I lose my footing and fall directly into the flames.

And the smell. Sweet, like burning newspaper. Campfire.

Melted plastic. Scorched metal. Burning flesh. Singed hair. My own voice, calm and collected.

> *Be careful, this is really hot, you could burn yourself, okay?*
> *Get away from there!*

Oh my God. Oh my God. This poor woman.

> *Why don't you get the fuck up? Why don't you help?*
> *Why didn't you save her?*
> *Hey, don't touch this, okay? It's really hot.*

She's been through so much.
Your mom is one tough cookie, that's for sure!

> *She's in the woods, Krystal. I know she's there!*
> *I've forgotten something. What was it?*
> *Mom, what really happened in there?*
> *She was already gone when I got there.*

I have to get away from here.
I have to get away.
Fuck you, don't touch me. Fuck you. Fuck off. Don't say that.
Don't you ever fucking say that to me.
You can help stir, but just remember this part is really hot, okay?

"Mom? Katie? MOM?!"

> *She's crying and tries to touch me.*

"Fuck you. Fuck YOU. Fuck OFF!!"

"Krystal. Krystal, shhh. Hey. Hey. It's okay."

I'm abruptly aware that I've been yelling in my sleep. I'm breathing very heavily, and the rush of adrenaline slowly leaves my body as I try to actively slow my own heartbeat.

"You were yelling in your sleep again."

I feel my face go hot at the thought of what I may have been saying involuntarily. I'd prefer for everyone around me to think that I don't experience big, negative emotions like grief and rage. I'm just a chilled-out, easy-going, cool young woman with a sort of dark past, sure, but I'm not some drama queen who can't get on with things in life anyway. I can handle my shit.

"Oh, oh," I put my hands on my chest. "Sorry." I breathe sharply inwards. I can breathe. The air is cool and neutral. The only sound is of cars beeping on the street and mariachi music coming from the apartment across the alleyway. New York City's version of silence.

"Fire dream again?" Stuart asks, yawning. Stuart is my boyfriend, Scottish, a chef who was working for Gordon Ramsay when we met a year ago, is now a chef at a private members' club in midtown. He got me a job as a waitress and bartender there.

"No, no. Just like . . . dreaming of punching Renee in the face," I smile and laugh. Hoping that's convincing enough. Renee is my current nemesis at the club.

"Hm. You said Katie a couple times," he says sleepily, rubbing my shoulder.

"Oh. Well. Maybe that was part of it." I laugh, unconvincingly.

Please, don't ask me any more questions, I think. He doesn't. I'm not ready yet to fully realize the thoughts that are brewing in my brain without my consent, let alone share them with anyone else.

At least we're in the dark, I think.

Part One

1.

"Okay, so. If you could eat anything in the world right now, what would it be?" Mom said, strewn out across the entire length of the couch, head propped up on her hand and bent elbow, which was propped up by three pillows.

We played this game a lot. Seemed as good a starting point as any to figure out what we should have for our next meal. Was it even possible? We'd start from the best possible scenario and go from there.

"Crab with garlic butter!" Katie piped up, balancing on the back of the couch, feet slipping off every two steps. Katie was my five-year-old little sister, and this was her most common response to the question. An answer that was both truthful and a bit of a suck-up to the rest of us, because we all loved seafood. We'd have it on Christmas instead of turkey or ham. A huge salmon, clams, crab. Garlic butter. Bread. Shrimp. It was expensive and rare, so it felt really special. Magical food from the sea that was to be savoured and you had to constantly remark upon how good it tasted while you were consuming it, because if you didn't, it felt as though it would be taken away.

On this occasion, though, Mom wanted cheeseburgers. "You know what I'm really in the mood for? *Burgerville*," she said with those wide eyes adults give to children when they're trying to hype them up for something that the child won't be inherently enthused about.

Burgerville was a chain of fast-food restaurants that had shrunk over the years to only a few locations in Oregon and Washington. We were in the north of Washington state – a three-hour drive from the nearest Burgerville. It was July, and it was hot. Sweltering. Summer vacation. Mom struggled with what to do with us in the summer holidays, a not uncommon issue for most parents.

"Let's just go!" she said.

Ah, one of these days, I thought.

No game plan was discussed, nothing was packed. We didn't think about when we would get home, what we'd do on the way there and back, where we would sleep. She just decided we would go, and presumably we had no other plans, so why not? (Of course, there were many reasons why not, but they didn't seem to cross anyone's mind.)

Our red '89 Ford Aerostar minivan was born three years after me and had no air-conditioning. We'd roll the windows down and feel the wind whip our hair around while Mom drove and blasted the radio. The Judds, James Taylor, Dolly Parton, Carole King or whatever was playing on Star 101.5 or WARM 106.9.

The journey down was long, seemingly endless. We stopped at a rest stop for snacks but tried not to spoil our appetites for the titular Town of Burgers we were to shortly arrive at. It took longer to get there than anticipated, and when we finally drove up to the underwhelming fast-food branch in Centralia, we were starving.

We stepped out of the car. Burgerville's layout was like any McDonald's in the rest of America. A wrap-around asphalt parking lot, an angled roof with plastic "tiles", an outdoor play park for kids that was unacceptable for anyone to play on in this heat, because touching any part of the equipment would be accompanied by a trip to the local burn unit.

We followed Mom, zombie-like, into the restaurant. She always wore sweatpants and a sweatshirt, usually with the collar literally cut or ripped out, because seams in clothing near her neck made her feel "like she was choking". Her hair was always very greasy and pulled back tight, dyed an unnatural shade of red from a home-dye kit from Safeway. Whenever we walked into any premises, every eye turned to look at us. I already knew the first thing she'd say to the person behind the counter at the Burgerville. I could have recited it myself.

"We just drove three-and-a-half hours to get here! We love Burgerville that much!" She leaned towards the person behind the counter to say this with the top half of her body, the bottom half pointed towards the end of the long line, body cheating towards the people in the queue, like she was talking to the person behind the counter in a staged play, unnaturally facing the wrong way so that the crowd could still see her facial expressions.

A woman in the line said something inaudible to me and Mom's face lit up as she said, "Oh, are you offering me your place in line? That's so sweet of you! Oh no, it's fine, thanks so much! What's your name? Linda? Oh my God, I had a best friend in high school named Linda! You're way prettier than her though, hahaha. Nice to meet you, Linda, I'm Tracy." Mom forced a huge smile, and her voice went higher pitched and louder, as it always did when she spoke to strangers.

"Mom, let's just get in line," I said. But I knew this wouldn't work. I also knew that if Mom got lost in a conversation with this woman, we'd be here for even longer than we were already destined to be.

I don't believe psychics are a real thing, but Mom was as close as you could get. When she was desperate, she would summon some sort of deep dark superpower which let her know things she couldn't possibly have known. She could look at someone and just know they'd been through a divorce recently and give them advice that would make them start crying tears of gratitude, and they'd pay our restaurant bill. She could make an overdrawn bank charge disappear by connecting with the teller about their toddler's learning disability. A nurse in a doctor's office would get a prescription sorted quickly because Mom guessed, correctly, that she was a huge Joan Jett fan. Mom's spontaneous conversations with strangers were epic. They had the potential to turn into hours, ending with one of them breaking down into happy tears. They could finish with us getting a lift from them, or going to their house, or with Mom at the very least exchanging phone numbers. She could garner connection and laughs from the most hardened human, and she knew it.

She knew things about me, too. "You're lying, Krystal," she'd say, her eyelids halfway shut over her grey irises, one eyebrow raised to a perfect point – the spitting image of the wicked witch from *Snow White*, except in a grey tracksuit. And I sometimes *was* lying, but I knew there was no way she could know this for sure, so I'd stick to my guns, but eventually start sobbing and confess that no, I hadn't wiped down the counters with bleach spray, only antibac.

But these moments of connection with strangers made me feel queasy and uncomfortable. I knew this person didn't know Mom like I did. I knew where every relationship she cultivated was fated to end.

"Mom," I said again from the back of the queue, "we're gonna lose our place in the line."

"It's okay, honey, I'm just talking to Linda!" She laughed and pulled me and Katie towards the woman, introducing us to her. The woman beamed, hesitant because of Mom's manic energy, but also captivated by it. Another part of the ritual was to insist that our "chance meeting" with this person was some sort of fate.

"Oh my God, Krystal – she has a 13-year-old son, same age as you! 1986, right? What's his name? That's crazy! What's his birthday? 11th February?! THAT'S MY SISTER'S BIRTHDAY! OH MY GOD I CANNOT BELIEVE THIS!" I went completely numb inside every time she did this. It would be exhausting to let myself feel the weight of humiliation as often as the situation warranted it. The best thing to do was just wait it out. I knew this, but at age 13 there was a teen indignation rising in me that frequently pushed me to the end of whatever rope of patience remained within. I'd seen enough of other adults and families at this point to know her behaviour was, at best, abnormal and humiliating. I didn't yet know what the worst of it could be, but in any case, it didn't feel like it had anything to do with our welfare. It fed something inside her, and that only made me angrier.

We sat down to eat, relieved by the air-conditioned restaurant, the smell and taste of fries and burgers and milkshakes filling us up from the inside out.

Okay, I thought. *Mom was right.* These burgers were the bomb. Thin, not too greasy, American melty cheese. The "special sauce" tasted like a combo of ketchup, mayo and mustard with Worcestershire, with teeny tiny onions and pickles chopped up through it. Hell, yes. For all of Mom's faults, she had great taste in food and would go to great lengths to get and enjoy it.

After we ate, we got back in the car. Mom stared at the dashboard and quietly, sharply, said, "Shit."

"What?" I asked.

We only had a quarter of a tank of gas left. Not enough to get all the way home. It was Saturday. Payday wasn't until Monday. "Shit, shit," she said again. She looked inside the restaurant and scanned the parking lot. Linda had already left.

Thank God, I thought.

We found a campsite nearby with an outdoor swimming pool that was only $20 a night to park and camp. But of course, we hadn't planned on staying anywhere overnight, let alone camping, so we had no spare clothes or swimsuits. We splashed water on our faces and used handheld fans to try and cool ourselves down, fruitlessly, while Mom tried to think of what to do. A classic situation.

"Look, look! I found a snail!" Katie exclaimed. She played in the dirt, dragging sticks through it and digging and making trails with stones. Other families were doing barbecues or coming back from the pool in big towels, laughing and being normal.

Watching the other families, and then looking back at us gathered around our red van, something in me ached. A hot, acid-like fluid seeped into my stomach. *I can't stand this any more*, I thought. Years of getting into situations like this piled on top of me. The heat also helped in fuelling the ball of anger forming in my throat. I couldn't decide if I wanted to scream or cry. I was too old for this bullshit. I didn't dare start yelling or swearing at Mom, because I knew her rage was fierce, and she could be unpredictable, so I had to balance my feelings and channel my anger to try to reason with her, calmly. I thought this in my head, but when I tried, instead, my feelings of rage came out as a desperate plea.

"Mom . . . I hate this," I whined. "I'm so hot . . . and . . . tired, and . . . I just want to go home."

Mom stared at me, mouth open slightly, a blank expression on her face, beads of sweat rolling down from her hairline to her eyebrows.

"I don't want to be here any more! I'm just. So. HOT." I broke down in sobs.

Mom continued to stare at me, fruitlessly searching for something to say. Her face was a deer in the headlights. I rarely questioned her lack of planning and saying it straight up like this made her freeze. She looked to the side, searching for some words of wisdom, but her face conveyed, *I've got nothing.*

She blinked, shook her head to bring herself back into the moment.

"Well. I'll tell you what works," Mom said, as she threw some water into the handheld fan and it sprayed across her face. "Really cools you off." She gave a little nod.

I stared at her, brows furrowed. She did it again, demonstrating how much this technique *really worked*. I was not budging. She then did it to me, and I tried to keep my face neutral, despite the fact that the water and fan combo actually did feel pretty good.

"Me! My turn! I want to do it!" Katie jumped back and forth between the two of us and Mom indulged her by spraying her in the face, as if Katie was running back and forth through the world's smallest, most pathetic garden sprinkler. Katie yelled, "Again!"

Mom and I stared at each other as the water spritzed over all three of us and the buzz of the handheld fan hummed its insipid whir. The laughter came simultaneously from all of us. We were doubled over, my sides hurt. Katie was laughing a lot too, despite not completely getting the joke. Laughing helped.

All for fucking Burgerville? Wow. For a moment, laughing meant everything was okay.

In 1987, when I was one year old, so the story goes, I would sit in the front of a shopping cart with Mom in Everett, Washington, and say, "Hi!" to every single person in the store we'd go past. Some would say, "Hi" back; some wouldn't. "She's just really friendly," Mom would laugh. "You're just so friendly, aren't you?" From then onwards, her nickname for me became Friendly. She called me this since before I can remember, so it wouldn't even register when people would ask years later, "Why is your mom calling you Friendly?"

When I was very young, up until age eight or so, I remember Mom being beautiful and vibrant. She was a gymnast before I was born, had dark chocolatey hair, grey eyes and perfect porcelain skin, and looked a bit like Linda Ronstadt. People always commented on Mom's skin, and how young she looked, and Mom told us all about this with pride. I don't blame her; as a girl, I soon came to recognize the apparently universal truth that our looks, especially our youth, are the most valuable thing we could have going for us.

Mom only played chords on guitar but was especially good at finger picking – "Which always impresses people who don't know how to play," she'd whisper, winking at me. Along with playing, she had a gentle, wispy singing voice that was uncharacteristically quiet compared to her speaking voice and her entire personality. She had a knack for harmonizing by ear. She passed this skill on to me, and we'd practise doing songs by the Judds (a mother-daughter country singing duo popular in the 1980s and '90s) together, with our own harmony arrangements. "I want us to be like the Judds when I grow up!" I'd tell Mom, and everyone who would listen, as a little girl.

Mom wrote her own songs as well – they were folksy and country, and she wrote them about anything and everything. Just walking around the house, a tune would drop into her head and she'd pick up the guitar and figure out the chords. Many were children's songs, inspired by me. One song that I always loved went:

> *I love your eyes, and I like your smile*
> *I want to be your friend all the while*

THE HOTTEST GIRL AT BURN CAMP

Every day I'll treat you kind
Because a friend like Krystal's hard to find!

She'd replace "Krystal" with whoever's name she was singing about. My friends, other friends' kids or anyone who happened to be around. I loved this. Mom was so fun and animated. Mom was like a child herself.

Kids loved Mom most of all. She had a way with children, like a secret language only she knew how to speak. She'd see a young girl in a store having a tantrum and the desperate mother struggling to get her under control. Mom would calmly walk over and say, "Oh, well, hello there. Now let me guess, are you four years old?" The child would stop crying and look at her, fascinated and a little taken aback, and then she'd nod. "I thought so. You know how I can tell?" The child would hold back a smirk and shake her head. "It's your teeth! Those are four-year-old teeth if I ever saw them. Now can you smile, let me see them? Wow! Wait a second – you haven't lost any of your teeth yet, have you?" The girl would shake her head again and clutch her mother's leg, smiling. "Well, hey, my name's Tracy and it's really nice to meet you! I'll betcha you're such a big helper to your mom. I bet you could help put the next thing in the cart for her, because you look very strong. Have a nice day!" The mother would look at Mom with grateful eyes and say, "Say thanks, Sadie, thank you to this nice lady."

"Oh what an absolute doll," Mom would say, as we walked away. "You're doing a great job," she'd wink to the mother.

*

Mom's presence was gargantuan. Everything about her was simultaneously loud, excitable and fragile. Her booming, vociferous laughter or her painful, choked tears that were always simmering just under the surface. The long, drawn-out conversations she'd indulge in with people wherever we went, her eyes searing into people's very souls, her face showing that she knew something about this person intuitively, and they could feel that. She made people feel seen, and special, which made her magnetic. She had this apparent innocence and a way of looking at someone and immediately knowing that they were very tired, had been working a double shift, that they were taking care of a sick sibling, that they had recently got a divorce, that their mother just died, that they were having trouble with their asshole boss. Mom just knew. She could get people to open up as easily as look at them. It was incredible, sure, but also exhausting for us, her children, who just wanted to get back home.

It would be like having a mom who could levitate things with her mind; sounds good on paper, but must she constantly do it in public?

2.

When Mom left Dad for good, in 1987, I was one year old. We moved to a few different locations, mostly still in the Seattle area, and Dad would see me every other weekend, sometimes more, sometimes less.

In the early '90s, Mom met a cop named Mike and married him quickly, moving us both to his home state of Arizona, a state that borders Mexico, which was a three-hour plane ride away from the rest of our family in Washington state (which is in the north, bordering Canada). Dad told me later he was devastated when Mom moved me away, but there wasn't much he could do about it. Dad didn't see me the entire time we lived in Arizona.

I was six years old when we moved there, in 1992. One of my earliest memories is playing in the Arizona desert with another little girl, under giant cactuses. The kind you'd see in Warner Brothers cartoons, with a torso and two green spiky arms sticking up at the sides. Garbage would blow into the cul de sac we lived in, surrounded by sand, and we'd take the plastic tarps and cans and boxes and make cool forts out of them around the cactuses and play pretend games in the 100+ degree heat. The natural environment was in stark contrast to Washington state, with its evergreens, white-capped mountains and fresh sea air.

Mike looked like Freddie Mercury: slim, Caucasian, complete with white wife-beater vest (a garment named a little too on-the-nose for this man, if you ask me), tight blue jeans and a thick, bushy 'tache covering his whole upper lip and most of the lower.

Mom and Mike would fight a lot, screaming fights, and I would get scared and hide, but also spy because I wanted to make sure Mom was okay. One night I was sat in the living room, hearing them shouting. I can still see the bedroom door swinging open and Mike having a hold of Mom by the shoulders and shoving her out of the room, hard, then her losing her footing and falling down into the hallway. Another time, they thought

I was asleep, but I heard yelling so ran into the hall and saw Mike dragging Mom across the kitchen floor by her hair.

Mom had a black eye the next day, and she called the police on Mike, but it was pointless because he was a cop, so the other cops that turned up were all his pals. I remember them laughing outside together before driving off, and Mike coming back into the house all smug. Mom never even got to speak to them.

Mike then clapped his hands together, patted me on the head and said casually, "So, what's for dinner?" Then, keeping eye contact with Mom, he went into their bedroom and slammed the door.

I was so happy to see my Uncle Guy when he came to help us move away. Guy was the designated peacekeeper of Mom's family. Mom's younger brother, he was the youngest of the four, and the only boy. He was about 5 foot 10, stalky and athletic, with piercing blue eyes, black hair, a baby face and a cutting, dark sense of humour. He was quieter than his older sisters (which wasn't hard), and more laid back. Guy was very sensitive; women loved him, although he got his heart broken regularly. I always thought to myself, when I was a little girl, how pretty all of Guy's girlfriends were.

Mom had called Guy so he could help us move. He was only 20 years old at the time, but he brought a male friend to sort of intimidate Mike into letting us leave. He did, thankfully. We were in Arizona only three months or so, but it seemed longer.

Guy was very protective over his older sisters. When they were kids there had been – let's cut to the chase here – physical and emotional abuse, from my grandfather. I've heard a lot of arguments over the years about how much or how little abuse truly occurred. Very traumatic, upsetting scenes described, that another sibling will roll their eyes at and say the other had dreamed or imagined. Remembering the same events completely differently seems to be a common occurrence in families where abuse happens to kids. One thing they all agree on, though, is that there was hitting, and the girls all got it way worse than Guy. Guy would always try to stop it, even as a little boy. He lived with a lot of guilt over this, and wanted everyone to get along as adults. He was the favourite, and he knew it. I remember the feeling of him putting me up on his shoulders, being so high up and knowing I was safe with this sturdy man beneath me.

We drove away from Arizona in Guy's car, safe from Mike.

Having escaped from the evil policeman, Mom and I re-established ourselves in Washington state, this time near city-centre Seattle. Mom soon befriended a man named Henry, a very thin guy with very long, greasy black hair who lived near us. He was delightfully sarcastic, very intellectual and fearful of being in public. His job was delivering newspapers in his car. His apartment smelled like rubber bands and wet cardboard. Mom left me in his care sometimes, while she went to work or out in the evenings. Meanwhile, he would spend a lot of time on his computer.

I have one clear memory of Henry looking after me at his apartment and being in the shower. I was seven. I said to him, "Are you naked in there?"

"Yes," he said.

"Can I see?" The shower turned off, and he loudly raked the shower curtain open, showing me his fully naked, grown male body. I had no idea what I was seeing, and I covered my eyes and screamed and ran out of the room.

Mom liked using very early chatrooms on Henry's computer and soon started speaking to Henry's brother, Robert, who was in prison. They started a relationship, despite protests from everyone who knew what was going on, and Mom began to visit him in prison.

There's no easy way to write what he was in prison for, so I'm just going to come out with it. It involved the death of an infant. Shaken baby syndrome. To be fair, he claimed he was innocent. And immediately after he was released, he got a job as a manager at Jack in the Box, another fast-food chain. Quite a catch.

Robert had short, spiky blond hair, and wore a buttoned-up white shirt tucked into ironed slacks and a dark visor with a black, shiny, rectangular plastic nametag with indented white writing that said "Robert T, Senior JitB Manager". The dark visor was a standard part of the uniform for all staff. Robert would come home, regale us with a story about firing someone, which he did often, usually mocking their foreign accent, and the story would always end with him saying, "So I said, 'You're fired. Give me your hat.'"

Robert had an immature macho-ness about him, like he was always trying to prove he wasn't stupid. He bossed Mom around, and I hated that. She would sometimes make a joke about it, and the line between him laughing along or getting angrier was always a thin one to tread.

Robert was from Wisconsin and wanted us to move there with him after he was released from prison so that he could be closer to his family. Wisconsin was most of the way across the country, a four-hour flight from Seattle. Mom hesitated, and at first flat-out refused, probably because she had moved me across the country so recently, and it had been a disaster.

But shortly after their relationship started, Mom and I came home to find our apartment completely ransacked. The place had been trashed, every drawer emptied and our TV, furniture and all valuables had been stolen. Robert capitalized on this as an opportunity to convince Mom that the area where we were living was not safe and that Wisconsin was a way better place to raise kids. So she agreed to go. They got married very quickly after we arrived in Wisconsin: a hasty courthouse wedding that included Robert's immediate family, me and no one else.

Truesdell, Wisconsin, was so strange compared to the places we'd lived in in Washington. The trees in Wisconsin weren't all evergreens, and some of the streets were lined with broken cobblestone (not in a deliberate, quaint way – more like a "we've never bothered relaying this road this since the 1910s" way), which caused problems for me as a seven-year-old, as it made it impossible to ride my scooter without severe whiplash.

On my first day in a new class in second grade, my teacher gave us all a handout and I tried to write my name in cursive at the top. I didn't realize it, but she was right behind me and slammed her hand down on my desk, screeching, "WRITE IT SO THEY CAN READ IT, KRYSTAL!" She grabbed the paper, crumpled it up and tossed it onto the floor. I jumped halfway out of my seat at the loud BANG that exploded in front of my face as her hand hit the desk again, but I didn't dare say anything back. Within the same ten-minute period, she also whacked a kid on the back of the head with a ruler for chatting. I was utterly terrified. I'd never seen a school where the teachers were allowed to put their hands on the kids. I made a note to myself to remain small and invisible.

Later that same day, I saw a lady wandering around the lunchroom with a lanyard on (the cafeteria bouncer, I suppose) pick a kid up by his collar, lift him off the ground and press him up against the cafeteria wall. She spat a warning into his face, and the kid, a young black boy with short dreadlocks, looked shocked. The cafeteria bouncer looked exactly like Miss Trunchbull from *Matilda*, in that scene where she is wearing a tracksuit, only this woman had thin, greasy, salt-and-pepper hair that was sprouting out every which way like a homeless Medusa.

I told Mom. A school that still hit kids as punishment was quite a throwback, even in 1993.

The first Christmas in Truesdell, Mom and Robert brought home a puppy. It was grey, short-haired, with pointy ears and extremely sharp puppy teeth.

"It's a wolf hybrid," Robert said, excitedly. "My buddy had a litter! What you wanna name it, Krystal? You can pick! Anything but Wolf. Because it reminds me of my ex-wife." He bellowed with laughter at his own joke.

He shouldn't have said that, because from that moment on I'd settle for nothing but Wolf as the name of this creature. Something that upset Robert and delighted me no end.

But the name turned out to be spectacularly accurate. As the weeks and months progressed, it gradually dawned on us that this "dog" was in no way a "wolf hybrid" as we'd been told but was, in fact, in no way discernible from *Canis lupus* – in other words, an actual *wolf*. Wolf was very aggressive and territorial and lacked the affection present in domesticated dogs. He barked all day and howled all night. We'd come home from school and work, and he would have ripped the couch to shreds, cotton fluff everywhere.

To be fair on him, he was never walked or exercised in any form, which would surely result in any animal flipping its shit out of frustration.

As in many lower-income upbringings, pets in our home were used as a temporary relief and distraction from being poor and unable to afford luxuries. When people say, "A dog isn't just for Christmas", they are definitely talking about people like us.

One day during a playful wrestle, Wolf bit Robert's hand and left two bloody marks on his palm like a teeny furry vampire. Mom started having meltdowns and screaming at Wolf, and it all came to a head one day when she'd left a $20 bill on the coffee table, only to come in and find he'd ripped it to shreds.

"Oh, that's fucking IT," she screamed. "This animal is SO. GONE."

When Robert came home she told him he needed to get rid of it, and he did, although I don't know how. I wasn't upset in the least. Wolf was cute, but he was a pain in the ass, and anything that lowered the stress levels in the household was fine by me.

We moved over the Wisconsin border to Illinois, to a very small town called Lindenhurst. This school was in a way better area (they didn't hit kids! Score!), although we were still poor as dirt, so the trade-off was that wealthier kids in this school made fun of my clothes and Mom's car.

Mom and Robert fought a lot – constant screaming fights, just like the last time, and even though I was only seven, I'd sometimes get involved too. I didn't want another man hitting Mom like what happened with Mike. I never saw Robert hit Mom, but there was evidence of it; she started having bruises again.

Meanwhile, I was labelled as having a "lying problem" and maybe I did. I now know that all children go through a stage where they discover lying and how useful it can be, and my suspicion is that I was just going through that normal stage of development, but Mom and Robert would not let me forget it. I cried a lot and was very angry. I'd kick things and scream, alone, in my room. I secretly hated Robert and, in my little child brain, I truly believed romantic relationships never lasted; I had yet to see one succeed, at least with either of my parents, so all I had to do was wait and eventually Robert would be out of our lives, just like all the others.

3.

"You're gonna be a big sister!" Mom told me, her eyes shining.

She also told me later that this was the only period of her relationship with Robert when he didn't hit her.

"He only cared about his precious sperm," she'd joke.

I had longed for a sibling my whole young life, and asked Mom about it consistently for years, probably annoyingly, not fully understanding all the circumstances required for a little brother or sister to come into the world. So, when she told me that she was pregnant, a grateful seven-year-old me burst into wet, happy tears. I'd wanted this for so long.

I suggested Katie for the new baby's name if it was a girl, after a book I loved reading, *Katie the Kitten*. If it was a boy, he would be called Kyle, in the grand tradition of K-names. I wasn't too keen on Kyle, so I was overjoyed when, on 9 February 1994, Katie was born.

I was immediately in love. She was the most precious thing I had ever seen. All my classmates had siblings, and I'd felt like the only one who didn't. I took a photo of her into school to share at Show and Tell. I helped with the baby every day, holding her, playing with her, even helping with changing her diapers. "I love you and I'll always look out for you," I whispered into her little baby ear, under her silky brown baby hair that smelled that way that only babies smell. I'd sometimes go into her room and pick her up when she was crying, before

Mom got there, and try to rock her back to sleep, frustrated that my skinny little eight-year-old arms couldn't comfort her like Mom's.

It felt like it took forever for her to start talking. I could not wait for her to say my name. When she did, she always pronounced it "Kwithto".

Katie was unbearably cute from the moment she popped into the world. Other things she was, right from the start, were loud, demanding and feral.

"The reason I wanted a second child is that Krystal was so perfect and angelic," Mom would repeat to people again and again, "and now we've been blessed with this little banshee."

Katie was a classic second kid (I know this dynamic myself now that I have two). Her screams could wake the dead. I can still see her perfect little round baby head, a few strands of wispy hair poking out of her little pink headband with a single pale-pink silk rose glued onto the side, her face turning as deep red as a beetroot, her mouth open as wide as it could go, eyes clenched and fists waving wildly. And Mom, rushing around stressing, not knowing why this baby was crying, and running out of ideas of how to get her to stop. Robert was at work. We'd discovered that the car sometimes put her to sleep, but that wasn't always an option, so Mom figured that the noise of the extractor fan above the stove might do the trick. Katie would sit, strapped into her car seat, and I would squat below it and rock it ever so gently back and forth, with the extractor fan going full blast, to simulate the motion and sound of a car. I'd put my eight-year-old index finger inside her tiny baby fist and watch her eyes slowly droop, open, fall, open, fall . . . then finally close, her sweet little fist closed around my finger all the while.

We made up a song about Katie (Mom's lead, her being the family songwriter) that seemed to pop out of nowhere from sheer desperation if nothing else:

> Kate-sy Kate
> Kate-sy Kate
> Katesy Kate doesn't like to wait
> Wait for food or wait for lovin'
> Sometimes we have to put her on the oven.

There are many, many other verses to this song that I won't subject you to, but trust me when I tell you that they're all just as impressive.

I'd slip away from rocking Katie and say, "Mom, I did it! She's asleep!"

"Oh thank God, good job, sweety! That's such a big help to me. She loves you so much." I'd beam.

I felt that I was the only one who could help Mom with the baby. Everyone else who tried would end up frustrated, Robert included. I knew her little quirks and desires, even before she could talk. She'd be crying and I knew what she wanted was her pacifier and a gentle rock in her car seat, not a bottle and to be held. I took pride in this, smugly. I knew what

I was doing, I knew what Katie needed and nothing would ever change that.

Uncle Guy was diagnosed with cancer a few months after Katie's birth. Lymphoma. Guy was a long-haul truck driver and had chewed tobacco for years. They planned an aggressive course of chemotherapy, but the prognosis wasn't good. Six months was their best guess. He still lived back in Washington state, and Mom desperately wanted to move home to be with him, but Robert refused. He started hitting her again, as his precious sperm was now in baby form and separate from her body.

During one of their many fights, Robert admitted to Mom that he had staged the robbery in Seattle just to convince her to move with him. He had sold all our belongings and kept the money for himself. What a guy. (To be fair, it was Mom who told me this and, although it is very believable to me, I feel the need to mention that it came from someone who turned out to be a very unreliable narrator.)

We needed help again, but this time Guy couldn't rescue us, what with having cancer. And so, it was my Aunt Kelley who came to our aid. Aunt Kelley is Mom's younger sister; the third child and youngest daughter. I know most of you reading this haven't met my Aunt Kelley and probably never will, but you must believe me when I tell you, she's the funniest person you'd ever meet. Imagine a very vulgar, more glamorous, way funnier Melissa McCarthy or Jayde Adams. She's been this way since, seemingly, birth. Kelley learned to play the piano by ear as a small child, and has a velvety, clear singing voice reminiscent of

Barbra Streisand (who happens to be her singing idol). Everyone loves Kelley. "The thing is," she whispered to me recently, leaning in, feigning a sarcastic arrogance with one eyebrow raised, "everyone always wants to be my friend, but I have to be picky because I can't be friends with everyone. It's like, I get it! I'm great." Kelley has always exuded confidence, a "don't fuck with me" type attitude. I taught her the modern buzzy phrase "body positivity" recently and she was like, "Oh yeah, I mean I've always been like that."

Kelley was the classic, rebellious, sardonic younger sibling, and has never lost her teenage insolence, rolling her eyes at the very predictable things her family around her does. While I was growing up, Kelley loved nothing more than getting a rise out of her prim and proper Mormon mother, father and older sisters. If anyone dared to mention Kelley's vulgar language, she'd pause, open-mouthed, furrow her brow at them, as though temporarily confused, then proceed to say, loud enough for everyone at the dinner table to hear, something like, "Oh, sorry! Well, anyway, as I was saying, Mom. I told the lady at the DMV to suck my dick." Her eyes would go wide, her mouth open in an evil cackling laugh. The table would erupt with our various reactions: Grandma Lora would roll her eyes and say, "Well I never." Grandpa Woody would stay silent but good humoured, sometimes adding a bad joke of his own, making Kelley then go, "Ew, Dad that's gross." Aunt Tina would go, "Good lord! Can you believe this language, Krystal?" and I'd half smile and blush, wanting to laugh too, but also not wanting Mom to ask if I knew what Kelley meant, specifically, which she sometimes would.

But no one argued with her, because that's just what Kelley's like and everyone knows challenging Kelley about her dirty jokes only makes it worse. Plus, we all secretly loved it, because – as we have established – everyone loves Kelley.

As the story goes, around 1980, my Aunt Tina (the oldest of the four siblings) had received her very special Mormon Mission Calling Letter in the mail, which details where in the world you're being sent for two years to be a missionary. Boys get to do this at 18, girls 21, because a woman's first duty is to get married and pregnant ASAP, but if you still haven't achieved this by the ripe old age of 21, then they'll allow you to go out and spread the truth about biblical times, which is that Jesus and Mary and all of them actually lived in North America. Go USA!

Luckily, Grandpa Woody had a habit that thoroughly annoyed the rest of the family where he would secretly record special family moments on his tape recorder, and this was one of those tapes. I've heard it many times, because Grandpa Woody used to get the old tapes out at family gatherings.

Everyone was gathered around the dining room table to watch as Tina opened her letter. All their Mormon cousins had got to go to exciting, exotic places like Spain, Mexico, France, Japan.

Tina pulled the letter from its big brown envelope.

"Des Moines, Iowa," she said, flatly.

The sound of 14-year-old Kelley's evil, cutting laughter filled the room, as the rest of the family tried to sound upbeat.

"Well, Iowa, that's where I went on my mission, sweetheart. You'll love it," Grandma assured her. Kelley's laughter was peaking.

"Des Moines IOWA HAHAHAHA. Oh my God, oh my God that's great. Wow."

Mom was reading over Tina's shoulder and said, "Shut up, Kelley, oh my gosh, you'll never believe who signed it!"

Fourteen-year-old Kelley said, in the perfect comic flatline, "Jesus?"

The room exploded with laughter.

When Kelley arrived at our flat in Lindenhurst, Illinois, Mom told her about the staged robbery. Kelley raised her eyebrows, half-smirked and said, "Wow. So weird that an ex-con would do something like that."

Mom was not amused.

Our getaway happened while Robert was at work one evening; we only had six hours to pack everything into a U-Haul van and get out before he came home. I was terrified. Mom was crying, the baby was crying, so I definitely could not cry, but though I was dry-eyed, I was in knots. What would happen if he came home early? I'd seen his temper before, and it wasn't pretty.

"Krystal, hand me the bottle for Katie," Mom instructed, her right arm full with the baby, trying to bounce and rock to calm her, and her left hand holding the diaper bag.

"Here, Katie, shhhh," I whispered while I gave her a bottle. We stood in the apartment, surrounded by boxes, Mom with tears in her eyes.

There was a moment of silence and Kelley said, "Well, I'm hungry. Hey, on the way out of town, should we get Jack in the

Box?" The perfect, most satisfying joke to punctuate this fucking mess. We all perished with laughter. It had been days since any of us had laughed.

I sometimes think I can trace my trajectory in life to becoming a comedian back to that very moment, that very joke. Through shock, sadness and terror, Kelley gave us all a gift. She made it funny.

I've always found it fascinating that in America they will just give the keys to a large utility vehicle to any person with a driver's licence. I suppose we also do that with worse things, like guns, so in comparison perhaps it's not that bad. Nevertheless, we all crammed into the car to which the big, clunky, orange and white U-Haul trailer was hitched: Mom, Kelley, me, an eight-year-old girl, and Katie, a six-month-old baby, with a diaper bag, my backpack and everything else we owned rammed into the trailer. It was a long drive back to Washington state; days, in fact, and Mom cried a lot.

We stopped for gas at rest stops many times and Mom and Kelley did various adult tasks while I held Katie. Mom had a routine at these rest stops. She'd run into the gas station shop, pay for the gas, say she needed to use the toilet and walk around the back of the building, coming back a few minutes later reeking of cigarettes, strong perfume and minty chewing gum. She didn't know that I knew she was smoking, as she always did it far away from me and (she thought) out of my sight. I just played along. She'd only deny it anyhow. Meanwhile, Kelley smoked within throwing distance of me and Katie. She'd give me a little smile and get us buckled back into the van while Mom returned from whatever she was doing out back.

We stayed with Aunt Kelley in her house in Renton, just south of Seattle, where she lived with a roommate, a gay guy called Steve. Steve was a skydiver and lead singer and guitarist in a band – the coolest guy I'd ever met in my life. Kelley was of course very musically talented too, so she and Steve were always bursting into song around the house, and sometimes Mom would join in, usually a Beatles or Monkees song, or an old Andrews Sisters tune; something with gorgeous harmonies that they were able to improvise around and they'd show off by creating their own arrangements. They also loved changing the lyrics to be silly or dirty, which would send me into fits of laughter (not an easy task).

Kelley and Steve's entire basement had been turned into a music studio, lined with foam spikes, where Steve's band would practise, and I would sit in the corner and listen, in awe of them all. Their long-haired golden retriever, Jerry, who always had a different-coloured bandana around his neck, would wander in and out of the rooms, cuddling up to me and breathing his stinky, warm dog breath in my general direction. If Willie Nelson had had a curse put on him that turned him into dog form, he'd have been Jerry. A general sense of just "Okay. So, I'm a dog now. Far out." His long, sandy-blond fur had created a permanent layer of fuzz over the contents of the entire house.

I loved staying at Kelley and Steve's, although we knew it was only supposed to be temporary. The house always had a faint hint of long-extinguished incense or candles which, blended with the scent of Jerry and the cats, gave it the feel of a beatnik café installed above a pet shop. It was packed with cool trinkets and memorabilia: a glass mermaid, an old music-festival poster, sand in a jar, black and white magnetic words on the fridge arranged to say something slightly risqué, weird musical instruments. Everything had a deep, meaningful or hilarious story behind it, and humour was top priority. It was delightfully cluttered, as though there were so many rich, complicated, fun aspects to their lives that there simply wasn't room for it all. Definitely not a child-friendly space, and not apologetic about it. It felt lived in.

Steve and Kelley taught me to play card games and make candles and would involve me in their evening games with their super-cool, bohemian Seattle friends. We played poker with chocolate coins. They'd sometimes busk in the Pike Place Market, Steve playing guitar and Kelley on keyboard. They were reminiscent of the B-52s, and did a mean "Love Shack", which always drew a crowd. They'd bring me along and encourage me to sing with them ("Come on, you're a cute kid, we'd make so much money!"). I was shy, because they were unimaginably talented in my eyes, but I relented and sang "Under the Boardwalk". A semicircle of people would gather quickly when I took the mic. They shared the tips with me, of course. They even took me to Bumbershoot, the Seattle music festival, which went on late into the night, and it never felt as if they were babysitting me – it was as though they genuinely liked my company and thought I was cool and wanted me to be around. I loved this feeling.

Kelley and Steve always treated me like an equal; they never talked down to me or censored swear words or said, "Whoops, sorry!" if they said something vulgar. When Steve brought home a guy he was dating, they'd make out in front of me. They'd tell very off-colour adult jokes and, when I didn't understand them and asked what they meant, they'd take the time to explain them to me. Since I always had to second guess everything Mom said, this honesty felt like safety; I could trust them. I felt so grown up and never wanted to leave.

At the local school I immediately struck up a friendship with a girl named Sana, another nine-year-old who lived right next door to Kelley and Steve's. She had also just moved to the area with her family from Pakistan. Her parents didn't speak English very well and so she and her sister had to be the translators most of the time.

"My sister is going to change her name to fit in more in America."

"Why? What's her name?" I asked.

"Nasia," she answered.

"What's wrong with that name? It's pretty!" I said.

"I mean, Nasia? Like, nausea, you know, feeling like you're going to throw up?" she said.

I stared at her, and we both burst out laughing. "Oh, I didn't even think of that!"

Her school lunches smelled strongly of spices, and contained goat, which she told me her father had slaughtered himself in their back garden.

"Yeah, I've seen them slaughter the goats out back. They scream like hell," Steve would say, giving a slight side eye. Sana would be made fun of for her packed lunches, and for the way she dressed, sometimes in traditional Pakistani clothes. We bonded over this, because I'd constantly get picked on for my clothes, too, which were just terrible, usually second-hand, and lacking any sense of fashion. Clothes were functional in our house, nothing more. It felt good to have a friend I liked, but I knew it wouldn't last.

In my mind, a friend was something you had for a few months, or a year at most, then something dramatic happened and you had to leave, sometimes not even saying goodbye. A friend was something that changed seasonally, like weather, or new seasons of a TV show. We never bothered to keep in touch with anybody we left behind. Why would we? Any adult friend Mom made always turned sour quicker than milk. We'd always "escaped their toxicity", "They weren't really our friend" or they'd stolen from us, or showed their true colours when we really needed them. Mom always looked at the past in a way that would build up where we were now, how far we'd come. "That was such a hard time. But we made it through," she would say, and lovingly squeeze my shoulder.

But, for now, for these few short months, I had Kelley and Steve, Sana and Katie, and no abusive boyfriends or husbands to speak of. Mom would disappear now and then, for days at a time. Sometimes she'd take Katie with her, sometimes she'd leave her with Kelley. And when Mom was home, she was messy. She left empty Diet Coke cans all over the house and was generally disrespectful of the communal living spaces, not cleaning up after herself or us kids. Kelley and Steve always looked out for me and made sure I got to school, fed me breakfast and dinner when Mom wasn't home, despite having jobs of their own.

But a few months into this, Kelley asked Mom how much

longer we'd need to be there. "I mean, it *is* Steve's house. It's just getting pretty cramped in here," Kelley said.

"Wow, what the fuck? Are you kicking me out?" Mom said.

"No, of course not, it's just Steve is pressuring me a little bit, he needs to know how much longer you'll be here with the two kids, that's all."

"Okay. Okay." Mom's eyes filled with tears instantly; she took a performative deep breath in through her nose, and blew it out through her mouth, over and over, like she was doing Lamaze. "I . . . I guess I just didn't know that was the situation. I mean I just escaped from a fucking abuser, and I have nowhere else to go." She gave a singular, sharp, high-pitched sob.

"It's been three months, Tracy. And you know we love you and the kids, but it's not exactly smooth sailing . . . It bothers Steve that the kids leave their messes everywhere, there's half-empty cans of soda all over the house, toys and clothes all over everything. I mean Krystal accidentally knocked over Steve's Mom's mermaid statue the other day, it's just really fucking crowded in here and . . ."

"Well . . . this is what kids are like, they make messes. I thought . . ." Mom started saying.

I was on the porch – they surely didn't know I could hear, but the window was wide open and I heard every word. Anyone around could sense it was two sisters fighting; neither held back. I hated this. Fights always signalled the beginning of the end. The end of a living situation, a relationship, a friendship. Sometimes that was a good thing, but not this time.

"We just want to know what your plan is! I'm not kicking you out, Jesus Christ, stop being so dramatic, and the mess thing, it's just about respecting other people's spaces, Tracy."

"I'm not fucking listening to this any more!"

Mom stormed out of the living room. I reached down and petted Jerry the dog, burying my small hand in his flowing waves of fur that smelled like corn chips. I started to walk back into the house, stopped, turned back and picked up my half-drunk can of Sprite off the porch, drained it down the sink before putting it into the recycling.

I thought, *I should probably start packing up my stuff.*

After the fight, Mom took off with Katie. I stayed at Kelley's, not knowing where Mom had gone. I wasn't too worried, because she always came back eventually. I just kept going to school as normal.

Two days later, Kelley got a phone call from Robert, the abusive ex-husband that she'd helped us escape from in Illinois. He told her that Mom had flown there and left Katie in his care, then flown back to Seattle.

"What should I do?" Robert asked.

"Well, I don't fucking know, she's your kid, right?" Kelley snapped.

Shortly after, Kelley got a call from Mom, hysterical and distressed, saying, "Kelley, I was THIS CLOSE to driving my car off the 520 Bridge. I'm at Henry's."

Henry. Robert's brother. The one I'd seen naked in the shower.

"Jesus Christ, Tracy. Where is Henry's apartment? And why did you take Katie to Illinois? How the fuck could you leave Katie with that asshole after you just got away?! Jesus!" Kelley was livid.

"Kelley." Mom was taking in laboured gasps of breath. Between sobs, she wailed, "I am not fit to be a mother. She's better off with him than with me. I just can't be here any longer."

Mom hung up on Kelley, but Kelley had the call traced, got Henry's address and sent emergency workers to his apartment. When they arrived, Henry told them Mom had just tried to jump out the window of his high-rise apartment, but he had stopped her.

Kelley and Henry checked Mom into the psych ward at Harborview Hospital in Seattle. Two days in, she convinced someone to let her use a phone (despite this being against their policy) and called her dad, my Grandpa Woody, saying Kelley had kicked her out of the house and she had nowhere else to go but the hospital. (She left out the part about the driving off the bridge/jumping out the window.) Grandpa Woody signed her out, despite the hospital's policy of suicide attempts requiring a minimum three-day stay.

Kelley phoned him, furious. "She tried to fucking kill herself, Dad. The psych ward is exactly where she needs to be."

Grandpa argued that Mom claimed Kelley had kicked her out, and that the staff weren't treating her well in there.

"Well, of course she said that, Dad! It's Tracy! Christ." She hung up the phone.

Meantime, after Mom had been checked out of the hospital, no one knew where she had gone.

Without speaking to anyone, Mom left the hospital, got Katie back from Illinois and picked me up from school one Friday (about a week after I'd last seen her), then moved the three of us into another house in the Renton area. She didn't speak to Kelley again for months. Kelley was worried sick and tried to find us, to no avail. To all intents and purposes, we had vanished into thin air.

In retrospect, I find many of the circumstances surrounding Mom's life events and the behaviour of people around her bewildering, especially the actions of supposed professionals. How could a woman who has just tried to commit suicide twice and got checked into the psych ward be allowed to leave the hospital, pick up her eight-year-old daughter from school and her six-month-old baby from the airport, then take them God knows where, without anyone checking up on them for months and months? Why didn't the authorities step in somehow? Why isn't there a system in place for a scenario such as this, which surely can't be that uncommon?

And what does a woman have to do to convince the people around her that she needs help, whether she wants to accept it or not?

For me, moving somewhere new with no notice was par for the course. I had learned to inure myself to the pain and confusion. The constant moving was perhaps even comforting. A fresh start was always around the corner, so I mostly welcomed it. Mom's mood swings were also routine, so it all felt like another day in the life.

"How are you so normal?" or some variation of this question gets thrown at me a lot, from people who grew up differently. I've found that people who have had more stable lives tend to be simultaneously admiring and judgemental of those who haven't.

The belief, whether conscious or not, seems to be that the people who have had trauma and instability as children must be the ones who are the most messed up – the ones who are damaged and, probably, the ones to be avoided. Amazing that you made it out, sure, but also, you must be a ticking time bomb. As a younger adult, I could see these judgements in people's eyes: sympathy mixed with caution. *There must be a monster lurking inside you somewhere*, their eyes and body language said. So, eventually, I stopped telling people about my past. My life started when I was 19 and moved to New York. "I grew up in Washington state, near where the *Twilight* series takes place, heard of it?" But there wasn't much else to tell, really. No more questions.

The truth is more complicated and usually seems like too much of an effort to share. Every fact or statement leads to more questions, which always lead to the truth, which is painful and corrosive to happy-go-lucky, light-hearted chats.

The truth is: growing up with someone with a mental illness is sort of like growing up in the ocean. You get really good at swimming. Then you meet someone else who can't even navigate a puddle and you're like, "Wow, okay, what ocean did you grow up in?" And they're like, "I grew up on dry land, Krystal. Just like everyone else. And we judge people who grew up in the ocean." Then you realize that it makes some people really sad and uncomfortable when you talk about growing up in the ocean. So, you stop telling people. And you avoid the ocean at all costs. You swear you'll never go back there again. But while you're in it, you think it's normal. You just keep treading water. Because that's all you can do.

4.

A couple of months after our great disappearing act, Mom was forced to make contact with the family to check on Guy. He was 28 years old, and the cancer had been aggressive: lymphoma, which caused him excruciating pain and spread throughout his body quickly. Intense chemotherapy, blood transfusions and radiology treatments did little to stave off the inevitable.

And so, after months missing in action, we moved to a house that was only about a ten-minute walk from Kelley and Steve's in Renton, so I could stay in the same school and visit them, and my friend Sana, anytime I wanted. It was 1994, and still acceptable for eight-year-olds to walk around local neighbourhoods on their own, so I took full advantage of this.

There were a few memorable holidays here, including Halloween 1994, when I wanted to be Princess Jasmine from *Aladdin* (like every other eight-year-old girl in my school, and presumably most of Planet Earth) and I begged Mom to buy me the costume sold at the Disney store in the mall. It was $35 and she refused, saying she could make me a better one at home. I threw a small fit, but to Mom's credit she pulled this costume off like it was some sort of *Project Runway* challenge. She took a pair of nylons, cut them up and stretched the legs over my arms and chest, then made a crop top out of a shiny blue scarf. She glued plastic jewels all over it, and did my makeup complete with cat eyeliner and hair all fluffed out and in a three-sectioned ponytail.

When I looked in the mirror, I gasped. All the kids at school complimented my costume, which stood out from the swathes of other girls whose parents had just caved and got the Disney-store version. This was classic Mom; her chaotic mind often led to disaster, but this time she nailed it.

The house we were renting in Renton had a lot of space, and so we would illegally sublet the basement to people. There was a guy named Mitch, a tall, white guy with black puffy hair that looked like Sideshow Bob from *The Simpsons*; the only memory I have of him is that Mom kicked him out because she found out he had been in prison for child molestation.

Then there was Brett. He had a mullet and a bushy moustache, and I remember him once saying to me, "Black people are just as prejudiced against white people as we are against them. And don't let anyone tell you different." Another time, Brett was helping me write a birthday card to someone, and he wrote, "With all are love." I corrected him, telling him it should be "our", not "are". He argued this point, and eight-year-old me thought, "Wow. This guy's a fucking idiot."

The third set of roommates we had were a mother with two kids, a boy and a girl, aged six and three. She spanked them in front of us, something that was shocking to me, as Mom never hit us. The young mother would often leave her six-year-old to look after the three-year-old while she went out for hours at a time, which really meant that she was leaving Mom to look after them, as they inevitably wandered upstairs to be with us.

This mother was late on her rent one month and, instead of paying it, packed up and left with her kids in the middle of the night. They left some boxes behind, and when we went through them I found a little baggy of white powder shoved into a baby shoe. Even Mom looked shocked. We took a break from looking for roommates for a while after that.

My grandparents on Mom's side were born in the 1930s. Grandma Lora – her maiden name was Lora Dunn – grew up in Utah, in a traditional Mormon family where everyone's hopes and dreams consisted of going to church, growing up, getting married in the Mormon temple, then having as many children as possible. Grandma Lora was a late bloomer. She didn't get married to Grandpa Woody until she was 32, and she didn't speak much of her life before this.

Grandpa Woody, real name Clyde Forrest Wixom Junior, grew up in several places in the US, most notably Florida. His mother was born in Mexico City, and came from a moderately wealthy family, a famous fact among us all. "Great Grandmommy had a nanny when she was growing up!" Mom would tell me. She had married Grandpa Woody's father, Clyde Senior, who didn't have money, and the wealth in the family didn't carry on. Clyde Senior was a cold, unlikeable character, with whispers among all about how abusive, both physically and mentally, he was to his kids. Grandpa Woody had a little sister who died of meningitis at age 16, in the 1940s. Her photograph was always sitting on his and Grandma Lora's piano, an old black and white photo that had been professionally colourized but had since faded again. Grandpa Woody had been raised without religion but he met Grandma Lora when they were 30 and 32 years old respectively, and converted to Mormonism. He fully committed himself to the church, stopping smoking and drinking forever when they got married. Although he immersed himself in the religion, not being raised in it meant that he always kept a slight side eye at some of the, in his view, more questionable teachings.

"There's a joke in the service," Grandpa said. "A group of men stood around, in Heaven, and one goes, 'Who are those guys over there in the corner?' and another guy goes, 'Oh they're Mormons. Shh, don't bother them. They think they're the only ones here.'" Then he'd wink at me. Being his granddaughter, I never saw Grandpa Woody's abusive side, only his very explosive anger, and only a few times at that. Most of the time, in my eyes, he was just a goofy, very large man who told slow, long-winded stories and loved drawing. He tried to keep up with his kids' sharp wit, but always fell flat and so settled for usually being the butt of everyone's jokes. I loved Grandpa Woody and Grandma Lora, but they were about 15 years older than Dad's parents, and that fact combined with their Mormon principles made their house boring and ancient in my eyes. Their four kids carried with them a resentment for the things they'd gone through as children, and it was apparent in the venomous and vitriolic way they spoke to their father.

There's no excuse for abuse, but I suppose what Mom and her siblings went through was a combination of that sort of thing being acceptable at the time, and generational trauma that had been passed down, as Grandpa Woody experienced even worse abuse and neglect from his own father. I have a clear memory of Grandpa Woody, who would have been in his sixties at this time, spending about a year making a model reconstruction of his dad's old farm where he'd grown up, as a surprise for Clyde Senior's birthday. Grandpa Woody lovingly carved every barn, every building. Crafted trees and little farm animals out of clay and felt. He worked from old photos, and he'd spend hours on it every day. It was huge – about 5 feet by 6 feet and three-dimensional, like a little model town that a toy train would run through. When it was finally ready, he spent hundreds of dollars getting it shipped to Florida, where his 90-year-old dad lived. My great-granddad barely acknowledged it, pointing out that some of it had broken in the shipping process, and telling Grandpa Woody everything he had gotten wrong. Even in his sixties, Grandpa Woody was trying to get his abusive dickhead father's approval – and failing. The next year, Grandpa Woody just sent him a voucher for Applebee's. The year after that, Great-Granddad died, and Grandpa Woody got the farm model back. He put it back into the same garage where he'd constructed it in the first place, and it gathered resentful dust for the next decade.

While Guy endured his cancer treatments, the whole family focused on him. Preconditioned to avoid showing emotion, Grandma Lora and Grandpa Woody would visit the hospital stoically, but nevertheless always emerged with eyes red and shiny. We spent so much time at Guy's bedside. His body and face went from slim, muscular and healthy to hugely swollen and grey, and he went bald. He fought on for about nine months.

Eventually the day came, in May 1995. Mom drove me to the hospital, crying, saying that it was "time to say goodbye to Guy".

It was dark outside. Mom sent me into Guy's hospital room, alone, and I walked up to his bed, not knowing what to say. I knew I was supposed to feel sad, but I just felt uncomfortable. The hospital smelled weird and the man in the bed didn't look like Guy. He wasn't the funny, strong man who had helped us move away from Arizona. He wasn't the smiling, romantic 20-something always with a new, pretty girlfriend on his arm who he was crazy over. He wasn't the man who had put me on his shoulders and carried me around his house just for fun.

I didn't know what to say. I stood at his bedside, looking at my feet and shifting around nervously. Guy said, "Hey, Krystal. I just wanted to tell you I love you. And I'm gonna miss you."

"Yeah. I love you too," I said, in a flatline little voice. "And I'm gonna miss you too." I just wanted to run away.

He gave a weak smile and there was a slight knowing laughter behind his eyes. "You can leave if you want."

"Okay."

I walked out. That was the last time I ever saw Guy.

The next day, Mom woke up early to the phone ringing. I stood at her bedside while she twisted sideways in bed, reaching for the cordless phone from underneath her big fluffy white duvet.

"Hello? Oh, okay." She pushed the receiver under her chin for a moment and said, with the tone of a secretary telling someone that the big boss unfortunately couldn't see them, "Guy's gone, honey."

Her emotions never fit the scenario. More often than not they were way too big, but if there was no one else around, she just seemed slightly annoyed, and they rarely reached the heights the situation seemed to warrant. I said nothing.

The funeral was held at Grandma Lora and Grandpa Woody's local Mormon church. This was a slight controversy in the family because Guy wasn't Mormon. Like all the siblings, he'd left the church the moment he moved out of his parents' house. But ultimately, everyone agreed that Grandma and Grandpa were hurting the worst, and they should get the funeral that they wanted for their son.

On the morning of the funeral, Mom was a wreck, working herself up into tears as we got ready. Little Katie was crying too, and I rocked her in her car seat. Mom put on her clothes and makeup and hairsprayed her fluffy bangs.

Mom's tears always made me extremely uncomfortable, especially when she'd do it in public. It made people look at us, and it felt like I was with an adult who couldn't handle the situation, and that was embarrassing. As a result, I never cried at the same things she cried at. After all, we couldn't both sit there crying.

Mom dragged Katie and me into the church more than 30 minutes late, very noisily, crying and sighing wildly, everyone turning to look at us. Aunt Kelley was at the podium. I still remember the words she was saying when we walked in.

"One thing that me and Guy bonded over was our love of music." She talked about how eclectic his musical tastes were; how his two favourite artists were AC/DC and Barry Manilow. I'd never seen Kelley look so sad. My Aunt Kelley, the funniest person I'd ever met, who used to skip Mormon primary at age 13 to go smoke out back, was standing inside a Mormon church telling everyone how much she loved her brother, and now he was gone. It broke my heart to look at her. She was so cool and expressive and honest, and had such a dirty sense of humour, and it felt like she didn't belong in a stuffy Mormon church.

I breathed in the aroma of the place – new carpet, crisp paint, new Bibles, freshly printed paper and wood varnish, with the combined smell of all the grownups' cologne and perfume. The pews were perfectly aligned, with a scratchy turquoise fabric against a dark-stained natural wood. The back wall held a pipe organ, made to look old-fashioned, but nothing in this church was more than 30 years old, as with almost all Mormon churches. A single American flag hung, motionless, on a golden pole next to the podium. It didn't surprise me to learn that every Mormon church across Planet Earth has an American flag on a golden pole, front and centre. Mormonism is, of course, the All-American religion, lest we forget.

I looked at one of Guy's friends, a big, muscular man who never cried. He was sitting with his head in his hands, sobbing, his white button-up shirt tucked into his slacks and his tie falling to rest on his knees. Grandpa Woody and Grandma Lora were red-faced and their eyes were puffy. Everyone I looked at was crying. But none as loudly as my mother. *I should be doing something to help Mom*, I thought. *I wish she would cry more quietly.* I just sat, completely silent. *Maybe my silence will counterbalance how loud she is. And then maybe people will stop turning to look at us.*

Mom took to the podium. "When I woke up this morning," she said through tears and choked sobs, "I picked up the phone and tried to call Guy and . . . and . . ." Her face contorted, and she couldn't finish her sentence for sobbing. This first sob-terruption lasted about 15 seconds. An eternity. She raised her hand to shield her eyes for a moment, before placing it back on the podium. In a high-pitched whimper, she spat out, "I forgot that he had died. I got in the car with the kids and . . . and . . . drove to the hospital to see him. Which is why we came in late. I drove in the wrong direction . . . When I realized, I turned around and . . . and . . . that's why we're late. I'm so sorry, Guy." She looked to the sky at this last statement. I took a glance at my two aunts, Kelley and Tina, making eye contact with each other and a barely perceptible eye roll. *Classic Tracy,* their eyes said, *making it about herself, even on the day of Guy's funeral.*

No one gives a sarcastic eye roll better than Aunt Tina. Tina is by far the most serious of the siblings. That doesn't mean she lacks a sense of humour, but her jokes always erupt from the middle of a feeling that you're about to be yelled at.

"Krystal, your Aunt Tina left a message on our machine. She sounds, like, *really mad,*" my husband once said to me, years later.

"Oh, no! That's just how Tina sounds," I explained.

Tina was a city bus driver for years, a job that suited her down to the ground, because she takes shit from no one. From around age 35 to 50, Tina got the daily comment from bus passengers that she looked like Gillian Anderson. She even had the medium-length ginger hair. "I know, I know, I'm Scully from *The X-Files,* you getting on?" Despite her hard exterior, Tina has a huge heart.

Back to Guy's funeral – Mom's crying continued, performative and way too loud. She didn't cry like the other adults cried; it was more like the way a devastated and frustrated four-year-old cries when someone has cut their toast wrong and they're fighting with themselves to express to the confused adult exactly what the problem is.

I do believe some real emotions existed inside her, standing at the podium at her little brother's funeral. But as always with Mom, it was as though she took that genuine feeling and poured gasoline on it, set it on fire and danced around it, demanding that everyone watch.

When I think, nowadays, of her hyper-emotional explosions at events like Guy's funeral, it leads me to the conclusion that she somehow couldn't help it and wasn't fully self-aware. I think some part of me also knew this back then, which was why I felt so bad for Mom, always childish in her need for sympathetic eyes. As long as people were looking, she didn't seem to care why.

5.

The bike was bright red, sparkly and had multicoloured plastic tassels bursting out of the handlebars. It had a white basket, and rainbow beads on all the spokes that rattled and slid up and down as the wheels turned. Across the middle bar (which slanted downwards, signalling a girl's bike – "So you can wear dresses on it!" I remember other girls saying), it said, in big bulky letters, PACIFIC. Ten speeds. *This is it*, I thought. *I can go anywhere.*

Mom had pooled together with Dad to get me this cool new bike for my ninth birthday.

It was the best thing to happen to me for a long time. After Guy's death, we had moved again, this time to a block of ugly brown apartments in another suburb of Renton. I started at a new school. It was a shitty neighbourhood. The type of place where little kids would be out way too late, unsupervised. The new bike was a way for me to zoom past weirdos and kids I wanted to avoid on the way to and from school.

I can still feel the cold plastic handlebars getting sweaty under my hands because of how tightly I was gripping them while jumping kurbs, skidding across the parking lot of the brown apartments. *And* it was red. And sparkly. Did I mention the tassels? Other kids asked for a shot on it, constantly. "Yeah, but only for a minute," I'd say. Wow, status. This bike had changed my life.

Diligently every night I locked it up at the base of the concrete staircase outside our flat, with a combination lock that no one knew the code to except me. Just another detail that made me, and my bike, cool as hell.

I looked forward to riding it to school every day, so when I noticed it was gone on a Tuesday morning at 8.15am, I ran back upstairs and told Mom, panicking and nearly in tears. She was silently livid, her eyes shut tightly, and I thought she was about to start yelling at me. She said, in a high-pitched tone, almost to herself, "Hm, okay," while exhaling sharply. She put on her jacket, walked somehow simultaneously full of rage and with an air of calm, down the stairs barefoot, looking wild with her thin wispy hair up in a teeny tiny bun and no makeup, braless, and her size G breasts swinging around in her ripped sweatshirt. I had no idea where she was going, but I silently followed. Her lips were pursed in an angry little circle, and she pounded on the door of the apartment downstairs from us. A boy, no older than 11, opened the door about six inches and just behind him I could see that the apartment was crammed from floor to ceiling with bikes of all colours, types and conditions. Before he said anything she shot out, in her best clear, bitchy secretary voice, "I'm here to get my daughter's bike back."

"Oh, uh, I don't know . . ." he stammered, eyes vague.

"Uh huh," she said sarcastically, shoving the door open and walking briskly past the confused boy.

Oh God, Mom, I thought to myself. *What exactly is your plan here?* There were hundreds of bikes in this apartment. It could be anywhere, if it was in there at all.

She looked left, then right. She confidently took two steps forwards, grabbed a red sparkly bike from a stack of a dozen or so that were leaned against the hallway wall. "This is it. Thank you," and as she was walking out of the apartment, the boy was mumbling, "Oh, we found it and were gonna give it back . . ." Mom slammed the door in his face.

She set the bike down one-handed, in front of me. "Here you go. Have a good day at school." She stalked back upstairs.

I blinked. *Oh. Wow. Okay.* Mom had summoned all her

psychic powers and got my bike back within 45 seconds of it being missing. I'll bet other people's moms can't do that.

"Go and give him your leftovers, *now*." Mom's left eyebrow was raised into a perfect point, her lips pursed into a tight little circle, nostrils flared. *I dare you to argue with me*, her face said. I knew that would be a futile exercise.

The three of us, Mom, Katie and me, were in Taco Bell, as we were a couple of times a week. Katie had shovelled through all her pintos and cheese and deconstructed tostada. Katie had a never-ending appetite and loved all food that kids weren't supposed to like – lettuce, fish, tomatoes, chickpeas, okra. Weird shit. I, on the other hand, liked about four foods until age 18, and I sat there with my half-eaten pintos and cheese and plain burrito with extra cheese that I hadn't touched, along with a Sprite which I'd taken two sips of, then declared to Mom I was finished. She sighed and said something about spending money she didn't have on things that then got wasted.

From our table we had witnessed a very dishevelled-looking man, thin, with long brown hair and a beard, dirty clothes and a limp, walk up to the counter and ask, in a soft, gravelly voice, for a cup of water. His voice sounded like he hadn't used it in days. He was obviously homeless. The person at the counter refused and told him to "please leave" unless he was going to buy something, and he turned, slowly, and started shuffling out the door. Mom witnessed the whole thing with mounting anger.

"Krystal," she said to me, in a sharp, loud whisper, never

taking her eyes off the man, "go and give him your leftovers." He was starting towards the door.

I felt bad for the guy, but I didn't want to walk up and speak to him. I was 11 and embarrassed by everything. "Nooo, Mom. I don't want to," I said, in a teenagerly whine of *don't make me*.

When she said it again, I picked up my tray and intercepted him as he reached the door.

"Um. Here you go," I said. He looked at the tray, and looked at me, and said, in a very genuine, soft voice, "Thank you."

6.

I stayed silent, waiting for the punchline.

Mom had just said, "We're going to get married!", but this statement was confusing at best.

"To who?" I said blankly. This was a genuine question. Mom wasn't dating anyone, as far as I knew. And she couldn't possibly mean the man I had in my brain.

"The thing is, I was talking to Grandma," I clearly remember her telling me in a hushed, giggly whisper, "and y'know, he's really old and he's probably going to die soon. And so, if we get married, we'll get this house, and all of his stuff!"

Oh, okay. So she does mean him.

I agreed that this was a good plan, because this was obviously what Mom wanted me to say. *It better be soon though*, I thought. *Because this house smells like sweet farts and piss.*

We had moved to Port Townsend, a middle-class hippy town on Washington state's Peninsula. Katie was two, and we were living with this 91-year-old who had a very nice house on top of a hill, overlooking the town. We were always moving in and out of towns, in with weird people, getting kicked out, kicking someone else out, so to be in the same house as this fossil of a human varied a little from the norm, but not enough for me to kick up a fuss about it. Besides, he had a pool table in his basement, and he was too old to climb all the way down the stairs, so I could play to my heart's content. Katie and I shared a room, and Mom enrolled me in the nearby school.

A month into living there, he and Mom got married in his living room. There were only a few people there, including Grandpa Woody and Grandma Lora, this man that looked like a melting wax figure of Charlton Heston, and his children, who were all way older than Mom, already in their fifties and sixties. I stood in the kitchen beside Mom, who wore a simple white, satiny professional-looking wedding dress, which only emphasized the fact that she viewed this as a business transaction. She held a bouquet of white flowers and was speaking with the female pastor about the vows as I leaned against the cupboards.

"Definitely make sure you emphasize *commitment*. But also taking things slowly, like not pressuring each other," Mom said. I had no idea what she was on about. "And if you could say 'Husband and wife', please. Definitely 'Husband and wife'. Not 'Man and wife'. Man and wife is sexist, y'know," said my mother, the woman marrying a man that she hoped with all her heart would die as soon as possible.

I hated this man from the moment I met him. He was thin, very wrinkled, tall, and wore a red dressing gown over his clothes around the house. A replica of Hugh Hefner, robe and all, only older.

When the pastor said, "You may kiss the bride," Father Time wrapped his arms around Mom as tightly as he could and pulled her into him, his lips pressing against hers very hard with his eyes closed, and her struggling to end the kiss as quickly as possible and laughing awkwardly when they broke apart.

Ewwwww. I wanted to puke. It was obvious to me that she hated this man, too. But I understood why she was marrying him, because she told me, and so I went along with it. I never questioned Mom's decisions at this age. She had a plan, and she was the adult, after all. I had no power anyway, so there was no point in me stewing over these things. This was the sort of thing people probably did all the time.

The day they got married, he told me, "I would be honoured if you would call me Dad," still wearing the type of suit that one would be buried in circa 1917, bow tie and all, tears gathering in his wrinkled eyes, and smiled, waiting for my response.

"Oh . . ." I said, not knowing what else to say. I was not expecting this. I looked at Mom for help, and she gave me a wide-eyed look, with her eyebrows in an exaggerated "worried" face, communicating silently, "Please just go along with this."

"Yeah, maybe," I said. *Please leave me alone. Please leave me alone.*

The moment she got me on my own, Mom said in a low voice, "I'm so sorry he said that to you, honey. You do not have to call him Dad. I'll talk to him about that, okay?"

Whether I called him Dad or not, that didn't stop him trying to give me antiquated advice regularly. There was an apple tree in the front garden that grew tart green apples, and he caught me and a friend climbing the tree and eating them one day and told me off, shouting from the front door, "Girls, don't eat them, they apples'll give you the runs." My friend burst out laughing. "Is that your dad? He's so old," she giggled, taking another bite out of the tart, rock-hard little apple.

"He's not my dad. We're just living with him," I said, blushing.

Over dinner one night, he said, "Never embarrass a chicken by picking at it with a fork. Just pick it up with your hands. That's more respectful." I ignored this.

At breakfast the next morning, he showed me his tin of black molasses and told me this was better for me than using brown sugar in my oatmeal. I tried it. It tasted how I imagined melted tyres would taste. Still, I was mostly polite to him, because I was a nice kid. I didn't like confrontation of any kind, and being rebellious took too much effort. *Just wait it out and he'll be gone like all the others*, I thought.

I don't know if Mom ever slept with the mummy of Tutankhamun, but she certainly never slept in his room, opting for the guest bedroom down the hall. Either out of guilt towards making me live with him, or just out of boredom, Mom started making fun of the old man behind his back, laughing with me at all the old-man things he would do and say. It was a fun running gag, a way for her to address the geriatric elephant in the room. I'd laugh along, of course, but subtlety was never one of Mom's greatest strengths.

The general air in the house became bitter and suspicious. The old man would come into the kitchen slowly, make his meals and potter back to his room or the living room, not talking to us, because he probably knew that, when he did, he would get mocked by his new wife.

Katie was still in diapers and was at the stage where she loved nothing more than banging a hard thing on another hard thing over and over to make the loudest noise possible. Pots and pans were acceptable, but something she wasn't supposed to do was even better. She'd sometimes deem the bashing noise to not be enough, so she'd add in a wild banshee yell between each bang. Using this method, she could achieve a sound velocity that I'm unable to do justice to in text; suffice to say that the zombie of Dwight D Eisenhower did not like it. His days of raising toddlers were supposed to be finished, and having a walking baby who raised hell and had a penchant for ripping her own dirty diapers off and leaving them in special places around the house wasn't his idea of a good time. The diapers would stay on the floor for longer than would be considered acceptable, similar to the Diet Coke cans back at Kelley and Steve's. To add to this, whenever we were out in public, Katie had a lovely habit of stripping all her clothes off and running around completely naked (her favourite place to do this was the supermarket, where Mom was busy with other things; I'd be the one who had to run after her and try to re-dress her, while other adults laughed and told me what a great big sister I was, which I secretly loved). I'd try to play with Katie and keep her occupied as best I could, but relations with the old man were tense.

Mom started antipsychotic medication around this time, raising and lowering her dosage at will, or sometimes stopping the meds completely, not trusting doctors to know as much about these things as she thought she did. "I was a hospital administrator," she'd remind me, and everyone who would listen, whenever she got the chance. "And trust me, doctors don't know what the fuck they're talking about. They don't listen."

One night during this period, Mom lost it on a completely different level from anything I'd ever seen previously. It was Halloween, and we were all dressed up, and I had a friend over. It was late, we'd come back from trick-or-treating and were sitting at the dining-room table. Mom had put Katie to bed and was loving having us as an audience and started going hard, making fun of the old man with me and my friend. He had already gone to bed. She was really hamming it up with the lowball jokes and my friend couldn't believe how cool my mom was. I revelled in this, laughing with my very chill mom and friend at the expense of the weird person whose house we were living in.

At one point, Mom took a Tootsie Roll and threw it across the hall towards his bedroom door. "He won't hear it. He's so deaf, he can't hear anything," she said. My friend's eyes went wide, and she covered her mouth to stifle more laughter. Mom took a bigger piece of candy and launched it. "Try it!" she said to us. My friend took a huge handful and launched it at the door. I did the same. We were all snickering with the evil laughter that little kids relish, Mom embodying the personality of a mischievous child along with us. What the hell was going on? I didn't care. This was so much fun. Mom grabbed an orange from the fruit bowl and threw it as hard as she possibly could at his door. That did it. The door flew open and he stormed out, puffy eyed, obviously having been woken up.

He screamed as loudly as his 91-year-old voice could, "Now that's enough!" He was shaking his fist as he yelled, and I was reminded of an old-timey steam-engine conductor, reprimanding us in black and white. We all froze, but Mom kept trying to suppress laughter.

The good feeling completely evaporated. This was not funny any more. It suddenly dawned on me that mocking an old man and throwing things at his door maybe wasn't the best thing to be doing. Maybe it was even cruel? Hot shame flowed through my face. My chest felt tight. We both looked to Mom, but she was still laughing, oblivious to how serious the mood had just become, and it became scary immediately, because that realization that I'd had so many times before, and would have so many times after this moment, rushed over me, like that dream you have where you're falling that suddenly wakes you up: there was no adult in this room. I was alone.

The old man went back into his bedroom and slammed the door, probably having a long hard think about his decision to marry a woman who was now throwing food at his door with two eleven-year-old girls.

We left that house shortly afterwards, the entirety of their relationship lasting about eight weeks. Mom got the marriage annulled, and we never spoke about it again except for her sometimes mentioning that she was "so fucked up back then. I don't know what I was thinking marrying that guy! He was completely insane."

I missed a lot of school growing up. If I were to put an estimate on it, I probably missed about half. There were various reasons for this: Mom wanting me to stay home and be her emotional support, sometimes Mom simply not wanting to take me to school or go to the effort to make me get ready. The more school I missed, the harder it was for me to go back. Every new school eventually became a scary place, a place where someone might question me about why I'd missed school, and I'd have to lie, because if I told the truth, it would make Mom look irresponsible or make me look lazy. And the other kids would start asking questions. One day in fourth grade, a girl who sat in front of me turned around and innocently asked, "Krystal, do you only come to school every other day?" I felt a knot in my stomach.

"Uhh, no, not really, I just miss some days. But I'm gonna start coming every day! I *am* gonna do it." I laughed to her about this, as though I'd just made a very relatable joke. She didn't laugh along with me.

After living with the old man in Port Townsend, we moved to Sequim (pronounced "Skwim"), Washington, to be nearer to Grandpa Woody and Grandma Lora, so that they could help us out more often. I wasn't ecstatic about this. Sequim is basically a retirement community, and the town seemed lifeless. With nearly every move that I mention, by the way, I started at a new school. People ask me now if this was tough, but the truth is, I *loved* starting at new schools. I loved being the "new kid". Any undone schoolwork, embarrassing absences or scenes made by Mom were all wiped clean; everyone was nice and helpful again, and I could be anything or anyone, because I was new.

Katie was nearly three, and she questioned why she couldn't come along to school with me. "I want to go too!" she would say. "I'll see you when I get back!" I'd answer, picking her up by her waist and turning her upside down, pretending that her feet were her face. "Wow, you look so cute today, Katie. Let me kiss that face!" I'd kiss her ankles and calves and she'd giggle uncontrollably, her hair falling downwards towards the floor. I'd then swing her back and forth, her head dangling towards the floor and say, "Tick, tock, Katie's a clock, tick, tock, Katie's a clock", with her laughing and laughing until she couldn't speak.

I knew that dealing with Katie alone, all day, was sometimes too much for Mom to face, so that was another reason to let me stay home. I didn't argue. Another day at home was another day I didn't have to face any repercussions. One more day that no one would ask me where I'd been. And if I waited it out long enough, we'd just move again.

I was a smart kid. I passed tests, but I never did my homework. When it was assigned I always had every intention of doing it, but as soon as I stepped off the school grounds and into my household, my memory of school was wiped clean and all that existed was me trying to navigate my homelife until the next morning. Then, on the bus to school, or maybe the moment my butt hit that cold, solid, plastic school chair, my stomach would sink. Shit. My homework. I forgot, again.

The schoolwork would pile up – sometimes I'd be given extra assignments to do over a holiday to catch up. Parent meetings would be arranged where the teacher would tell Mom how bright I was, and that I just needed to do the work and stop missing so much school. Sometimes, Mom would tell them that we were going through a hard time, she was on disability, and she would share with my teachers, in whispered tones, humiliating things about our personal lives – "I've just escaped two abusive marriages", "My brother just died of cancer", "We're going through a really hard time right now as a family" – that she hoped would make them sympathize with us and buy me more time.

Other times, she'd put the blame completely on me. "Yeah, we've gone through some procrastination at home as well. Avoidance is a huge issue, I think. Also lying has become a big thing." And she'd tilt her head to the side, looking at me, nodding slightly, putting on her "professional voice" that I hated. But at the time, I thought she was right and I was deeply embarrassed. What *was* wrong with me? Why did I never think about homework when I was at home? Why did I miss so much school?

I'm a lazy piece of shit, I'd think. *There's something very wrong with my brain.* I wanted to run away from these meetings with everything in my soul. Sometimes, the teacher would buy it, other times they'd look at me with a sort of knowing sympathy. Looking back, I'm sure these teachers had to deal with so many nutcase parents on a regular basis, they were probably experts.

*

Even as a child, I knew there was a sense of irony, that some of the worst fights between me and Mom would be over cleaning, because our house was always in absolute squalor, regardless of how much yelling there was. At the best of times, there would be countless piles of laundry all over the house: toys, books, magazines, garbage, shoved against walls to make paths for walking, the way trails occur in forests from animals naturally clearing out the grass in that route, showing you where to tread and where to avoid.

At the worst of times, there would be plates of food and half-full cups of coffee, gathering fuzz, moulding, sitting on bedside tables, hidden under beds. Piles of animal faeces (usually cat poo) would dry and decay in an undetected corner behind some side table that we'd all pretend not to notice. Someone would spill a can of Coke on the carpet, and it would be wet and sticky for a few days before it dried up and blended into everything else. Another reason it always felt so good to move was that a new house meant a fresh start, in every way. A clean house, a new school, new neighbours and friends and people who didn't know anything about us yet, so didn't give us weird looks or judge us or make Mom cry.

I'd gone to stay with Dad one week, a little respite from all the madness. When he was dropping me back, he walked me to the door. Mom opened it. Dad took one look at the inside of our apartment, and his body went totally stiff.

I never liked it when Mom and Dad spoke. It was two worlds colliding; and I knew that they hated each other, so it made me want to crawl into a hole and cover my ears. And I always felt like

I had done something wrong to cause them to fight, and I had no idea how to fix it. I had to tell each of them something that would calm everything down, but I could never come up with anything good enough.

I remember Dad saying, ". . . fucking disgusting" and me running to hide in my room. Afterwards, Mom was crying and told me that Dad had just called her a freak and told her that she "lives like a pig".

I asked him about this interaction later, as an adult, and he confirmed it. "When I saw that apartment, I just snapped," he told me. "I lost it. I felt like I couldn't leave you there. It was upsetting. Maybe I didn't handle it right, but I couldn't help it. I was furious."

Every now and then, Mom would have a day when it seemed like her eyes all of a sudden opened to how our house was, and she'd declare a "cleaning day". I dreaded these days more than any other, because it meant Mom yelling at us and screaming and stomping through the house like a roided up Yosemite Sam, shouting punishments at us and then when we didn't clean to her (usually non-existent) standards, she'd yell more.

"It's fucking ridiculous that you don't know how to clean a toilet at your age," she'd say. "This is exactly why this house is a fucking disaster! I have no fucking help around here."

Through red faces and streams of tears, we'd keep cleaning somehow, and that would be the entire day. The result of these days would sometimes be a clean house at the end, but even if it was, in my eyes it was not worth it. All I knew for sure was that cleaning was the thing I dreaded most in the world. Mom in a manic cleaning mode was the worst version of Mom. I even preferred "public breakdown" Mom over cleaning Mom. At least when she had a total meltdown in public, I wouldn't have to clean. Mom would be freaking out, and I'd just be thinking about how this was going to affect me and my immediate future.

As a direct result of this, my living environment as a young adult was always at best cluttered, and at worst trashed. As long as there weren't piles of cat poo and moulding food, I felt like I was killing it at life. I just didn't see the mess. It wasn't a priority in my mind. A messy house that no one mentioned meant comfort. A messy house meant peace and quiet. Safety. I could go out and ride my bike and not worry about what state of mind Mom would be in when I got home.

Mom didn't work at all by the time we moved to Sequim. The way we survived was a combination of her getting disability pay from the government, and child maintenance from my dad and Katie's dad. We were still always broke, and Mom's mental health was getting more unstable by the time I was approaching my eleventh birthday. She was on full disability, because of a dresser that supposedly fell on her back while we were moving out of the big house in Renton, near Kelley and Steve's. No one saw this happen, and I don't remember any physical ramifications like Mom recovering from it, but nevertheless she secured medical disability checks monthly because she was unfit to work.

Shortly after this, she began staying in bed for long stretches of time. At first, she couldn't get up in the mornings. I'd have to get myself ready for school, make my own breakfast and she'd put the TV on for three-year-old Katie so she could stay asleep.

On other days she would get up, get one or both of us off to school or daycare, and go back to bed until we got home. I'd come home from school and Mom would often still be in bed.

I slept in the same bed as Mom sporadically from a very young age, all the way up to 12 or so. I'd sometimes fall asleep watching *David Letterman* or *Conan* with her, or other times I'd start off in my own bed and then crawl into hers. I craved the comfort of cuddling up with Mom at night. It made me feel safe and looked after. When I got old enough to realize that this was weird, I stopped doing it and I never mentioned it to anyone. I also called her Mommy until age 11, and again, when I realized it was odd for me to be doing this (everyone else had moved on to saying "Mom" long ago), I simply didn't call her anything for many months, only to pop out with "Mom" one day and hope she didn't mention it. The same thing happened with Dad, calling him Daddy, then nothing for about a year, then coming out with "Dad". Dad had no reaction. Mom said, "Ohhhh, so I'm 'Mom' now, huh?!", smiling. Damn. Thought I got away with it.

7.

My arm hurt because it was being forced, hard, into Ashley's arm who sat beside me. The car then changed direction, and I was forced the other way, into Mom's arm. *I don't remember the car ever going this fast on this road*, I thought. The rain pelted the front of the car's windscreen in sheets, the wipers working like maniacs, on full speed, to clear the water away fast enough for us to see out the front, but it was futile.

There was a lump in my throat. This wasn't right. I had to say something. "Mom, can you slow down? I have a feeling we're going to get into an accident," I heard my own small voice plead. The car sped onwards, revving around the tight corners whose shoulders were sheer cliff faces, with no signs of slowing.

The first house we lived in near Sequim was way out in the countryside, in an area called Diamond Point. It was a picturesque A-frame structure, exposed wood on the inside, ceiling-to-floor windows on the front looking out all the way to the water. It was the nicest house we had ever lived in. It wasn't big – there was one bedroom, and a loft above the living room, where Mom slept. We were renting, of course, and the rent was cheap because it was so far away from any town. It was about a 20-minute drive from this house into Sequim town centre, so this period of my life consisted of a lot of time with me sitting in the passenger's seat of a car, staring out the windows at the evergreens whizzing by, as tall as skyscrapers, blocking out most of the natural light at all times of year. We had cats here, as we almost always did. They would get into fights with raccoons, other cats, foxes and God knows what else, and come home with injuries. One night we came home to find a raccoon had got into the house through the cat flap, and our cat immediately came in and fought it out, ending with the raccoon rushing out the door, defeated. We all cheered for our cat, Spot (I named her after Data's cat from *Star Trek Next Gen*), who managed to come away from the scrap with only one slightly bloody paw.

Mom had started what was to become a lifelong pattern of making friends with young women on a regular basis. She'd meet them anywhere and everywhere. At a shop, doctors' offices, the bank, wherever. They always had similar characteristics; they'd be around age 15–25, estranged from their family or going through some sort of a hard time and in desperate need of a mother figure in their lives. A couple of them had just been released from prison, or juvey (juvenile hall – kids' jail). She'd get close with them very, very quickly, opening up to them about the deepest, darkest things in her life, and they'd reciprocate – something I now know as "trauma dumping".

It was always the same. Mom would go on and on about how special their connection was, how she'd never made a friend this quickly and that their meeting must have been "meant to be". There were always so many coincidences, and she pointed them out as though it was proof of her making correct decisions.

"There are no coincidences," she'd say, which I found a bit rich considering they were her favourite thing in the whole entire world. What she meant by this was that a coincidence is just God, or The Universe, giving you a sign. The sign always meant whatever she wanted it to mean. They rarely seemed particularly special to me.

"Oh my God, Krystal, I was literally just thinking about Guy and then a Barry Manilow song came on. He must have put it on! Guy is watching over us!" I know that this is one of the main reasons why I'm such a cynical adult. My knee-jerk reaction to people trying to point out some weird occurrence is that they're trying to be manipulative, and I get very suspicious.

These young women that Mom befriended would frequently move in with us for long periods of time, usually because they had nowhere else to go. They'd sleep in the living room. Sometimes they'd run errands, or babysit us, but they'd just generally always be there, rotting on the couch between going outside to smoke.

A young woman named Ashley, about 17 years old, who in my memory looked just like Avril Lavigne, was staying with us for a few weeks when Mom came home and caught her doing drugs in the house. I remember she was smoking, so it must have just been weed, but she had also come home drunk several times, and Mom was losing patience. Prescription pills were one thing, but Mom, for whatever reason, had a short fuse when it came to alcohol and illegal drugs.

"I can't have this around my kids!" she'd shout. Sometimes this would be the catalyst in kicking the person out. They'd be our friend from anywhere between a few weeks to a few months, before there was a terrible fallout and we'd never see them again. Rinse, repeat.

With Ashley, though, Mom forgave her, and so she stuck around a bit longer. Hindsight's a bitch, because she definitely should have left.

Orange pill bottles with white lids started appearing everywhere. All over the dining table, needing to be shoved aside when we ate. On the counter in the bathroom. On Mom's bedside table.

She didn't tell me what she was taking, of course, and even if I had read the labels, I wouldn't have known what the substances were.

There were antidepressants/antipsychotics, as well as pain pills. I had heard Mom speaking about her meds with Grandma Lora, and her teenage friends, and many people who would listen. Mom always had a very good technique when it came to getting what she wanted from doctors: she went to one doctor, and if they didn't play ball, she went to a different one until they did. I have a theory that the reason Mom hates medical professionals so much, especially doctors, is that they tend to be some of the hardest people to manipulate. Many of them are numb to sob stories and tales about her past; they want facts. Some are not afraid to say no.

"They're fucking idiots" was Mom's favourite thing to say about doctors. This was her way of saying, "No more questions."

One night at the A-frame house in Diamond Point, after Katie had gone to bed, I was up with Mom and Ashley. We were chatting about normal things, like school and movies, and out of nowhere Mom started saying things that didn't make sense. She asked Ashley to get a broom, so that she could swipe all the spiders off the walls. We were confused. We looked at each other.

Within a few minutes, Mom started crying, then screaming and saying that there were tigers and animals crawling up the walls. She was fully sobbing when I noticed Ashley start crying too. I immediately ran to the phone and called 911, telling the person on the line that my mom was hallucinating. I then called Grandma Lora and Grandpa Woody, who arrived before the ambulance. They stayed with us for a couple of nights while Mom went to the hospital to sort out her medication.

"Those fucking idiot doctors prescribed me the wrong dosage" was the given explanation. Everyone accepted this, because there was no other option. But no one spent as much time with Mom as I did, and I could tell things were going in the wrong direction.

And so, one very stormy night, I found myself in the front seat of the car with Mom driving home late with Ashley. Katie was now nearly four years old and was in Illinois visiting her Dad, Robert the Jack in the Box manager, which she did a few times a year.

We were all sitting up front, Mom driving, me in the middle, Ashley in the passenger's seat. Mom's demeanour was anxious; she was breathing heavily, forcing her eyes wide every few seconds, then squinting. I had nodded off, this journey had become so familiar, but this time a sharp fear pierced through my neck and chest and woke me.

"Mom, I'm scared. Can you slow down? I have a feeling we're going to get into an accident." I phrased this carefully – "I have a feeling" was a turn of phrase that Mom used a lot, because trusting her gut feelings was something that she did, and believed in, and respected. In response, she said something along the lines of telling me to relax and stop distracting her from driving. The car wound dramatically through the pitch black, evergreens in every direction around us illuminated momentarily by our headlights. Sporadic cliff edges appeared next to the car's slippery tyres, and I imagined us plummeting over the edge to our deaths. In my mind's eye I could see the wheels leaving the road and sense the free-falling feeling before smashing into the strong tree trunks that would crunch the grille of the car without remorse. Every turn felt like the end.

She was just going so fast... *Please slow down, please slow down*, I said to myself. Every muscle in my body was tight, bracing for impact. Mom then did slow down a bit, and this eased my fears, temporarily. I closed my eyes for a moment, not drifting off, but it was late and the comfort of the knowledge that we were almost home made my muscles release. Nearly there.

In what seemed like three seconds after my eyelids shut, a deafening *SMASH* flooded my senses. The sound of shattering glass, crunching metal and screaming came at me from all directions. I was thrown towards the windscreen and must have put my knees up out of instinct to protect myself, as my injuries would later suggest. I know I didn't really say this out loud, but the words that pummelled through my brain were, "I TOLD YOU!!!" *I told you. I told you. I fucking told you. I was right. I fucking called it. I tried to stop this. And you didn't listen to me. I TOLD YOU.*

Everything was still for a moment, and my head swam. I saw the windscreen had cracked and a huge piece of glass, the size of a large oven tray, had come down and sliced my right knee open. I'd never seen a cut this deep, and in my memory I can see down to the bone. I saw something white, anyway. It didn't hurt. But I was bleeding, and I knew that was bad news. Mom and Ashley didn't look obviously hurt, but their faces were cut, and Mom was crying. We all got out of the car, and I saw that we had hit a telephone pole. It was wooden, the impact of the car had caused the base to bend at an odd angle, it had cracked horizontally, and splinters were sticking out of it in all directions, but it was still standing. The front grille of our Oldsmobile Cutlass Supreme was wrapped around it, hood crunched up as though it were made of tinfoil.

There was nothing but forest around, and this was before cell phones. In the far-off distance, maybe about a ten-minute walk away across a field, we saw a tiny house with lights on. Ashley ran to the house and called 911. As I'd come to be very familiar with, ambulances took their sweet time getting to Diamond Point, because it was so far away from civilization. I limped back to the car and sat in it to wait. I wasn't in pain, but walking was hard. We waited 30 minutes for an ambulance, Mom moaning and sobbing the entire time.

At the hospital, I got stitches in my knee. Mom had suffered a back injury. We thought Ashley had gotten off scot free, until she started fainting a few days later and we realized she had a concussion. She disappeared from our lives shortly after the accident, never to be spoken of again.

The telephone pole got a huge metal brace on its base, and I saw it for years every time we'd drive past. I'd tell people the story, even wrote a report about it at school, until Mom started asking me not to. Mom's side of the story was that she had thought she was pressing down the brake, but accidentally pressed the accelerator.

"My medication dosage was all wrong then, that stupid fucking doctor," she'd say. I nodded, but I felt that, for me and Katie, life was increasingly like being in the back of a car climbing a steep hill, not knowing what was just over the crest.

Part Two

8.

"We can just have some quick sandwiches and pops before we head back," Dad said to his new friend from Blue Cross, the insurance company where he worked in the cafeteria. "You can meet my wife and baby daughter!"

"Great," the friend said. Dad opened the door to his house, smiling, his new pal beside him. The door swung slowly open, revealing a completely empty living room. No furniture, a few papers and plastic wrappers littering the carpet.

The two men stood, silent. Staring. Dad's new friend turned to him and said, "Oh, have you guys . . . just moved in?" He said this delicately, because neither of them wanted to state the obvious: Mom had taken me, and all their possessions, packed them up in the morning and left Dad for good.

"I never saw him again, you can bet on that," Dad told me, decades later.

My parents, Tracy and Dave, met in their hometown of Corvallis, Oregon, at age 14. That summer of 1975, they were attending the same camp, collecting bugs for farmers because a bright yellow plant called tansy ragweed would take over and destroy crops. The bugs they collected fed off the tansy ragweed, and that helped. They got paid for the bugs they'd collect. They were friends as teenagers, and into adulthood. I can very easily imagine young Tracy and Dave being like a classic Manic Pixie situation, him being a dark, brooding young teen craving the bubbly positivity Mom radiated. Mom had taught herself to play guitar and, when they were 14, she taught Dad some chords.

"Then he totally overtook me! He practised way more than me and could play all the riffs to AC/DC within a few years," Mom told me.

Mom was engulfed by her Mormon religion while growing up. When she and Dad turned 19, she convinced him to convert, so that they could get married. He did, but within a year of starting going to church, Dad read a bunch of stuff about Mormonism he didn't agree with, and – in what must have been a devastating blow for the Mormon church – decided he wanted out. He duly persuaded Mom to leave too. They had me in 1986, when she was 24 and he was 23.

"You were three weeks overdue. I thought I was going to be pregnant forever!" Mom said. There's a photo of her sitting in a rocking chair, resting a coffee mug on her stomach. Her bump is humongous. "I was so desperate. The day before you were born, I tried taking a spoonful of castor oil, and it worked! I immediately started having contractions. And you were huge! Nine pounds six ounces." Mom gave birth to me naturally and lost so much blood that she fell unconscious and, she claims, saw the white light leading her into Heaven. "I floated above my own body, and I saw the doctors and nurses hurrying to try and get me a blood transfusion, and I saw myself with my eyes closed. I saw Dave holding you and knew that you were going to be fine, so I just let go." Then, she says, something strongly pulled her back into her body, and she woke up and took a huge breath and she was alive again. Just one of many near-death experiences and spiritual awakenings in Mom's life.

Mom and Dad's relationship was never perfect, even at the beginning. Dad always drank a lot. He started drinking and doing drugs as a teenager, stopped when he converted to Mormonism, then began drinking again after they left the church.

"He'd drink beers on the way home from work, then hide the bottles in the bushes so that I wouldn't see them, but I always knew," Mom would say.

If you ask Mom about this period of her life, she will tell you she was living with a man who drank beer and watched football all day long, and she decided she had to get out of this toxic situation. If you ask Dad, all that was true, but he didn't know that any of it was a huge problem, and certainly had no idea at all that Mom was thinking of leaving him. Hence, the humiliating story about bringing the colleague home from work to meet his wife and newborn child and finding the house completely empty.

A few months after she had taken me away, Dad called her crying. "I want to see my baby," he said. To this day, I have never, ever seen Dad cry. This wasn't one of the stories that Mom told me again and again – this was one she told me in one of the rare moments when she was trying to endear him to me, for some reason long forgotten. Her motives over the years changed many times, but this story stuck with me: the fact that, in this situation, she held all the power and wielded it by keeping me away from him, at least for a time. It seemed, at best, cruel.

As I grew up, I'd visit Dad at most every other weekend. Sometimes it would be a long weekend, or an extended school holiday when he'd take me to his mom's house, Grandma Sharon, in Corvallis. In the years when we lived far away, in Illinois or Arizona, the visits would be cut down to once or twice per year. It upset Dad, of course, but he had no control over Mom's actions and, short of making a huge federal case about it, he had to let her do whatever she was going to do.

Dad's a mellow guy. He's average height, and his dad was half Native American, something he inherited in his looks more than his siblings did, having very dark skin and hair and dark brown eyes. I cringe when I remember saying to him at age three or four, noticing his hands were a much darker shade than mine, "Daddy, your hands look so dirty!"

"Really?" Dad answered. "Hm, that's weird. I just washed them." Dad is a nice guy and very chilled out, so he never would have followed this up with what I probably deserved, which would have been, "Ya racist little shit."

He's one of those racially ambiguous-looking people; Mom says when he was growing up a lot of people asked if he was Samoan, or Hawaiian. In Mexican restaurants, waiters would speak Spanish to him. At airports, he gets profiled, and his bags get searched, more often than the average person's – especially since 9/11. I've never once heard him comment about this. It's just something all the women who care about him in his life (his mother, daughter and wife) have noticed, and we sometimes talk about it behind his back. He's the silent type, rarely expressing strong feelings except towards certain foods that he gets really excited about. The way Dad and I have bonded most over the years is by sending each other pictures of great meals we've cooked or eaten recently. Dad mostly sends pictures of epic sandwiches. He drank a lot when I was growing up. His drink of choice has been Bud Light for as long as I can remember. He would get two 24-packs of cans from Safeway, the ones in cardboard with a nifty handle built right in, bring them home, along with whatever he had picked up for our dinner that night, and attempt to drink them all over the course of a weekend. Sometimes he'd go back to the shop and buy two more and crack into a third pack before Sunday. Drunk Dad isn't volatile or destructive – mostly his eyes go foggy, he slurs his words and he laughs a lot more than usual. At his worst, Dad could be mean. "Your Mom's family are all nutcases," he'd say, with me sitting there not knowing how to respond.

In my younger years, Dad was a bachelor. He was 23 when I was born, which is insane to think about now. He took me on many adventures when I was a little girl that maybe weren't the most appropriate – gold panning, hiking, fishing and white-water rafting, to name a few. Kudos to him for including me in his crazy outings, but I remember being cold and bored a lot of the time. Despite this, I remember Dad's house as a normal place. There was no yelling. The house was always clean. And Dad always cooked me a nice dinner.

Dad's frustration with Mom was obvious. He hated dealing with her, and Mom tried to turn me against him several times. She'd tell me he was an alcoholic, and that I should speak to him about his drinking, or else he'd probably die. I have a flash of being in a supermarket with Dad when I was five or six years old, him picking up a 24-pack of Bud Light, and me pulling it away from him and telling him that, if he bought it, he was gonna die. "Krystal! Stop it! You are embarrassing me," he said. I told Mom about this later, and she raised one single knowing eyebrow in judgement.

The truth is, Dad always drank a lot. He got drunk most nights of my childhood, even drove drunk regularly and, to tell you the truth, he's always been great at it. Dad has never, ever been in an accident. I'd gladly fall asleep in the car with Dad, drunk or sober. But Dad's drinking paled in comparison to the issues Mom had. If Mom had not had major mental health problems, Dad's drinking probably would be front and centre in my life. But everything is about perspective, so I laugh at the idea that Dad's drinking has affected me in any major way. Is that how all family problems are? Is there a version of me in another universe who has a dad who is Jeffrey Dahmer or something, so then Mom's mental illness seems benign? Or maybe another version of my life where Mom and Dad have the exact same issues, but we live in an active war zone, like during the Holocaust, so their flaws don't affect me because we have bigger problems, like hiding from Nazis?

For the vast majority of my childhood, my favourite place in the entire world to go was Grandma Sharon's, my dad's mother, who I would always refer to as Grandma in Oregon. She had a house near the railroad tracks in Corvallis, and had had the same phone number since the 1970s. Grandma Sharon taught me her phone number when I was very young. In my late teens, she told me, "Sweety, I always made sure you knew my number so that you could call me if you were ever in trouble."

Her house smelled like baby lotion and fresh towels. It was always warm, and there were eternally amazing smells coming from the kitchen. No one ever yelled in this house. I could eat whatever I wanted, whenever I wanted, and my favourite foods were always at hand. For breakfast, I'd alternate between Lucky Charms, Cocoa Pebbles and Fruity Pebbles. I'd eat a huge bowl of them, sometimes two, and then go and play Super Nintendo. To this day, if I ever indulge in a sugary cereal from my childhood, my mind is whisked back to playing Donkey Kong at Grandma's house. Grandma was always doing cross-stitch or playing Zelda or one of the Final Fantasies. We'd go together into GameStop in the mall, and she'd go up to a young male worker, Grandma wearing a light pink sweater with her short curly hair and glasses. Then she'd say, in her grandmotherly voice, "I'm looking for a turn-based RPG. I can't handle live-action fighting. I get too excited!" and she'd giggle. The young man would stare at her incredulously and recommend some games to her. "Oh, I loved Chrono Trigger," she'd say. "Something like that would be great."

One Christmas, she bought me Mortal Kombat on the PS1, a bloody, violent fighting game (for 1995) that I had specifically asked for. Mom saw five minutes of it, said she didn't want it in her house and mailed it back to Grandma Sharon with a note saying it wasn't appropriate. I only played it at Grandma's after that.

When I was very young, Grandma Sharon's husband, Grandpa Melvin, hadn't retired yet and was in the Coast Guard. He would be gone nine out of twelve months of the year, so it would mostly just be me and Grandma home alone together. There were pictures of big, vast ships on wild seas hung all over Grandma's house. Some watercolour, some oil painting, others embroidered or cross-stitched and, of course, there was a ship in a bottle. I would stare and stare at these pictures of ships and sometimes imagine they were moving, right before my eyes.

Her kitchen had a very high shelf going around the whole perimeter that had hundreds of salt and pepper shakers on it. Buddhas and Hindu statues, Japanese figurines, little thimbles and delightful clutter covered every inch of free surface. Grandpa Melvin brought all these things back from his travels in the Coast Guard as gifts for Grandma Sharon.

In no uncertain terms, Grandma Sharon's house was Heaven. She had known Mom since Mom was 14 years old, and though she knew that things weren't great with Mom at home, she never, ever spoke badly about her to me. This was a major relief, as I never felt judged by Grandma Sharon. Her intentions always seemed pure. She just wanted to love me and keep me safe and make me happy. I felt that, and I could truly let go and fully be a kid while I was there.

When Mom took me away to Illinois, to live with Robert the Jack in the Box manager, Grandma Sharon told me later that she thought she was never going to see me again. Mom drove away from her house and I remember seeing tears in Grandma's eyes as she waved frantically, and I didn't know why she was so upset. My Uncle Terry, Dad's brother, was there to see me off too.

"I burst into tears as you drove away from me. Terry held me while I cried," Grandma said to me when I was older, smiling. "I was so worried about you. I've always loved you more than anything and I just wanted you to be safe."

My favourite treasure at this heavenly house was Grandma Sharon's collection of bells. She had about 40 of them, and when I was a very little girl she'd pick me up and let me ring each bell every morning. When she died, she left me the bells and I now let my little boys ring them now and then, if I'm in a good mood – although I mostly tell them not to touch them because they're mine.

Whenever a new baby was born in the family, Grandma made a beautiful cross-stitch with the baby's name, their date of birth and birth weight sewn into the picture. I have one, and my first son, Sonny, has one as well. Coming to the end of her life, Grandma Sharon knitted several baby blankets because she knew she wouldn't be around to do it for the new babies that would arrive after she passed away. When I got pregnant with my second son, after she was gone, I chose a pink and green blanket from her special stash, and I still put it under my younger son Jesse every night. I'm not superstitious, or religious or anything, but I feel like Grandma Sharon's blanket somehow keeps him safe. The love from her passed into the blanket that she made, and he can feel it when he sleeps. At the very least, whenever I see him sleeping gently, safely, without a care in the world, I think of her.

9.

After the car accident, things were never quite the same again. Mom, Katie and I soon moved again, this time closer to Sequim's city centre, and the Diamond Point house was history.

Dungeness Meadows was a housing complex set amid a golf course, with winding man-made hills, paths with little sand dunes, carefully manicured lawns and, as with everywhere in Washington state, evergreens covering every inch of ground that wasn't a road, a yard, a driveway or someone's house. Some houses were nicer than others, but most of them were mobile homes. I live in the UK now and it's hard to describe to British people the type of house it was because there's not really an equivalent over here. It was nicer than a trailer or a caravan, but not as good as a stand-alone house.

Ours was a double wide, very much set into the ground, with a porch, a driveway, a wrap-around yard and all the features of a house – but also, it could easily be split into two; each half could be hitched onto a truck, hauled away and br replaced with another house in the space of a day. Ours was built in the 1970s, I learned later – which is old for an American house, but even older for a mobile home.

We had a trampoline out back and this was before the days when they made you have those huge safety-net things around the outside, so we bounced happily, 10 feet or more into the air, hoping like hell to land on the small black surface beneath us surrounded by blue plastic.

One hot summer night when I was 13, I was bouncing out there, alone. It was very dark, and there was a full moon, partially covered by clouds. I had a book on witchcraft that said you should pick herbs and plants under the light of a full moon for maximum potency, and I wondered if the dandelions and blackberry bushes that covered the chain-link fence along the back of our yard could be used in any sort of concoction. Bounce, fall, bounce, fall, bounce. Bounce... I started falling, farther than I should have. It didn't feel real – like I had accidentally slipped into dreaming while looking up at the sky and thinking about brewing potions. Then, THUD. I slammed onto the cold, hard, grassy earth, pain shooting up my tailbone where I'd landed. Ouch. I was too old to start crying for Mom about this, so I took the pain in my stride and sulked back into the house.

Katie idolized me by this point, and at the same time was solidifying herself as the rebel of our household – she was once out with Mom at Safeway and asked if Mom would buy Spice World for me ("Krithtal loves the Spice Girls! Can we get this for her?"). Mom said no, not today, but when they got home we found she had stolen it, placing it inside her backpack without telling anyone. I laughed and thanked her, but told her she probably shouldn't steal.

I cried a lot at Dungeness Meadows. I was now a teenager, and Mom's mere presence made me angry all the time. I couldn't put my finger exactly on why. We'd fight over everything. Screaming fights at the top of our lungs that would always end in me sobbing so hard that I couldn't speak. I could never articulate what I wanted to say during fights; it would come out something like, "This isn't normal!", "I can't fucking live like this any more!", "I don't know what you mean! You're not making any sense!"

"Krystal, you're 14 years old, you should know how to clean out the fucking tub . . . there's no fucking way you're leaving this house for the rest of the week. You will come straight home from school. This place is a disaster, and I have no help around here."

I rarely dared to say the real thoughts that crept into my head in this time period, but they lay there, right behind my lips, muttered as quietly as I could while I ran past her sobbing, gasping for breath, rage and sadness fighting within me, and me desperately rooting for the rage to win. Thoughts like *You're a psycho* and *You're a crazy bitch and I can't wait to get the fuck away from you, Fuck you fuck you fuck you, I fucking hate you.* The words didn't do justice to how I felt, but these sharply whispered swear words were the only small power I felt I had at the time. Something was bubbling up inside me. I knew that something wasn't right with Mom, but I had also never known life without her, so I felt caught.

Katie had started kindergarten. She was an adorable five-year-old with perfectly round glasses and a very pronounced lisp, especially on the *s* sound, which came out like a *th*. She had shaggy, frizzy-brown hair that Mom had cut herself, and Aunt Kelley would say she looked like Rod Stewart. I'd take Katie on long walks in the woods and along the railroad tracks behind our house; we'd pick flowers and play games, usually involving us pretending to be cats. My patience for these games was short, but still longer than Mom's, so I'd indulge her.

Katie was obsessed with our cat, Spot. Spot was an outdoor cat and would come and go as she pleased. I taught Katie how to pet Spot nicely, so that she'd like it, and I told her that petting animals reminds them of their mom licking them as babies. She stared at me for a moment, said, "Hey can you look that way for a minute? And cover your eyes."

I raised a sceptical teenage eyebrow. "Why?"

"Just do it!" she said.

I pretended to, and she immediately got on all fours and started licking Spot.

"Katie, ewww, don't lick the cat!"

"I told you not to look!" she screamed.

I'd have nightly cries, in my bed, alone, after brushing my teeth. Clean, minty crying. I'd fantasize about Katie dying, a lot. *What if she died?* I'd think. *What if she got hit by a car? What if she got murdered?* Gruesome, intrusive thoughts would play out like a projector in my brain; my eyes felt like they were being held open and forced to watch it all, like that scene in *A Clockwork Orange*. I'd welcome the tears, letting myself grieve over something I knew hadn't happened, and was unlikely to ever happen. *What the hell is wrong with me?* I'd wonder.

Katie and I shared a room in the mobile home in Dungeness Meadows. We had bunk beds – I had the top and Katie had the bottom. It was out of necessity, of course, but even though I loved Katie to bits, as a teen I could not stand sharing a room with her. I craved my own space. I'd spend the night on the couch sometimes so that she wouldn't wake me up at 6am, as little kids tend to do.

I started feeling sick when I became a teen – constant stomach aches and back aches and weird leg pain that was put down to growing pains by all the adults around me. I also felt very faint in the mornings, and when I yawned and stretched my body after waking up, my eyesight would sometimes temporarily disappear. One morning, I stretched, everything went white and the next thing I knew I was waking up on the floor wedged between my bed and side table with a sore head. I'd fainted. I told Mom, and she took me to the doctor, who informed us that I was severely anaemic. She asked me how many portions of vegetables I ate in a week, and the real answer was none. I lived off boxed cereal, Top Ramen, delivery pizza, goldfish crackers, Kraft Velveeta Mac 'n' cheese and, if Mom was really in the mood for cooking, lemon chicken, which was frozen boneless skinless chicken breasts fried in a pan of oil with lemon juice out of a plastic bottle (shaped like a lemon) squirted over them. Sometimes she'd add in kielbasa sausages. Now and then, we'd go to Taco Bell. But I said to the doctor, "Around three." She looked horrified. I got prescribed iron tablets.

At 14, fighting with Mom became volatile. We'd scream at each other and Katie would run into her room and shut the door. The tears felt like they would never end. I'd reach deep inside myself and try to find the source of the anger, and the solution, and how to articulate it all. The problem was, there was no way to bring up Mom's mental state to her face without her transforming into Medusa right before my eyes. There were a few buttons that could be pushed that would make everyone's life hell. One was calling her crazy. If anyone pulled out the crazy card, they were out of our lives, immediately. Questioning Mom's sanity touched something deep, something raw and unhealed, and I witnessed this again and again.

"You're fuckin nuts, you know that?" a boyfriend would say, beer bottle in hand.

"You *cannot* say that to me," she'd sputter, tears in her eyes. "Do not. Ever. Say that to me. Get out. I'm calling the police."

The other was comparing her to her father. She was a lot like Grandpa Woody, and she knew it, and hated him. They were both very funny, extremely emotional and sensitive.

"You're just like your fucking father," I said to her during one fight, knowing the backlash that would follow. It was a dramatic sentence, like one from a soap opera, and I knew how dangerous it was to say it, but I wanted to see the look in her eyes when presented with the truth.

Punishment and much cleaning would surely follow either of these comments, so most of the time I chose my words carefully. But as I got older, I became more and more bold. Fuelled by my teenage hormones most likely, I was determined to make my voice heard.

During one of Mom's mentally low points at Dungeness Meadows, she was trying to clean the bathtub by herself. A self-induced cleaning day, so Katie and I were staying well out of her way. We were playing Crash Bandicoot on the PlayStation 1, with me trying to teach Katie how to jump over gaps, which she was generally terrible at. She'd fall down the same gap every time, after the big stone roller rolled across the screen, and we'd collapse into laughter. Falling down the gap became a bit that she'd do on purpose to make me laugh again and again, the little orange bandicoot character an eternal sacrifice to the Gods of Comedy.

Katie would eventually get frustrated and say, "Can you jutht do it? Jutht get me patht thith part though and I'll do the retht." Her lisp was still going strong, and between that, her glasses and her mullet (Mom's handiwork), she was a scrappy-looking six-year-old, and too cute for words.

As Katie jumped Crash Bandicoot down the gap again, we heard a bloodcurdling scream from the bathroom. I jumped up to see what was wrong and Mom ran out, limping. She held her foot up to me to reveal that the metal bathtub filter that normally sat at the bottom of the tub to catch hair and things – with six metal spikes on the bottom that held it in place – was fully stuck into her foot.

She screamed again, in pain and terror. Her eyes expressed wild panic. I knew this routine. The adult was gone again, and instead of my 38-year-old mother there was a scared child in front of me. "Get it out!" she howled, taking in huge gasps between yells to make them as loud as possible.

I screamed too. "Mom, I don't know what to do!"

"Get it ooooouuuutttt!! Oh my God, oh my God, pleeeease." Tears streamed down her face.

I somehow managed to get the metal filter out of her foot, it fell to the floor and six holes in a perfect circle appeared on her heel and started gushing blood. I called 911, then Grandma Lora and Grandpa Woody. She was taken to the hospital and had her wounds cleaned out and was then given a tetanus shot; I waited at home with Katie for Grandma and Grandpa to arrive.

As we watched Mom get into the ambulance and drive away, I held Katie's hand while she cried.

"It's okay, Katie," I said. "Mom will be back later, she just has to get her foot fixed. C'mon, let's go inside." We casually sat back on the couch and un-paused Crash Bandicoot, which had been waiting patiently for us. Katie jumped down the gap again. We looked at each other and laughed.

10.

The number of wanderers Mom took in at Dungeness Meadows was at an all-time high. There was a woman named Cassie who moved in with us after being in prison for a year for assaulting her boyfriend. Katie and I had gone with Mom to visit her in prison a few times, Mom speaking to her through glass via a corded plastic phone, Cassie in a brown jumpsuit, me running around after Katie trying to keep her away from the unused telephones.

Cassie had piercings and at least half a dozen men's names tattooed all over her body. "Sean" on her wrist, "Tyler" on her throat, "Chris" on her left breast. A lesson that refused to be learned, voluntarily on display forever. Cassie would bring home weird guys, and they'd have sex on our couch, which I could hear at night. She eventually went back to prison, and we never saw her again.

Then came Tiffany and Willow, a single mother and her 18-month-old daughter. Mom met them in line at the DMV (Department of Motor Vehicles, where you go to get your driver's licence renewed and so forth). Tiffany was a very tall, modelish brunette with a short brown bob and a face like Sarah Jessica Parker. She was stylish, feminine and very insecure. Mom gave her psychic readings and general life advice about how to pick the right sort of partner, instead of the toxic men she'd been with up to this point. As with all of Mom's lost souls, after they became friends, Tiffany and Willow were over at our house almost daily. Willow was a shy, still-nearly-bald baby, toddling around with a few tiny wisps of blonde hair. Her smile was very coy. When I tried to make her laugh, she'd tighten her lips and look as if she was trying very desperately not to laugh, though you could see her eyes cracking up while she buried her head into her mom. As far as lost souls went, they were tolerable.

Early in 2000, Mom's mother, Grandma Lora, was diagnosed with breast cancer at age 70. Grandma suddenly became the focus of the whole family, and my aunts frequently came back and forth to Sequim from Seattle (a three-hour journey) to be with her. Grandma Lora was scheduled in for a double mastectomy only a month after she was diagnosed, and she was to be in the hospital from 17 March, a Friday, for at least a few days. The whole family came over to Sequim to support her, help care for her when she was released and help Grandpa Woody with anything he needed. Aunt Kelley was staying at ours with her boyfriend. She had a grey plastic boot on her foot, up to her calf, from a recent ankle surgery. Tiffany and Willow were also staying with us, so the house was very crowded, and we were all getting on each other's last nerve. Sleeping arrangements were tight. Little Willow was in a travel cot in our room, Tiffany on the bottom bunk beside her (normally Katie's bed), Katie on the top bunk (normally my bed), me in Mom's bed with her, and Kelley and her boyfriend on the couches.

The day of 18 March, because we were all at each other's throats, Mom and Kelley had the idea to have us all sit in a circle and have each person in turn go round the circle and say one thing we liked about each of the others. A lot of people said I was smart, and a lot of people said Katie was funny.

"You have a beautiful singing voice! You just learned how to harmonize, and you're so great at it, especially on 'Truly Madly Deeply' by Savage Garden," Mom said, sort of to me, but mainly to everyone else. I rolled my eyes.

It was a Saturday, and the adults had all decided they wanted to go to a karaoke bar in Port Angeles that night. They were going to leave us kids at home, with me in charge of Willow and Katie, but Mom decided at the last minute to stay home too because she "wasn't up to it". We watched *Peter Pan* on VHS in the living room before bed, with Willow and Mom on the couch, and me and Katie in our PJs on the floor, level with the TV, under a blanket together, leaning against the couch. "I want more popcorn!" Katie said as I passed her the bowl, now mainly white crumbs and buttery hard kernels that she'd slowly suck all the butter and salt off before throwing them back into the bowl.

I caught her doing this, realized that she'd probably been doing it all night and that we'd all inadvertently been eating popcorn covered in Katie's spit. "Aw ewww . . ." I said, laughing. Katie laughed back at me. I kissed her on the forehead.

I went to bed in Mom's room. It was the bigger of the two bedrooms and had an added-on bathroom. The master bedroom and bathroom together took up the entire back section of the house. The bed was pushed up against the back wall, with a TV on the long side of the bed, facing it. This looked odd, but with the way the cable plugs were situated on the walls it was the only way to have a TV in that room. I hadn't slept in Mom's bed for at least a few months, and was glad to have an excuse to feel this familiar comfort again. After watching a Conan O'Brien rerun on cable, we both fell asleep at about 12.30am.

This is the last thing I remember before the house was on fire.

Screaming. Blood-curdling screaming. Female screaming.

Roaring, deafening crackling. A blinding light coming from the hallway, too painful to look towards. Unimaginable heat. The wave of heat you feel on your face for a split second when you open the oven, but around my entire body.

I am in the oven. I am on the surface of the sun.

An adult figure running out of the bedroom and into the hallway, only to vanish immediately into pure white and yellow. The screaming continues but is drowned out by the roar of a thousand different substances burning, each with its own unique smell and sound, indiscernible from one other.

I jump out of bed and there's no air. The inhale mechanism

isn't working. Either there's no oxygen around me, or my lungs don't work. I drop instinctively to the floor, where I find I can draw a singular, searing hot breath. The breath stings my throat, but it's a breath, nonetheless. I throw myself under a desk pressed up against the back wall. Flames pour into the room from the hallway and cover the bedroom ceiling, the doorway having turned into a huge flaming mouth coming closer to me every second to try and swallow me. There are no thoughts in my mind at all. The only thing in the world that exists is what's going on directly outside of my body, in this room. I take a deep, smoky breath, get out from under the desk and grab the bulky white HP printer from the top of it.

The windows in this mobile home are triple-levelled (from top to bottom) and double-paned, with a handle you can spin to open them, in the style of a Venetian blind. The panels spin sideways to let in air, and you spin the crank again the opposite way to close them. Each panel is about 2 feet wide, and 6 inches tall. I realized later that had I been any larger than I was – a barely 100-pound, 14-year-old girl – there'd have been no way of getting through those windows.

The printer is burning hot to the touch. I hurl it forwards as hard as I can, into the first panel of glass on the bottom layer. I am standing with the left-hand side of my body facing the window, and the right-hand side facing the flames. As soon as I feel the *SMASH* of the glass, I let go. The fabric on my pyjama shirt boils like prickling stings of metal against my shoulder.

When the first layer of glass shatters with the impact of the printer, the printer and shards of the window pane fall to the floor. One more pane to go. There's no time to get the printer again – it is covered in glass and is on the floor. I grab a drawer out of the desk and do the same movement to the second pane. Another *SMASH*. I feel cool air on my face and, when I turn towards the flames, it is as though the oxygen from the window has given them new life. They shoot towards me, and I feel them licking my calf as I brace my right arm on the metal frame and pull myself, head first, through the broken window and into the relief of the cold night air.

I hit the ground, hands and knees first. The fall was about 6ft. I don't feel any pain, only panic and urgency and my own shaky breath. It is quieter outside, and the sky is dark. I hear myself shakily breathing in and out. I run, barefoot, across the cold gravel of our driveway and along the side of the house, past the front door.

The smell of that night is something that, to this day, I can recall at will. I have never smelled it again, in all the years since. I've gotten whiffs of certain ingredients of it, but never that exact smell. It was the scent of burning plastic, burning wood. Hot ash and cold, corroded metal. My singed clothes, my singed eyebrows. The smell of a tea towel that goes on fire in the kitchen; the smell of burning hair and flesh, coming from my own body. The smell of an open wound. The smell of panic and the smell that nothing will ever be all right again. The smell of everything in my world being put into a pile and burned in front of me.

I reached the front of the house and saw many things simultaneously; Mom was lying on the ground in the middle of the street. She was wearing only a t-shirt and was on her back, her legs bent, covered with blood that had streaked down her thighs and calves as her knees moved back and forth, front to back, in slow motion. Her eyes half shut, she moaned, in a low, deep voice, "Oh my God, nooooo." She was sobbing, as hard as I've ever seen her sob, intermittently letting out a scream as though she was waking from a nightmare in a horror movie. The little toddler, Willow, was walking around the grass at a steady pace, arms outstretched, red-faced, and mouth open as wide as it would go, crying full pelt, her head bald and red on top, in her white zip-up onesie, not knowing what was going on and presumably looking for any adult to comfort her.

Then I raised my eyes to the front of the house. It had a wide, sloped roof, coming to a point in the middle. Two large windows took up the entire front of the structure. Every day when I came home from school, I'd see our red curtains hanging inside, our couch and TV on the left, and our bookshelf and dining table on the right. All they contained now was screaming, angry flames and black smoke. The entire house was a pyre. Something on the inside went *CRACK, SMASH*. Each window coughed out flames that reached 15 feet into the air. And in the middle of it all was a huge, black, twisting, billowing smokestack that rose up, up, into the blackness of the sky and into infinity, blocking out the stars and moon. I heard later that some people saw the smoke from more than 30 miles away that night.

I saw our home, ablaze in front of me, felt the heat beating against the front of my body despite me being 25 feet away from it, our house being taken by fire, and I knew.

It was only a split second, because that's all the time I could spare, but I knew. It wasn't even a fully formed thought. It was already there. As though the thought had always been there.

Katie's dead. Katie's gone.

That's done now, I thought. *I was right. I always knew she'd die. I always knew this would happen.*

I'd cry for her in my bed because I knew it was inevitable. There was never anything wrong with me. I was right.

I WAS RIGHT. FUCK YOU.

My sister, who I gave a ride to on my bike to the bus stop every morning, in the dark, in the rain, who balanced on a couch cushion that lay across the middle bar, who I'd tell to hold on tight to the handlebars or else she'd fall off.

"Okay!" she'd answer, excitement in her voice every time. "Faster, Krythtal, go faster!"

HOW THE FUCK COULD YOU LET THIS HAPPEN?

Katie, who wore glasses and told me, in her lispy six-year-old voice, that there was a little boy on her bus who was bullying her every day before school, and I got on the little kids' bus with her to speak to this boy and tell him to leave her the fuck alone – to protect her, because that was my job, as her big sister.

I FUCKING TOLD YOU.

The little baby Katie who I was so desperate to meet. The little baby I held when I was eight years old, who I kissed and held her hand until she fell asleep. The little baby I'd whispered to that I'd always keep her safe. The little girl who people would stare at in restaurants because she loved crab legs and clams and baby corn and okra and chickpeas and a bunch of other weird stuff that kids aren't supposed to like. Katie, who stood up in church when the choir got up to sing for the third time and shouted, "NOOOO, NOT ANOTHER SONG," cue the whole congregation erupting with laughter at the four-year-old with no filter.

WHY DON'T YOU GET THE FUCK UP?

Katie, who I named after my favourite book when I was very little. Katie, the sister I'd always dreamed of having.

WHY DIDN'T YOU KEEP HER SAFE?

Katie, the face I see whenever anyone asks me if I have any siblings, and the choice I have to make at that moment, to acknowledge her and make someone feel sad or awkward or guilty, or pretend she never existed, and make myself sad and feel like a small part of me has quietly died again, and hoping that Katie can't see somehow that I said to them, "No, I'm an only child."

WHY DIDN'T YOU LISTEN TO ME?

A part of me did die in that fraction of a second. Something came alive too; I was changed. It wasn't when I woke up and the house was on fire around me. It wasn't when I broke the window or dove out head first. It wasn't when I saw Mom or called 911 from the neighbour's house or called Grandpa Woody or woke up and cried in the hospital or went to Katie's funeral or talked about it in therapy.

It was this second; looking at the front of the house, smelling my own flesh burning and hearing my mother writhe and cry on the ground and knowing Katie was gone forever. *That's done now*, I thought. *Okay*. An inhale, and I had to move on.

I ran to the house directly to the right of ours; it was

surrounded by evergreens and I banged as hard as I could on the door. A man answered, and I burst past him and told him I needed to use his phone to call 911. "They're already on the way," the dispatcher woman on the other end of the line said.

I then called Grandpa Woody. He lived a 20-minute drive away. I still, to this day, have Grandma Lora and Grandpa Woody's phone number memorized.

"Grandpa, the house is on fire," I said.

"Hold on, give me a second to wake up," he said.

Because Mom is the living embodiment of the Boy Who Cried Wolf, Grandpa understandably didn't have the sense of urgency the situation required at that moment. I said something else, trying to convey to him how serious this was, and he asked, "Well, are you all out, and are you all okay?"

I hesitated.

"Yeah," I lied.

Wow. Why did I say that? I wondered, even at that very moment.

I was 14. The weight of escaping from a house fire, getting burned, losing Katie, phoning 911. I couldn't explain all that to Grandpa Woody. I'd done enough.

I ran out of that house and back across the street, to where Mom still lay on the ground, moaning, with her hands up to her face, covered in blood. I tried to herd the little girl Willow out of the street. An old lady, about 70, who lived directly across from us and was out of her house and visibly upset, told me to come into her house to "run your hands under cold water". I did as she said and stepped into this mobile home I'd never seen the interior of before, and into her very small bathroom. I looked in the mirror. My long brown hair hung around my face, singed at the top, and my face was blackened with soot and ash, my forehead dark and shiny. I ran the tap and as I put my hands under the water, I looked down at them more clearly.

There are countless movies and TV shows where someone runs through flames, or is caught in an explosion, or a horror movie where someone is on fire, or a superhero movie where Two-Face the Batman villain has half of his face burned off. Even in films where gore is a big part of the entertainment, none of the depictions of freshly burned skin look anywhere near the way my hands looked, standing there in this bathroom. The skin was completely off, singed around the edges of the back of them, and stopping at the knuckles where my fingers started. The middle was bright pink and shiny, and there were hundreds of little white circles equally spaced out where my skin used to be. Like teeny tiny doughnuts. *These must be my pores*, I thought. I was surprised. I had no idea I was burned at all, let alone that my skin was off.

Still, I felt no pain. I ran the tap and shakily put my hands underneath them. I walked back outside and Mom was in her same spot, continuing her episode.

This was another moment when something in me snapped. The culmination of everything I'd had to do in my childhood came to a head. Here I was, burned, shocked, a child with no parent, and I ran around calling emergency services, calling Grandpa, herding the toddler out of the street, rinsing my hands under the cold tap, trying desperately to do the next right thing. And here was Mom, also burned, yes, also shocked, surely. But as usual, there was no adult here. The sight of her lying down crying wasn't surprising; it was typical. Everyone always felt so bad for Mom. But I couldn't any more. Of all the things I felt, my sympathy for Mom was spent. She could lie there crying if she wanted. I wasn't helping her any more. I was done.

When I looked up at the house, I saw that Aunt Kelley had just arrived back from karaoke with the other adults: Tiffany, Willow's mom, and Kelley's boyfriend. Kelley was at the back door, screaming and trying to kick it down with her grey plastic boot. She told me later that she had driven up and only seen Mom and Willow, and thought that both me and Katie were still inside.

"Kelley!" I cried out. She came away from the door thinking that we were both out, and then realized it was only me.

Tiffany ran out of her car up to her little girl, yelling, "Oh my God! Oh my God!"

I glanced at the side of our house and the man whose phone I had used to call 911 was standing in our driveway, with his garden hose, pointing it at the house and spraying water into it. He looked nonchalant, and it struck me as utterly ridiculous.

Two ambulances arrived. Medics led me onto a gurney, and I was given an oxygen mask and secured before they lifted me into the aid car. I turned my head sideways on the gurney to take one more look at my house before it was gone forever. Once in, I was immediately put under sedation. I can see now why they sedate people who have just suffered trauma. I could pretend the bad dream was over, at least for now. The last thing I saw was the female medic's face, blonde hair pulled back in a ponytail.

"Okay, Krystal, I'm going to ask you to count down from a hundred."

"Okay. One hundred... ninety-ni—" Everything went black.

11.

A completely white room came into fuzzy focus. White walls, white sheets, white sky outside. *Too bright*, I thought. My hands and arms were bandaged. I felt bandages on my forehead. Tube in my arm. I was dizzy and confused. Kelley and Dad were there. Kelley had tears in her eyes, looked at me and said, "Katie's gone, honey."

I knew this, of course, but at this point there was still a very slim chance that it had all been a bad dream. I sobbed. "Oh... oh, what am I gonna do without Katie?" I said. Kelley hugged me and we cried together. Dad put his arm around me too. "I know, I know," he said.

I don't know how long the three of us stood there crying, but it's all I remember until I fell asleep again.

I was in the ICU for two days. This is where they put people who are very badly injured and need constant care and supervision; when they can be sure the patient is healing and recovering satisfactorily, they move them to another injury-specific ward. They had me pumped full of pain meds when I was in the ICU, so I only remember flashes of this time. Crying with Dad and Kelley, and doctors and nurses coming in to check my vitals, and being given apple juice to drink even though I kept asking for water.

"We can't let you drink water, unfortunately," they said.

Apparently, it was because even digestion reduces your body focusing on healing, and when digestion happens, they need it to be something with sugar and vitamins as well as hydration so that your body gets a three-for-one for its efforts. I can't stomach apple juice to this day because it reminds me of this time in the ICU.

After about 48 hours, they moved me to the children's burn unit. I was in a large-ish room with a couple of other patients who never made much noise. There were curtains between me and them, so they remained mystery patients, and I didn't care anyway.

Dad was there beside me, every day. He'd come and sit with me, and we'd watch TV or talk. I'd sleep most of the time.

On the third day, when I'd been moved out of the ICU, they asked me if I wanted to go and see Mom. She was also in the ICU and stayed there for two weeks in total; for the first few days, they weren't sure she would make it, so they kept her unconscious.

"You must really want to see her, but we need to make sure she's stabilized before she has any visitors. I know it's hard, but you'll hopefully get to see her soon," the nurse would say, eyebrows raised in the middle and a tone of empathy in her voice.

I'd smile and nod, but in reality I really, really didn't want to. I hoped she was never well enough for visitors. I had no idea what

I'd say to her. But of course there was no way I could say this out loud, so when the time came I just sucked it up and went.

Let's get this over with, I thought.

I walked into Mom's room and saw a red-faced woman with no hair and with tubes coming out of her body from every direction. There were countless monitors doing their duty of rhythmic beeping. Her face was mostly covered by an oxygen mask, and her eyes were closed. The room smelled awful. I wanted to leave, and never come back.

"Tracy," a nurse said, "Krystal's here to see you." A weak, scratchy, high-pitched voice came from behind the mask, fogging it up as it squeaked, "Hi, honey..."

"Hi, Mom." *Please don't expect me to say anything more than this*, I prayed. I kept my face completely neutral.

I knew that all of human society would agree that there was only one emotion that was appropriate to feel in this moment: pity. Overwhelming pity. It cascaded towards Mom like a gas, flooding this hospital room and infecting everyone who gazed upon her. The nurses, her sisters, the beeping machines, the bed and the plastic sterilized tubes all felt bad for this poor woman. The caring faces whose eyebrows scrunched in the middle and whose mouths asked what more they could do to help.

This poor woman. This unimaginable tragedy. What else could you feel? She'd been through so much and now here she lay, burned, with an oxygen mask, barely able to speak to her one remaining living daughter. What a tragedy, what a loss. Life is so unfair.

But I didn't feel pity. I felt anger. I was old enough to know that this was the wrong thing to feel, so I kept my face blank and my body went numb. *If you can't feel the right thing,* I thought, *better to feel nothing.* I had a lot of practice going numb in my early years, but after the fire, I perfected it.

In *Star Trek: First Contact,* there's a scene where Picard and Data are about to go in and fight the Borg, and Data starts feeling fear, so he flips a switch on his head and turns off his little emotion chip, to the envy of his crew mates. When I saw that, I recognized myself.

I felt as though everyone wanted me to say something to Mom, as I stared at her in her hospital bed. Maybe they expected me to break down crying at the sight of her, or tell her about Katie, or apologize that I couldn't do more, or just anything that resembled a scene from a Hollywood movie. *Well, fuck that,* I thought. *You can wait as long as you want, but you're getting nothing out of me.* When it became obvious that I was just going to stand there saying as little as possible, they let me leave, to my relief.

I went back to my own room, where I spent countless hours in bed in between Dad and other family members sitting with me. My daily routine was showering with clingfilm on my open wounds to keep water off them, and then stepping out of the shower while a nurse held up a towel in front of my body to give me some privacy. After that I'd sit on a stool while she applied the most soothing white cream I'd ever felt all over my back, hands, right arm and right leg. It was called Silvadene, and I loved it. It smelled like paraffin and soap and was white with a silvery sheen to it, and it instantly soothed my skin. The nice nurses sent me home with tubs and tubs of this stuff, because they knew I liked it so much (and probably because it was medically necessary).

I had been in the hospital four days total when I got a phone call to my bedside. It was a girl in my grade, who I hadn't spoken to in a few years, and she could barely speak through sobbing and gasping. "H-hi, Krystal . . . I . . . just wanted to say . . . I'm s-so sorry for what happened to you and . . . and . . . to hear about K-Katie . . . I remember when we – we played tag in your back yard, she was . . . so c-c-cute, and . . ." she broke down into sobbing. "I just wanted to tell you . . . I remember her."

My throat and face felt like they were on fire, not from sadness, but from embarrassment. Oh my God. Did the whole school know now? I hadn't thought about this. I had no idea what to say to her.

"Thanks," I said. "Yeah, I remember that." We hung up.

Please don't let this become a trend, I thought. I hung up the phone without saying more than five words to her.

On day five, a young woman, maybe about 21, came in and told me she was a volunteer and asked if I wanted her to read to me. I was obviously a bit old for this, but I felt like it would be rude to say no. I was reading *Harry Potter and the Prisoner of Azkaban*, and told her to go ahead and pick up where I'd left off. She read with gusto and feeling, giving all the characters voices, and I immediately realized I should have told her no, it's fine, and freed up her time to go and read to some eight-year-old who would enjoy this a lot more. Dad came in while she was reading at my bedside, and made a face like "Whoops, didn't mean to interrupt" and after a few minutes he gave me a wide-eyed, raised eyebrow look that communicated, "Wow, even I know you're too old for this." The girl asked if I wanted her to stop so Dad could visit, and I said, "Yeah, that's enough, thanks."

She left and Dad said, "What the hell was that?" We both burst out laughing.

12.

When I'd been in the hospital for about a week, Dad came to my bedside and woke me up at about 6am.

"Hey, Krystal," he whispered. I could detect a glint of childlike excitement in his voice. I, however, was literally lying in a hospital bed, extremely tired and groggy. "Krystal. Krystal, hey. So, they're about to blow up the Kingdome. I was thinking we could go watch it from the parking garage."

"The what?" I yawned. I didn't fully understand what he meant. The Kingdome was the big sports stadium in the city centre of Seattle. I always thought it looked like a giant boob.

"The Kingdome!" Dad said, urgency in his voice mounting. "They're demolishing it. In, like, 15 minutes. No one's allowed near it and the best view is from here in Harborview because we're up on the hill." Dad seemed genuinely excited.

"Nooo, Dad, I don't want to." I turned over.

"No, seriously, Krystal, c'mon, c'mon, c'mon, it's gonna be really cool, let's go." He shook my shoulder very gently, stepped towards the door and pointed at it with his head and left hand, urging me to hurry.

We wandered to the parking garage, me being flabbergasted that no one stopped us. Me, a 14-year-old burned girl in a hospital gown and slippers, trailing behind a 37-year-old man in a baseball hat. The nurses smiled at us as we left; they must have known Dad by sight now. We stood at the edge of a concrete barrier, looking out towards the Kingdome and the entire city centre of Seattle. Beyond the Kingdome was Puget Sound, a huge body of water that was now filled with boats and yachts of rich people who wanted the best possible view of the demolition. Long, low-pitched foghorns sounded from the stationary boats, everyone announcing their anticipation of watching the 24-year-old sports stadium that was about to be obliterated.

We waited, Dad checking his watch.

"Five more minutes," he said. That seemed like an eternity. While we stood, I started shivering, and Dad wrapped his coat around me.

We heard a sound like a gunshot, followed immediately by another, and another, and another. The huge, grey-domed structure started pelting up smoke from the rafters, each loud *SNAP* coming two to three full seconds after we saw the corresponding cloud of dust, because of how slowly sound travels and we must have been at least a mile away. I recall one single plastic banner being shot very high into the air, as though the stadium was waving a white flag, saying goodbye.

The sonic boom was intense and went through my body like a poltergeist. While I was feeling so numb, this was welcome.

The dome imploded, folding in on itself while dust poured upwards and outwards in every direction. An intense wave of sound and air radiated through the city, and I heard far-off applause and whooping, and all the foghorns blasting from their boats again and again, sounding everyone's approval of the big explosion.

The white-grey dust travelled outwards, as though a giant had smashed the hamburger-shaped structure with its fist, then upwards, becoming just another slow-moving cloud in the atmosphere, blending in with the rest of the air on earth. The materials that made up the Kingdome were now unbound from their mould, and wherever they settled, no one would know or care where they'd come from. It didn't matter. They could become something else now. Being a part of the Kingdome had been just a blip in their existence. The microscopic pieces could settle on the side of a mountain, or sink to the bottom of an ocean, or gather in the corner of someone's back porch, listening forever to the sounds of a family laughing and fighting and a dog shaking off its wet back after the kids had sprayed it down with the hose. The dust could float up into the atmosphere, and be rained down upon me as I stood, years from now, wondering what more I could have done. Thinking daily, weekly, of how I could have saved her. Standing there looking out at the Kingdome implosion was the first time my brain involuntarily attempted to solve this problem that it couldn't grasp had no solution.

I could have wrapped myself in the blanket, I thought, looking out to the sea. *I could have wrapped myself up and it would have protected my skin from the flames and I could have grabbed her and thrown her out the window before me. Yes. That's what I should have done.* I played the scenario out in my mind, as I'd do thousands of times after this. *I'd have wrapped her inside the blanket too, so we were both protected.*

I stood, red-faced, scrawny, in my light-blue hospital gown tied at the back, next to Dad. We stood in silence, watching the cloud of dust disappear completely. The falling Kingdome and the entire city of Seattle were unaware of me or anything I'd gone through. It was comforting, and thrilling. "It's the End of the World" by REM started playing in my head. Dad played this in his car a lot, so I associated it with him, and with Seattle. And as the Kingdome dust was fading away from all sight and the thoughts of what I could have done pushed to the back of my mind, I felt fine.

13.

Dad's side of the family all stood in a row together, at the foot of my bed, facing me, early-morning light streaming in through the windows and lighting up everyone's left side. I was grateful to see them all, but hoped they wouldn't run into any of Mom's side of the family while they were here. Grandma Sharon and Grandpa Melvin, Dad's two brothers, Uncle Chuck and Uncle Terry, and Dad's sister, Aunt Janet, all looked at me, telling me they loved me and would be there for anything I needed.

Mom's parents, Grandpa Woody and Grandma Lora, couldn't come to see us because Grandma Lora was still recovering in Sequim from her mastectomy and needed constant care from Grandpa Woody.

After three weeks in the children's burn unit of Harborview Hospital, they released me into Dad's care. The nurses trained Dad on how to treat and redress my bandages every day, and I was to come back to the hospital weekly for checkups to see how I was healing. Dad lived about a 40-minute drive from the hospital, in an apartment in Mountlake Terrace. He had taken a lot of time off work and had to get back while I was living with him, so most days I spent on my own in his apartment, which I didn't mind at all. We'd wake up, Dad would clingfilm my back so I could shower, then he'd put the lovely Silvadene cream on my wounds, tape fresh bandages to my back and leave me to my big day of watching TV and eating whatever the hell I wanted out of his cupboards until he got back in the evening and cooked us dinner.

My weekly checkups at Harborview consisted of me going to an outpatient children's care unit. All the staff there had some sort of disability. The secretary was in a wheelchair, another worker had burn scars, and the administrator who would take my information and have a big chat with me before I was examined by the nurse was a very sweet, quiet, black man with muscular dystrophy whose hands and arms were constricted in such a way that it was difficult for him to type on a normal computer, so he had a special keyboard. I guess this was all to make the children visiting feel more comfortable, and I suppose in a way it worked.

I definitely felt more at ease coming into a ward with my beet-red face, covered in bandages, speaking frankly to people who had to live with disabilities their whole lives.

They always had different child experts speaking with me while I visited: someone to check on my mental health, someone who came in with a selection of free books about trauma, someone asking if I was interested in joining a softball team for disabled kids. But a lot of it felt like it was geared at kids younger than me. I smiled and nodded and left, taking almost none of what they were offering.

There was one woman, however, who was a makeup expert and offered to show me how to cover my scarring and redness with thick stage makeup. I accepted this. Finally, something age-appropriate. This woman had short, jet-black hair and dramatic makeup. She looked like Liza Minnelli and was just as intense. She was very glamorous and obviously passionate about her job. "We have a trick in the makeup industry to cover redness – you use a green base to counteract it!" she beamed, her eyes widening.

She had a huge selection of skin-toned pots of makeup, and she used a little white spatula to choose one that most matched my natural (non-burned) skin tone. She slid some onto my face, and used her sponges to blend, blend, blend. I thought it looked excellent.

Oh, this is the shit, I thought. *I can totally go back to school now. Just need to put this stuff on my face every day forever and no one will know the difference.* She gave me loads of products for free.

When I took them home and tried to do the makeup myself, it looked a bit like thick pottery clay sitting atop raw ham. To say it didn't look natural was an understatement, and as for if it made me look better or not, that was very debatable. People who wear makeup tend to look back on their teen years and even their early twenties and cringe at the way they used to do it before they learned proper technique – but I'm going to go out on a limb and say my heavy-duty industrial-grade stage makeup looked a lot more insane than your average experimental teen's.

Mom stayed in the hospital for over three months. She got skin grafts on her back, a major surgery that extended her time there.

After nearly two months of me living with Dad, Grandma Sharon and Grandpa Melvin came up from Oregon to stay with me in Sequim. Grandma Sharon was a month away from retirement, but left her job of more than 25 years working in the hospital cafeteria early to help us. They rented a house in Sequim's town centre and lived with me for five weeks before Mom was released. They bought furniture for the house, cutlery, towels, toiletries, everything we needed.

I felt a deep, inner calm settle over me during the time I stayed with Dad, and then with Grandma Sharon and Grandpa Melvin. Of course I'd stayed with them all before, but never more than a week or two. Something was very different this time.

It was as though I had been wandering through snow, not wearing proper clothes, wind constantly beating my face, and having to turn away from icicles hitting my eyes, then coming into a warm house to take shelter, finally able to take off my wet clothes and warm up by the fire. My body had been through something intense, and at last I felt able to relax and unclench my muscles, which I was unaware had been tensed at all. Someone else was taking care of everything. The feeling I had sleeping in bed at night, someone making me breakfast, lunch, dinner; there always being clean clothes in my drawers, the house always being tidy, no one screaming at anyone else. Was this *really* how they lived, all the time? Do other people live like this too? The thought was there, not fully formed, but the seed of anger that lived in my chest, planted on the night of the fire, rooted itself more firmly.

If I let myself fully feel it, the truth was, I didn't want Mom to come back. I wanted to stay with Dad, or with Grandma Sharon and Grandpa Melvin.

I shouldn't feel like this. I am supposed to miss Mom and be desperate for her to come home. I should want to hug her and talk to her and be with her.

This was why, the week Mom was meant to come home, when her vitals dipped and she was advised to stay in for another week at least, which my Aunt Kelley told me, with sad eyes and a regretful voice – my insides danced a jig.

The thing that absolutely terrified me about Mom coming home, more than anything else, was that she might want to talk to me about what had happened. I say "might". I mean "definitely". I knew she'd want to talk about the night of the fire, in great detail, Katie dying and, most worryingly of all, what had gone on in the time between her running out of the bedroom into the flames in the hallway and her lying bleeding and moaning on the street in front of our house.

Speaking to her about this was the worst thing I could think of. It made me feel physically sick to think of her talking to me, telling me what she remembered, with dramatic flourishes, through weepy eyes and her high-pitched, scratchy, "crying" voice, explaining why she saved the one-year-old, Willow, but couldn't save Katie. I didn't want to know. I couldn't listen to it. I'd rather shove ice picks in my eyes. *Please, please, please, don't make me talk about it. Not to her.*

I dreaded, regularly, the day that Mom would come home.

14.

I was having a good go on my still very red face with the thick stage makeup given to me by the Liza Minnelli woman at the hospital. The other attempts were dress rehearsals, but today was the real deal. I applied it with a small white spatula, like she did, tried to blend it in with my fingers (I didn't have a sponge) and then covered it with a white finishing powder to hide the shininess. I topped it all off with a rectangular white gauze patch that I taped to my forehead to hide the worst of the burns, which were still a bit swollen and very dark red. So, part of the makeup job I'd done was covered by the white patch, but the area surrounding it was sufficiently coated in chalky foundation.

This would be my first day returning to school – in June, close to the end of eighth grade – so I had to get it right. The other major areas of my body that I felt needed to be hidden from view were my right arm and right shoulder, which both had keloidal burns, a type of scarring in which the skin looks swollen and puffy. I never failed to wear a long-sleeved t-shirt over these, no matter how hot it was.

The Sequim Middle School building had just been built the year before; the walls were stark white and it smelled like fresh paint and plastering. The halls felt huge, and the teenage voices echoed, booming around the high ceilings. I stayed silent, sticking with my best friend Chelsea, who stayed by my side and glared at anyone who looked at me. She'd been my best friend for about a year. I was grateful for her, if a little embarrassed sometimes by her performative anger in my defence.

Curious eyes looked at me, some judgemental, some pitying, both equally nauseating to me. There were whispers as I walked by, no one daring to say anything, even though the natural instinct of all 14-year-olds is to shout differences loudly, to proclaim that they've noticed this weird bird among their flock, which needed to be highlighted to confirm their own normality. Of course they knew. Everyone knew. *Why didn't I think of that?* And why was no one saying anything about it? Would someone say something about my burns, or mention my sister? I wouldn't put it past middle schoolers – surely the cruellest creatures produced by the miracle of human evolution.

At lunch, on my first day back, I was standing outside beside Chelsea and the tension became too much for a group of tall, popular jock boys gathered nearby. I heard snickering as one of them glanced towards me and then back at his friends.

Okay, here we go, I thought. *Brace yourself.* The tallest boy took a step out of his circle, started walking towards me, followed by his crew, and said loudly, for the benefit of his friends, "Hey, what happened to your head?", immediately falling into a fit of laughter as if he'd made the quip of the century.

His friends gave light laughs, and they sauntered away. *So, it starts*, I thought. I said absolutely nothing. I felt blank and numb, and I planned to keep it that way.

"FUCK YOU!" Chelsea screamed after them. A little late, I'd say. They were already back inside. Still, a nice gesture.

"I think this is for you." My choir teacher softly smiled, handing me a white plastic Safeway bag, stuffed to the brim with clothes. *Oh, what the fuck now?* I thought. I was sat at the tail end of the front row. He'd come up to me before class started, while people were still finding their seats. All eyes turned to look at me, and at the bag, and I felt my face go red and what felt like a brick sink down my throat and settle in my stomach.

"Oh. Thanks," I said, frowning, looking at the floor. I shoved the plastic bag under my chair, where it remained until the end of class when I abandoned it, enraged that this situation had occurred at all. I didn't fully comprehend this at the time, but someone's mom must have made them take that to school to give to me, because everyone knew that we'd lost everything in the fire, but the student was obviously too embarrassed to do it themself, so made our choir teacher do it. *Moments like this can fuck off*, I thought to myself. *I'd rather have the popular rich jock ask what happened to my head in the courtyard again.*

15.

"Honey, when I heard what had happened, my first thought was, *She needs us, and she needs us now.* There was no question that we would drop everything to come to you and help," Grandma Sharon told me while staying with me, after I'd thanked her for the millionth time. Grandma was delicate and comforting. She smelled like baby powder and her voice sounded like coming home.

To her credit, even though I was a tough egg to crack emotionally, Grandma Sharon tried very hard to speak to me about the fire and Katie.

"What you went through was very hard, and it's normal to feel sad about it. You'll need to let these feelings out eventually," she told me. "You might not be ready now, but just be open to it." She'd smile and give me a big hug, squeezing me hard at the end of it like she was trying to transfer all her love to me in that embrace. When I came home from school, she'd be there, cooking or cleaning, and smile at me, asking how my day was and if I had any homework. I'd get it out and we'd go through it together on the dining-room table which was almost always clear of clutter.

It was about three and a half months from the night of the fire before they finally released Mom. She was to move into the duplex that Grandma Sharon and Grandpa Melvin had rented for us.

The day she came home, my stomach was in knots. I didn't want Mom interacting with Grandma Sharon and Grandpa Melvin. These two alternate dimensions were never meant to meet. Everything she did and said was embarrassing and wrong and felt like a reflection on me.

In classic Mom fashion, she was salty towards Grandma Sharon and Grandpa Melvin as soon as she arrived. Her eyebrows raised sceptically at the furniture they'd bought; she walked around the house, criticizing little things that they'd done. "I can't really have this here because it makes it difficult for me to put my feet up. I have to have my feet elevated while I'm sitting. Oh, there's a TV in Krystal's room? Yeah, we don't allow that. It makes it hard for her to sleep. We don't really watch that much TV." (My insides churned at this statement specifically. We watched *so much* TV. It's basically all we did.) My face went red, and I forced my insides to numb out.

Of course, they couldn't fight back in any way. This woman was burned and had just lost a child and her remaining daughter (me) was horribly injured. The only correct response was quiet acceptance and polite nodding.

When I got a moment alone with Grandma Sharon that day, I could tell she was upset, and I felt like I needed to explain Mom's awful behaviour.

"We love you so much. And we did all of this for you and to help, we don't expect anything in return. I guess we thought she'd at least say thank you," Grandma laughed.

"I know. I think she feels a little sad that you guys have been the ones who have taken care of me so well after the fire, and that she couldn't," I said. I don't know where I got these sage words of wisdom from, but they sounded good. The best possible explanation.

"Ah . . . I actually didn't consider that," Grandma said. "Okay. Of course. She probably feels like we've come in and taken over a little bit." Grandma's brows were furrowed like she was trying to take this explanation on board and let the words relieve her internal resentment. It doesn't feel good to be angry at a woman who has gone through trauma, no matter how difficult she's being, and I helped to make everyone feel better.

Grandpa Melvin packed all their belongings into their minivan himself while Grandma Sharon spoke to me and said goodbye and Mom pottered around in the kitchen. Grandpa Melvin would never, ever let a woman lift things while he was around, and besides, if he was packing up the car, he didn't need to make small talk with Mom. I hugged them both and told them I'd see them at Thanksgiving. Grandma kissed me and waved goodbye from the van as I stood in the doorway, watching them drive away in the warm, early summer afternoon.

They were gone.

Now it's just Mom and me. Great.

As I walked back inside to join Mom, I felt a stomach ache developing.

16.

The house felt cold, and there was an elephant in the room. Well, not so much an elephant as a brontosaurus. There was a blue whale in the room. The Loch Ness Monster was in the room, and we ignored the hell out of it. I liked this – I wanted it to stay that way as long as possible.

What was also in the room was a second-hand, big white plastic computer that I loaded AOL onto, and downloaded Napster. I was so excited to be illegally downloading "Truly, Madly, Deeply" by Savage Garden and that song by Alanis Morissette where she says "fuck". We were back to eating delivery pizza and watching endless television. Back to no laundry ever getting done and the house slowly slipping into chaos and looking like a frat house, but instead of beer bottles, it was pill bottles.

Now and then, Mom would point at the Loch Ness Monster and say, "How are you feeling? Do you want to talk about Katie?" She would sometimes ask point blank like that, with tears welling up in her eyes, eager to see my emotions spill over like hers. She'd put her hand on mine, squeezing slightly in an attempt to get me to "open up".

My neck would clench and my stomach churn. The touch of her hand was clammy and repulsive. *Never*, I thought. *I would rather eat broken glass than share a vulnerable emotion with you.* The thought of it made me feel nauseous. I couldn't say any of this, though. I knew I needed to give her something to get her off my back. Saying any of this would be dramatic (the opposite of my goal) and, similarly, crying and "letting it all out" was unthinkable, so I had to play a predictable middle ground.

"I do feel depressed," I'd say, not making eye contact and giving very little detail, just wanting this conversation to end. She took me to my paediatric doctor in Sequim and encouraged me to tell her what I'd said.

"I feel depressed," I said, sitting on the thin paper cover that lay over the squishy plastic exam table. Just those three words, nothing else. No detail. I didn't know if this doctor knew what we'd been through, or anything about our lives. Although our red skin and scars should have given a clue and, since it was such a small town, presumably everyone knew.

"Okay, well, we can give you something for that. I'd recommend 20mg of Zoloft to start," she said, clipboard in hand. No follow-up questions, no asking about my past or current situations, nothing about diet or exercise or if, I don't know, maybe I'd just escaped a housefire and my only sibling had just died. Nothing.

"Okay," I said. Mom nodded, approvingly. And that was that.

They may very well have been sugar pills for all they affected me. I felt completely numb anyway, so if Mom said I should be taking these pills, and it made her somehow feel like she was doing something proactive, then fine.

Back at the doctor's six weeks later, with Mom, for the follow-up appointment, the same doctor, standing there with her white coat and clipboard, said, "And how is it going on the Zoloft?"

"I still feel pretty depressed," I said. Mom nodded, looking again at the doctor.

"Okay, well, why don't we try doubling the dose?" And that was that. These appointments never lasted more than three minutes, maximum. The doctor was very busy, I'm sure.

I was down in Oregon visiting Grandma Sharon and Grandpa Melvin for Thanksgiving, a yearly tradition for me, when Grandma told me that she had found the Zoloft while she was unpacking my bag for me.

"Sweety, I just feel like I need to say that it's normal that you're feeling depressed. What you went through was so awful. It's important to feel your feelings about this."

I was annoyed with her, despite her being obviously right. I didn't want anyone in my personal business, and I didn't want to have to explain my choices. Besides, both Mom and the doctor said that I should be taking these pills, so surely that was the right thing to do.

"I know," I said. I didn't want to implicate Mom as the reason I was on them, either. I couldn't give Grandma and Grandpa any more fuel to hate Mom, because I'd learned that that only made it more difficult for me. I couldn't stand Mom either, but I wasn't going to join in on a hate fest against her. I had to live with her. I had no choice. "It's not that big of a deal. And I won't be on them forever," I said to Grandma Sharon. Subtext: leave me alone.

I stayed on Zoloft for about a year and then I just stopped taking them, cold turkey. I never discussed it with Mom, or a doctor, or anyone, and no one ever followed up with me about it. I didn't feel any ill effects from stopping them, which, looking back, was miraculous.

17.

"No, please, Mom, please, I'll do anything, just please don't make me go, I just really don't want to see it! PLEASE!" I wailed, I pleaded. I hadn't cried in front of Mom since the fire, but the tears came freely now. They weren't tears of sadness. It was pure fear. Complete terror.

Mom looked at Tiffany, sitting beside her in the van as she slowly navigated the suburban streets. I saw the look Mom gave her. It was a look of hesitation, not being completely sure this was the right thing to do.

"It's just, honey . . . they're going to tear it down in the next couple of days, so this is our last chance to see it. It would really help you, I think, to get some closure if you saw it."

I was scared, but also infuriated. The fear was winning, but I couldn't believe Mom had tricked me into getting into this van on the promise that we were going to get Taco Bell.

"We will still get Taco Bell," she said. "We're just going to stop there real quick."

It was nearly four months after the fire, and the destruction hadn't been cleared away yet for legal reasons.

I sat in the back seat, wailing. *What would it look like? Would it smell the same? Would it be obvious where Katie had been?* But I knew when Mom wasn't backing down. She had obviously decided this was what was best for me, to see the burned-down house as some sort of finality for my psyche, and her mind was set on taking me there. We were almost at Dungeness Meadows.

"I'm not getting out of the van," I said, insolently, my eyes swollen and red.

"That's fine, we can just drive by it," Mom said, then she added, "I want to see if anything is left and maybe get our stuff out of the shed if we can."

We drove the winding road around the golf course through the entrance of Dungeness Meadows, past the clubhouse that resembled a very old Swiss chalet. I held my breath as we approached the space where our mobile home was. Holding my breath only seemed to bring on the feeling that I was going to throw up more strongly, so I allowed breath in again.

The line of trees parted and grey sky showed through the gap in the mobile homes where ours had been, like a row of jagged teeth with one missing. All that remained of the structure was the floor. Mounds of flat, black ash. No walls stood, except for one or two wooden pillars at the back of the house, hinting at the shape the interior once took. Black, shiny, charred bits of wood with grey edges lay in random places everywhere. I looked straight through the space we used to live in, all the way to the woods in the back.

The washer and dryer remained, hilariously I thought, still

looking relatively normal except for the fact they were black now and slightly dented.

The centrepiece of it all was the gnarled shape of the metal frame of the bunk beds Katie and I had shared. It was twisted around itself, like a dead spider. The entire space was surrounded with striped blue-and-white police tape that clearly said, "POLICE LINE DO NOT CROSS". I knew Mom would ignore this.

Seeing it all lifted the dread inside me, slightly. The anticipation of the unknown had been the worst bit, it seemed.

Mom pulled over. She and Tiffany got out of the van and started wandering around the property. As predicted, Mom lifted the police tape over her head and stepped through it casually.

After a few moments, I found some courage and got out, too.

The sweet smell of burned wood, cooled coals and forest surrounded me. *How are these people next to our place living their day-to-day lives with this monstrosity next to them?* I thought.

"This is where our photo albums would have been," Mom said, pointing to a particularly high pile of black ash and coals beside what would have been our front window. She said this, then walked in another direction.

I stood where the cabinet containing our photos would have stood. I kicked some ash aside and felt something solid at the toe of my shoe. "Hey," I said. "Maybe some of the cabinet is still here..." I started shoving ashes away with my feet, not wanting to get my hands dirty, when a dark blue cover showed itself from beneath the ashes. I reached down and opened it up to see a photo, burned only around the edges, of Mom holding me when I was about two years old. "Oh my God. Mom! MOM!"

"What?!" She walked over.

"Look, look, Mom! Some of the pictures are here!" We all dug with our hands and found remnants of half a dozen photo albums. The photos seemed to have somehow miraculously just been burned around the edges like a pirate's map, but the middle of nearly every photo was intact. I still have no idea how this was possible when everything – the walls, the couches, *everything* – had been destroyed. Photo albums from the 1980s. They don't make 'em like that any more.

We took them away and cut away the burned bits, and Mom stuck them inside new albums. The photos have never lost the smell of the fire, and whenever I look at them now, the smell always brings me back to that day.

18.

The daycare nursery that Katie used to attend planted a tree in her memory and put a plaque next to it and invited Mom and me to the ceremony. Mom cried uncontrollably at it. I just stood, dry-eyed, waiting for the ceremony to end. I had had quite enough of Mom's self-indulgent scenes, and the empathy section of my brain seemed to have taken a permanent vacation.

Katie's kindergarten class did a penny drive for us and donated $400 into a savings account to help us get back on our feet. A local orthodontist, who I'd had an initial appointment with before the fire (and who'd mailed us an estimate that was just way more than we could afford), wrote to me offering me free braces which of course we accepted. I don't remember Mom saying thank you for any of this – she'd avoid phone calls. "Don't answer that – I don't have the energy to talk to him right now" or "Just let it go to voicemail, I can't stand that woman", and so it went.

It's such a huge deal in America to have straight teeth – having a messed-up mouth is a sign of being extremely low class and can make you a social pariah. Many jokes in movies, TV shows and stand-up routines confirm this. I was already getting teased at school for my one very high snaggle tooth – my left canine that sat up a full tooth length above the rest of my teeth. And one of my two top front teeth overlapped the other. Because I knew we'd never have enough money to get them fixed, I thought I was destined to basically never smile until I was old enough to have my own money and get them done myself.

There was a sense of the town coming together to help us, which I mostly found embarrassing, but yes, I was mega happy about the free braces. The social potential of not having fucked-up teeth outweighed the social risk of people finding out I got them free because of a family tragedy and because I was poor.

"Thanks so much for this," I said to the orthodontist on my first appointment. "I really appreciate it."

"Well, with what your family's gone through, we thought it

was the least we could do." He was a middle-aged, very thin man with wiry glasses, and he smiled warmly when he said this, a little awkward in his own skin.

After the initial visit Mom never came to the appointments and I was perhaps a little on the silent side, just taking my braces adjustments and walking straight out the door. I wasn't rude, but I was also still technically a child and lacked the awareness of humility and gratefulness that I maybe should have shown. Plus, parents probably usually accompanied their kids to the ortho, getting feedback on how well their teeth were doing, but my parent was nowhere to be seen. In retrospect, it may not have come across so well.

After about 11 months, the orthodontist seemed to have had enough. "Well, I'd say these are ready to come off," he said, sort of to himself, while he ran his latex-covered fingers over the inside of my mouth, poking and prodding. I couldn't believe this. Although there had been an improvement, they definitely weren't totally straight yet, and I knew that the standard amount of time for teens to have braces on was two years. I said none of this, though. I got the distinct impression he was sick of giving thousands of dollars of free treatment to a family that wasn't showing much gratitude. But I was mostly happy with my halfway straightened teeth. It was a huge improvement from where they'd been before. Eventually, though, I broke my retainer, and we never bothered to get a new one (they cost $300, an impossible amount of money for us at any stage of my childhood), so by the time I was 17 my teeth had mostly slipped back to where they were before.

"Well . . . thanks!" I said on my last visit, over the moon that these horrible metal cages were off my teeth forever. *Now I can eat caramel corn.* I was already eating caramel corn, of course, but now it would just be easier.

19.

Oh absolutely fuck this, I thought.

In July 2000, Mom had connected with a man who ran a teen support group in the next city over, Port Angeles, and he had heard what we'd been through and offered me a free spot in the group. The group was called GUTS for Teens, and was owned and run by a man named Glenn Goldberg (who I found out later was a very prolific writer and psychologist; he wrote the foreword for the best-selling book *A Child Called It*) and his group was partially funded by local government schemes, so most of the teens in the group were there by court order, funded by the state. It was a four-day seminar held over summer vacation.

These kids were rough. Some were goths or punks with loads of piercings, most obviously very poor and many fresh out of juvey. Many were in foster care. It was only four months after the fire, and my forehead was still red and shiny, and I still attempted daily to do the makeup the volunteer makeup lady in the hospital had taught me, to little avail. But on the upside, it felt good not to be the most fucked-up kid in the room for once.

There were about 20 of us. The course was in the basement of a church, and we all sat on the carpet, nearly everyone keeping to themselves and trying desperately to take a seat at the back, which was obviously impossible. Everyone's arms were crossed and faces wordlessly expressed, "Fuck this shit", so at least we all had that in common.

Glenn was a very large man with a big salt-and-pepper beard and round eyeglasses; he had rosy red cheeks and a big, bright smile, like a young Santa Claus. He looked genuinely happy to see all of us surly, grumpy, pissed-off teenagers. He perched himself on a high stool at the front of the room, his large body covering most of it and, along with his jovial demeanour, giving the illusion he was floating.

"So, welcome, everyone, welcome!" Glenn beamed. "Just a few rules up top. Firstly, you don't have to participate in anything you don't want to. We're not forcing anyone to do anything, but of course we would love it if you did. Also, no sarcasm in here. If you say something, mean it! I'll tell you a little bit about me and my background." He told us about his training as a counsellor and that he specialized in helping teens. "One of the first assignments I got as a state counsellor was to help men in prison. Oh, by the way, does anyone mind swearing? Is it okay if I swear?" No one made a peep. *Smart move*, I thought. Just imagine any teenager saying they "minded swearing".

"Okay, great. Well, I'll be honest." Glenn's face turned very earnest, and he made eye contact with all of us individually while he spoke. "I didn't really want anything to do with – and pardon my language – these fucking monsters. My dad was abusive to me and my mom, and I wanted nothing to do with these men. I didn't think they could be helped, and I wasn't interested in trying." We were listening.

"I had to do it, though. Because it was my job. And I was shocked, because, as I spoke to these men, and they told me about their own childhoods, I found that almost every single one of them had been abused as a child themselves, and they'd sworn up and down that they would never, ever abuse their families the way they were abused. But as hard as they tried, the cycle of abuse continued." Already, some of the kids obviously related to this.

Later that afternoon, some of the teen counsellors and Glenn did a sketch at the front of the room, with the rest of us seated and watching on the carpet. It involved a dad (played by Glenn), a mom, one teenage kid and the kid's friend. It went something like this:

DAD: (*storms in from work*) These fucking assholes at work I swear to God, fucking idiots all of them, I'm so sick of it. Where's my dinner?

MOM: Oh, honey, you work so hard, you're right, here, have a beer. (*Dad takes the beer and starts guzzling.*)

DAD: You look like shit as well. When I come home, I expect dinner to be on the table and maybe you can try and clean yourself up a little bit too.

MOM: I'm sorry, honey, it's just been a busy day . . .

DAD: I'm going to the bar. (*Dad leaves and slams the door.*)

TEENAGE KID: Mom, why do you let Dad talk to you like that? You don't deserve that.

MOM: Well, what the fuck do you know? You lay around here all day not helping, you have no idea what it's like to have all that I have on my plate, you're an ungrateful little shit, so don't you tell me what to do! I don't need it from you too! (*Mom storms out.*)

TEEN: (*starts pacing angrily, picks up a teddy bear and slams it to the floor*) Shit.

(*Teen picks up the phone and dials.*)

FRIEND: Hello?

TEEN: Hey, what you doing?

FRIEND: Just smoking a bowl.

TEEN: Sweet, can I come over?

FRIEND: Yeah, come on over. See you soon.

(*Teen leaves.*)

END

The sketch was stupidly simple, but very effective. Glenn came over to us and asked, "Can anyone relate to the sketch we just saw?" Most hands in the room went up. Glenn nodded. "In therapy, we call this the Cycle of Abuse." He drew a triangle on the whiteboard at the front of the room: at one point was "Enabler", at another "Abuser", at the other "Victim".

He asked us to label the characters in what roles we thought they all played, and how there was crossover in the roles. The father character was an abuser but was probably a victim when he was a child, Glenn pointed out. The mother played all roles at some point in the sketch – Enabler, Victim and Abuser. He also pointed out that the teddy bear could have been a family pet. For a bunch of surly teens, we were shook.

We each took turns sitting in the front of the group while Glenn asked us questions. What was our relationship with our mother, our father? Had we ever been in trouble with the law? What's the happiest we've ever felt? And so on. When it was my turn, he came to the inevitable question, "And do you have any siblings?" He smiled softly.

I said, in my best matter-of-fact voice, "I had a sister, but my house burned down in March and she died in the fire." You could have felt a pin drop in the room.

"Wow. So, is that where you got these burns on your forehead and arm?" Glenn asked.

"Yes," I said.

"Okay, well, that must have been really hard for you to go through." His eyes were warm and sympathetic, inviting me to feel any emotion I chose.

I felt bubbles in my throat and my eyes stung with tears.

"Yeah," I said, in a high-pitched whisper, feeling all the eyes in the room burning into me. I kept my eyes on Glenn. Even though this did feel safe, I was still a 14-year-old girl and I knew this was, on some level, extremely humiliating in front of these other teenagers. But it felt like a release, because I hadn't cried about Katie since I woke up in the hospital. Having them look at me and feel their reaction to what I'd been through woke me up to the reality of just how sad it all was. I took a small glance at the other teens and saw a young goth girl's eyes look at me, filled with tears.

"What was your sister's name?" Glenn asked.

"Katie," I said.

"Thanks so much for sharing this with us, Krystal." Glenn nodded, smiling. "You can sit back down now. Who's next?"

After I had shared, it seemed to break open a barrier for everyone else to share their trauma. A very slim girl in ripped jeans talked about how she'd been sexually abused by her father and then had been in and out of hospital for anorexia. A boy shared that he'd started doing drugs at age ten and had been selling them to get food for his little brother. Endless tales of abuse, drugs, foster care and homelessness. It built trust among all of us; a huge weight had been lifted and we all relaxed.

After all that sad shit was out of the way, we had a lot of fun. We did team-building exercises and laughed about stupid, normal stuff that teens bond over, like Beavis and Butt-Head and who in the group we had a crush on.

It was over all too soon, and most of us never saw each other after that; but I'm pretty sure that this was a key point in my teen years that was essential to me not remaining emotionally blocked and dead inside.

"I love working with teenagers more than any other age group," Glenn would say. "Because they're old enough to understand things, but not completely jaded by life yet. Teens are children and are still open to learning. And people grow up and forget how hard it is to be a teen."

When I think of my teen self today, I don't feel like such a different person. I don't understand when people talk about teens as though they're a different species, like they're so different from us as adults. I'm still that girl, and I will never, ever forget how hard it was to be a teenager. As I write this, I'm 38, but when I'm feeling intimidated or shy or angry or hurt, 14-year-old me is right there, and I have to remind her, *You're okay. I've got this. You're safe.*

20.

We drove up to the summer camp on a hot, sticky, August day in our van, the red, melted Ford Aerostar. This van had been parked on the right-hand side of the house when it burned down, so the side of it had a lot of heat damage. The wing mirrors, handles, anything plastic was melted and bubbly, then cooled off in the melted shape. The paint was peeled and brown on one side – the car version of the Phantom of the Opera with his mask off. Every time I got into this van, I had to touch the melted handle to open it. I'd get questions from kids at school, "What happened to your mom's van?" and sometimes I'd pretend not to hear, but if it was unavoidable I'd just say, "It got burned" and walk in the other direction. Best to keep things mysterious.

Following in the tradition of teen groups, especially after how much she saw I loved GUTS, Mom had signed us up for something called "Burn Camp" – a regular American summer camp for kids, the only difference being all the kids at the camp had been burned. A place for kids with burn scars to go and not feel self-conscious about showing their bodies while swimming and enjoying the normal summer activities that most kids can take part in freely. I was to be a teen participant, Mom a camp counsellor.

Mom had sold this Burn Camp to me as the same sort of vibe as GUTS, so I was open to it, even though having Mom there as one of the counsellors already put a damper on my mood. *Hopefully the place will be big enough that I can just avoid her*, I thought.

I wore my hair with bangs now, which covered my bright red, shiny forehead, and I was getting slightly better at using the makeup to cover the scars on my face. I still wore long sleeves, every day of my life, even in 100-degree heat, and held the edges of the sleeves over my hands too, which was uncomfortable but meant I didn't have to worry about anyone asking where I'd got my scars from. I knew that this might change at Burn Camp, because I wasn't the only one with burns, but on the day we arrived I still wore my usual long-sleeved attire.

When we drove up, a very tall, completely bald, Caucasian man greeted us. The scarring over his face was intense and shocking; it affected the shape of his eyelids, but his bright, light-blue eyes shone through when he smiled and greeted us. He then frowned when he looked at me, and I felt that he was thinking that I didn't look burned enough to be here. After all, the worst of my burns – my back, arms and forehead – were covered.

"You must be Tracy and Krystal," the man said.

"Hi! Yes, sorry we're late!" Mom said.

"Well, everyone's in the mess hall having dinner, but I'll show you to your beds so you can get unpacked," he said, still giving me the side eye. I picked up our bags and followed him. *What the hell is this dude's problem?* I thought.

Burn Camp was much like a regular camp, except it had group therapy talks. The first one included me and Mom, and we went around the circle and shared how we'd gotten burned. Mom's moment to shine. She regaled everyone with the story of what had happened to us a few months previous, complete with tears and sobbing, and her hand covering her face. It was all I could do not to roll my eyes.

The camp director, Shaughn, the bald guy who had been giving me side eye, had a look of suspicious about him while he listened to Mom. Most of the people in this group therapy session were children. It was unspoken, but the purpose of the group was for the children to have a safe space to share their stories, and for the adults to share their own stories of being burned in order to support the children. Not, as Mom demonstrably thought, to have a complete breakdown and expect the children next to her to give her support. My face stayed neutral. Everyone looked at her, then at me. *Fine*, I thought. I put a hand on Mom's back. All the burned kids and adults looked at us.

It was all inappropriate, and I sensed this immediately, urging her silently through my hand to stop so that the next child could speak. Shaughn the camp director was not impressed. He let Mom keep sobbing, took in a sharp breath and said, "Okay, we can move on" before she was finished, then moved on to the next child in the group. He had the general air that he had seen it all, been there, done that and wasn't going to let this woman steamroll the support that the children in the group needed. Mom and Shaughn clashed immediately. I knew right away this was going to be a problem; a time bomb ticking away, silently. But Mom seemed oblivious to this.

Mom latched herself on to quite a few teen camp members, telling them our story and having them express great sympathy, some in need of a parent figure themselves. It bothered me slightly, but was also a relief because it got her off my back. The adult camp staff noticed her seemingly codependent relationships with kids, and Mom seemed to know they knew, which only made her behaviour more erratic. She started having multiple breakdowns per day, including once when an ambulance had to be called because she had passed out.

"I'm sorry, I just felt really hot and I started having a flashback of the fire!" she wailed.

I tried my best to ignore her. I'd made friends with some older teens who drove, bringing me on secret beer runs and then ten or more of us piling into their room (some of them were staying in a hotel near the camp) to drink and listen to music. This was freeing – I could get away from Mom completely and she'd let me because we were basically in a large support group and everyone around us had the tone of helping and empathy. It wasn't like there would be any wild teen parties, so she thought. She suspected nothing. A perfect scenario. We'd sit in a hotel room drinking, listening to music too loudly, chatting about sex, and gossiping about hookups at camp and things the adults had got up to that the kids weren't supposed to know. Some of these counsellors had burns, and some didn't – they were just volunteering for school credits, which was why they weren't staying on site at the camp. One of the adult counsellors, a guy who wasn't burned, around age 22, drove me back to camp one night, drunk himself, and asked me, "Hey, if I were younger, or if you were older, would you date me?" I wasn't surprised he asked me this; we had been talking all night about other people hooking up and he had sat next to me and been very flirty. I wasn't attracted to this guy in the least; he reminded me of a real-life Eric Cartman, beanie and all. But he was driving me home and I needed to stay on his good side.

"Yeah, I think I would," I said enthusiastically.

He pumped his fist into the air. "Yesssss!"

I went back to my bunk, in my head "drunk" (in reality, I think I drank about one and a half Smirnoff Ices), and crawled into the bed next to Mom's thinking I was a certified badass.

On the fourth day of Burn Camp, there was an organized trip into town, and the camp director Shaughn wouldn't let anyone drive in the car with Mom, even though quite a few kids wanted to.

I stayed behind at camp. Shaughn took this opportunity to have a chat with me, as he'd noticed that I was silent a lot of the time, especially around Mom. We sat on the edge of a curbside on the edge of the mess hall, the summer heat pounding on my face, making me squint. My arms screamed to be set free from their long-sleeved prisons.

"I'm so sorry for what you and your mom have been through

this year," Shaughn said. "We're going to roast marshmallows in a bit if you want to join? And hey, the great thing about this camp is that we're all burned, so you can definitely wear clothes that you'd be cooler in if you wanted, and no one would care or say anything." I knew he was referring to my long-sleeved shirts and bell-bottomed jeans when everyone else in camp wore shorts and tank tops.

"I know. I'm just not used to them, I guess." Even though he was right, everyone here was burned, I felt like my burns stood out because they were still shiny and a deep shade of red; everyone else's scars were long healed, and the same colour as the rest of their skin.

"Honestly, when you drove up with your mom, I thought to myself, 'That girl doesn't look like she has any burns! She shouldn't be here!' I was worried you'd make the other kids self-conscious," he laughed, and I just looked at him. This completely confirmed what I'd thought when we'd first arrived, and he looked as though he immediately realized he shouldn't have said this and changed the subject.

"Well, this camp is for you to express yourself and feel comfortable, Krystal, so you let me or any of the other adults know if there's anything you need, okay?" I thanked him. Shaughn was all right, but I knew he didn't like Mom, and the ticking of the inevitable explosive that was to detonate at an unknown hour kept me guarded.

"He's such a fucking idiot," Mom said to me quietly about Shaughn. "He told me to stop telling the kids about the things we've been through. He literally said, 'This camp is not about you!'" Her eyebrows raised and her lips pursed, the inner corners of her eyes turning red, like they did multiple times per day at this point. She shook her head, closing her eyes tight and exhaling audibly. This wasn't good, I knew. He had challenged her victimhood, called her out on her act, and that was enough to send her into a panic. He was now the enemy, and I already knew how it would end, although I couldn't have predicted just how dramatic our exit would be.

The few of us who stayed behind at camp while the rest went into town were finishing up lunch in the cafeteria. It was a huge mess hall, relatively empty except for eight or nine of us sitting down with our trays and chatting. Mom was joined by two kids, both about 12 years old, and I sat at the next table over with a friend I had made. Shaughn walked in with a couple of the other adults, carrying bags from town. Mom started laughing loudly, uncontrollably. Mom has the loudest laugh of anyone in this universe, and in an echoey mess hall it was like an air-raid siren.

"Hey! Stop it!" Mom squealed with delight, embodying a giggling six-year-old. She was grabbing handfuls of food from her tray.

Oh God, no. No no no no. Please say she's not doing this. She's fucking lost it.

She pelted food at everyone in the mess hall, some of the kids looking confused, the youngest ones laughing and saying, "Tracy! Hey! Over here!" and flinging food back at her. If she had a right mind to begin with, it was now gone. Her eyes looked glazed, and she had a glint of rebellion like a small child. I froze where I sat, glancing over at Shaughn, who made a beeline for

Mom, accompanied by the camp assistant director and another adult manager.

"Tracy, stop. Stop this. Tracy, we need to ask you to leave the camp, immediately, okay? Please leave now," the woman said in the most hushed, measured, but stern voice she could muster. Her eyes were sober and determined. She held a hand over Shaughn's chest, as though she was assuring him that she would handle this.

Shaughn looked furious. His hands were clenched into fists. I was scared. He walked to the other side of the mess hall, seemingly to stop himself from doing or saying something he'd later regret.

"What? Why?" Mom's tears came thick and fast. "I'm just playing with the kids; I lost my daughter this year! You can't tell me what to do!" The adults ushered us outside. Our melted van was parked right next to the mess hall and our bunks nearby contained all our stuff, so we would have been able to just pick up and leave without much fanfare. But the scene was loud and reverberated quickly; a crowd started to gather.

"Tracy, what's happening? Where are you going?" One of Mom's 12-year-old friends came up and asked.

"They're telling me I have to leave and I don't know why! I'm so confused. He told me I can't talk about what I've been through, and he doesn't want me playing with you kids . . ."

The woman who had initially asked her to leave was now gently pulling the 12-year-old away from Mom and standing between them, saying, "Tracy, please. Just leave, okay? Stop talking to the kids, and just leave."

I jumped into the van and sat there while Mom tried to give

her phone number to a few teens, continuously stopped by the camp managers, who were now becoming increasingly irate. "Tracy, please, we don't want to have to call the authorities. Just leave, okay?"

They stood at the door of the mess hall, arms folded, watching our van as we drove it over to the house with our bunks, packed our stuff within two minutes, then hopped back into the van. They stood on the clay-coloured dirt road watching our van until it was out of sight.

I felt humiliated, but also relieved that we were leaving and would surely never see any of these people again. As I'd done so frequently before, I turned off the part of my brain that made connections with the other people at the camp. They were gone now, they were wrong, we were right and it was just us again.

Part Three

21.

I had my first date when I was starting freshman year of high school. I was 14 and he was 18. His name was John, he was Native American, had long brown hair and loads of piercings and tattoos. One of his tattoos depicted a very busty woman blindfolded, with blood coming out of her mouth. His two hobbies were doing drugs and making jokes about dead babies. This maybe wasn't the best choice of person for me to date, but he lived in a house with a few other guys his age, and a house without parents called to me like a beacon.

We had lived in three more places in Sequim by the time I started high school in the fall of the year 2000, the reasons for moving as wide-ranging as Mom's moods. We now lived next to the skate park at the west end of town, behind a large supermarket. Living behind big supermarkets is a great option if you're poor. It's generally cheap thanks to its undesirability because first, it's ugly, and second, the constant beeping of delivery trucks night and day is disruptive. But on the upside, you're in walking distance of a place to get loads of pretty cheap food.

Mom hated John immediately, which was one of the saner thoughts she had at that time. She forbade me from going over to his house. I was terrified of disobeying Mom, but I started testing the waters of sneaking around, lying, breaking the rules. She'd been accusing me of this anyway for years, so I thought I might as well go for it. She sensed this and started prying into my life in ways that pulled us apart more permanently.

One day while I was at school, she read my diary and confronted me about what I'd written about wanting to have sex, and then attempted to have humiliating chats with me, not just about safe sex, but about "good sex". I'd literally plug my ears and run out of the room telling her to stop. Any trust that existed between us was now completely gone, as far as I was concerned, and I was in no rush to earn any of it back.

I came home one day around dinner time after school and then a few hours hanging out with friends. I was sad and surly and wanted to be left alone, so I went to my room without speaking to her. She barged her way in, so I ran to the bathroom and locked the door, crying, telling her to leave me alone. She banged and banged on the door until I unlocked it, telling me through the door,
"Krystal, if you've been sexually assaulted you need to tell me!"

Where the hell is she getting this from? I hadn't been sexually assaulted. I just hated her and wanted to be left alone.

She's just desperate for something else horrible to happen so she can capitalize on it, I thought. *Aren't things fucked up enough?* To be fair, she was right to be suspicious about me keeping things from her because even if something had happened to me, there's absolutely no way I'd ever tell her about it. She couldn't be trusted with anything important, ever again.

John (the tattooed dead baby boyfriend) came over one night, spoke to me and Mom for five minutes or so, and then I walked him to his car. I didn't exactly tell Mom that I was planning on getting in the car with him, but I didn't not say that either. Truthfully, I absolutely knew she was unaware I planned on going to his place. I just waltzed out to the driveway, got into his car and we sped off. Thirty minutes later, I was sitting on his dirty, ripped, fluffy brown couch playing Crash Bandicoot, and I heard the unmistakable sound of the melted van revving up the driveway. I knew I'd be in deep shit, but I had a plan. A really great one. *I'll just tell her I assumed she knew I was leaving*, I thought. *Yeah.* Watertight teenage logic.

"Oh shit," John said.

His roommate came in.

"Krystal, I think that's your mom. She looks really mad."

John stood up, and it was the first time I'd seen him look truly terrified. He lit a cigarette, so he'd be smoking it as Mom stormed in from the driveway.

"Krystal!" I heard her scream from outside. "Get out of that house RIGHT! NOW!"

Her screams cut through me, and I wondered what I thought I was playing at just leaving the house from the driveway without her knowledge. What did I expect? For Mom to have a rational, calm response to me leaving without permission? *Just stick to the plan*, I thought.

I walked outside, over the porch, and stood there in the driveway looking at her wild grey eyes, framed by the puffy red burn scars on her forehead, topped with a few wisps of thinning brown hair pulled back in a tiny bun that was so tight she looked bald. Her grey sweatshirt with the collar ripped out was wet at the armpits.

Her eyes went wide, and one thin eyebrow was raised.

"Get in this car." She didn't touch me, but her body threatened that she wasn't above it. "Now." She enunciated the last word as though trying to teach someone how to speak English. Then "Now-wuh," she repeated, quieter, her nostrils flared. I obeyed. When we drove away, John watched us neutrally from the porch, smoking. I didn't fully meet his eyes.

Here we go. The plan.

"I'm sorry, I thought you knew I was going," I said, very unconvincingly. Only now, when I heard myself say it outloud, did I realize what a dumb thing this was to say. Mom gave an incredulous, single "Ha!"

"You know damn well I didn't want you going there. I don't ever want you going to that house. And you're not to see him again. EVER again. I cannot BELIEVE you would do something so stupid, Krystal."

To be fair, I couldn't believe it either. Did I really think there was a chance Mom wouldn't create a huge scene and get me to come home in the most dramatic way she could? Was I really that thick? But, for most of an hour, I had been playing video games and laughing in a house with friends where she wasn't present. In my head, that was worth it.

The next day at school, I told John that as far as Mom was concerned, we weren't dating any more.

"Wow, that really sucks," he said. "I hate lying and sneaking around." Quite a mature attitude for this guy to have, but I suppose he was 18.

After that, we pretty much ghosted each other. John and I never spoke again – no phone calls, no chatting at school. One of those endings of relationships that never officially ended. "So hey, maybe we're still dating," I'd sometimes joke to friends, years later.

In reality, I was glad it ended, even though I liked hanging out at his parentless house. He was a terrible kisser. One of those guys who thinks his tongue is the penis and my mouth is the vagina, thrusting in and outwards like a confused anaconda. And even though I was terribly inexperienced, I intuitively knew this was the wrong way to do it.

22.

"Hi, honey. Grandma's had a stroke," Mom said, sighing quickly, a slight annoyance to her voice. "She's in Olympic Memorial in Port Angeles. I just need to call Dad." I knew who she meant. She always referred to Grandpa Woody to me as "Dad". I had just walked in the door. I hadn't even taken off my backpack yet, but already sensed this was a tense day – Mom was dialling another number on the cordless, pacing back and forth. I was worried about Grandma, but knew I should wait to ask Mom for more details.

The family gathered around Grandma Lora once again, my two aunts, Kelley and Tina, coming back and forth to Sequim from Seattle, regularly making the three-hour trip.

I had made friends with a girl named Wynn in the year below me. We met in drama. She was funny, always wore ripped jeans and t-shirts like me, and we immediately hit it off. Her parents, and indeed her household, had a delightful hippy vibe. They were all vegetarian; their medium-sized white house sat on a cute row of houses among many trees in Sequim city centre and was filled with art and handmade knick-knacks. Her dad had hand-built a brick pizza oven in the back garden, which he would use at least weekly. The house always smelled like incense, or spices, or fresh bread. The smell of a house that had been occupied by the same people for years and years.

One cold, dry night in December 2000, Wynn was to have a sleepover at mine and Mom volunteered to drive all three of us to Deer Park Cinemas just outside Sequim to see the new remake of *The Grinch*, starring Jim Carrey.

All three of us had just visited Grandma Lora in the hospital in Port Angeles before heading to the cinema on the way back home. She was very weak, unable to grasp her cup of water or lift her arm or hold a conversation for more than a few minutes without falling asleep. It wasn't nice to see her like this. Grandpa Woody had gone home that day to get some things together and get a full night's sleep at their own house, so it felt a little wrong that we were leaving her alone. I gave her a big hug that she couldn't reciprocate fully, instead leaning her head towards mine and giving my arm a small squeeze.

Mom was sitting beside Grandma with her leg propped up on the bottom of the hospital bed. Mom's legs always needed to be elevated. She gave Grandma Lora a big hug, said, "Love you, Mom," and before we'd left the room, Grandma Lora's eyes were closed again.

We all loved *The Grinch*. Jim Carrey was my first celeb crush, and although he looked hideous in *The Grinch*, I still found this Canadian weirdo endlessly charming, and I hated anything that wasn't a comedy, so that was enough for me. Five stars. Successful movie night.

We left the cinema around 11pm. Wynn and I were finishing the industrial-sized popcorn on the way to the car. Before the movie started we'd poured extra butter from the big, metal squirting pump, available in most movie theatres in America, all over the approximately two-gallon-sized popcorn tub. They call it "butter", but God knows what this tangy, permanently liquid, bright orange substance actually is. It's chemically and sweet and fatty, and probably 99 per cent hydrogenated vegetable oil. Whatever it is, it somehow manages to remain a shimmery liquid until you eat it along with salt and popcorn kernels. Then is the moment it decides to solidify on every surface of your mouth, leaving a fatty coating all around it, feeling like your gums have been dipped in wax. The perfect antidote to this is a huge swig of fizzy dark soda, but then your mouth is covered in sugar, which salt is, of course, great for clearing, so you must start the whole process again.

We got in the car (Mom had now traded in the melted van for a small, used Toyota), and Wynn and I were still passing the trough-sized popcorn back and forth between us, digging determinedly for the M&Ms we'd dumped in it at the start of the movie (this gets them melty). The roads were mostly deserted, a car passing us in the other direction every minute or so. Only a few minutes into the journey, the road curved dramatically to the left and then hard to the right. Wynn and I were in the back seat, laughing about something, when a deafening *SMASH* exploded all around us. *BASH, CRACK.* Windshield broken. Metal crumpling. Our screaming, short but succinct. I knew this sound.

Our bodies shook violently, my head hit the seat in front of me, and then everything was still as quickly as it had started.

The car had halted at an odd angle in the middle-turn lane of a five-lane road. The sky was black. There were streetlights, and nothing but blackness and the tips of evergreens beyond. On the other side of the road was another car. Old, rusted, with its windshield also broken. I saw no one inside.

No sound, except for breathing. My breathing. It came in shaky gasps. I looked next to me. Wynn's face was bloody, and she was weeping.

"Are you okay?" I managed to get these words out, but I wasn't sure I could cope with saying anything else. I felt my heart beating, at what seemed like a million miles per hour. I lifted my hands to have a look, the way I'd done in the bathroom after the fire. They looked normal but were severely shaking. Wynn hadn't answered me so I said again, "Are you okay?! Are you okay!" I couldn't think of any other words. Wynn was breathing shallowly, but seemed unable to speak.

I touched my face and my hand came away, filled with bright red blood. My braces had caught on my lip.

The entire car was filled with glass, most of the windows were broken.

I'd been here before. *Not again.* This time I'd had no warning, no bad feeling. This time came, seemingly, from out of nowhere. I can usually predict dangerous things before they happen because of Mom's moods. She'd seemed fine today. It had seemed like a normal day.

"Mom... Mom? Are you okay? MOM."

No answer. My seat was diagonal behind Mom's, and her head was tilted backwards, leaned against the driver's seat, eyes closed. There was blood coming down her forehead. She was unconscious. "Oh my God... oh my God... oh my God..." I cried. I took a deep breath inwards.

The entire world and the air around us was completely still. The darkness seemed reverent, and the only sounds were my loud, shallow breath, and Wynn's crying. How could no one know that this had just happened? The other car still sat 40 feet away from ours, completely stationary just like ours, front left headlight smashed in and still on, shining in dim streetlights ahead to nothing, as though time had stopped.

Next. What's the next thing? I thought. *Help. I have to get help.*

I unbuckled my seat belt and opened the car door with my right hand. Twisting my body slightly sideways, I attempted to get out of the car. My legs not only wouldn't move, but a bolt of electric pain shot up my pelvis and into my abdomen. I screamed. Shit. *Something must be broken.*

A car finally passed by and a couple who looked like they were in their thirties stopped and called emergency services. We only had to wait ten minutes for them to arrive.

"Everything's going to be okay, an ambulance is on the way," the woman said. "Just don't move. Don't try to move, you may have broken something." I couldn't tell you, now, what this couple looked like, only that I was relieved they were present and helping.

"Mom . . . Mom?" I tried a couple more times to wake her, to no avail. She was out cold.

When the medics arrived, I finally felt like I could break down sobbing, and did. Mom didn't regain consciousness before I got put into the ambulance. I was in a separate ambulance to her, and as soon as the door slammed shut, I asked the medic, point blank, "Is my mom dead?" I felt I needed to know this now, in order to try and deal with the reality of it as quickly as possible. Rip off the Band-Aid, please.

"I don't know," she said, steadying the table of tools in sterilized wrappers beside her. "But I can tell you this. She's getting the best care possible right now."

I said nothing. What a bullshit answer.

She turned away from me and fiddled with my IV while saying, in a slightly brighter voice, "But hey, I do have some good news – you definitely won't have to go to school on Monday! Pretty good right?"

She did not just say that to me. Is this a standard line she uses on all severely injured children? I thought. I wondered how well this had worked for her in the past.

At this moment, she pumped some sort of pain medication

into my IV and I went all woozy. Luckily, when you're 14, and your pelvis is fractured and you think your mother might be dead, people don't really expect you to make much small talk. I lay back on my stretcher and stared at the ceiling of the ambulance, bright light encompassing me, making me squint. The smell of gauze and ointment and blood and latex filling the space. I relaxed, a little bit. For now, I knew my job was just to lie still. I could do that.

Every time I've been on a stretcher, I've felt a small sense of tranquillity. Something horrible has inevitably just happened, you're hurt and scared. Then, very strong, confident, infinitely calm and capable people are strapping you down, lifting you upwards, always perfectly level, making sure every inch of your body is stable and cared for. Their voices are reassuring and kind, telling you they're "going to lift you up now, okay, Krystal? Just relax." Their only priority is keeping you safe. The feeling of rescue. *They've got this.* Thinking of the ember of strength and relief that resides in me in those moments, I can almost understand why some people might seek it out. If you'd felt unloved or unseen, it might be a place that you'd reach for over and over. And just maybe, if it became an addiction, a stretcher would eventually not be enough, and you'd need more and more elaborate forms of care and attentiveness to feel that strength and hope again.

I was air-lifted to Harborview for the second time in ten months, this time straight to the children's ward. I was in hospital for two weeks following this accident, my most major injury being that I'd fractured my pelvis. While I was awake, they cut my orange Powerpuff t-shirt straight off my body in the ER, which I was extremely annoyed by.

I had a catheter in (a tube that leads directly into your urethra to drain your pee so that you don't piss yourself while asleep), I assume from when they'd put me under on the helicopter. They took it out when I woke up in the hospital and, after I was released two weeks later, I noticed that there was a huge hole in my labia. It didn't hurt; it was almost like a gauged piercing. *That must have happened while they were putting in my catheter*, I thought. I never told anyone about this as a kid, because I found it too embarrassing. I just lived with a weird hole in my labia for years. Sometimes tampons would get stuck in it, and I'd have to thread the string through like a needle to get the tampon to come out.

When I was pregnant with my first baby, I asked my midwife if this loop would affect childbirth. Would the baby get stuck in the hole like my tampons had?! She said no, but that I could probably just get it snipped if I politely asked the midwife while I was still under epidural. I did and she obliged, and it hasn't been a problem since. Thanks, NHS. Although now, I really wish I had said something back then. I hope as years pass that teenage girls will feel confident enough to speak up when a part of their body has been involuntarily pierced by a supposed medical professional while they're unconscious.

Wynn had internal injuries as well as a fractured spine, so had to wear a back brace for six weeks. Her parents were horrified and stayed close to us at first, feeling bad for Mom and me and helping us out here and there – we had dinners together and bonded over this shared misfortune. Then, slowly, they faded out of our lives. I felt them backing away from Mom, and Mom told me that they had said some very insensitive things to her, and that was that.

The other driver had had alcohol in his system, so was legally at fault for the accident. There was a trial, where I had to stand up and give my account of everything I remembered from start to finish, and we got compensation for it. It wasn't much, and almost all the money went to medical bills. The man didn't have much to his name anyway, so it wasn't the most lucrative of settlements. Our car was totalled, and Mom had broken a leg, requiring more hospital time and then months of recovery.

After being out of school for about a month, I returned on crutches, which I used for another month or so. There was a point where I didn't need them any more, but used them anyway because I still walked funny and crutches seemed less embarrassing. But no one at school said anything this time, weirdly. I guess making fun of burned-car-accident girl was old, perhaps even too easy.

I know that, at this point, you may be thinking that my life abounded with red flags. I didn't recognize them, of course, because I couldn't have. I'd known no other life but the one I was living. Sometimes I'm angry at other adults for not recognizing it back then. But then I think, what is it they would have been looking out for? This was the peak (or valley?) of Mom's mental illness. If a condition doesn't have a name, it's hard to conceive of it. I am angry, sure, but I don't blame any one person for not intervening, because the situations were always very complicated.

Nevertheless, at this point in my life, after the year of the fire and car accident, I knew I didn't want to be with Mom any more. Luckily, I was old enough to be able to navigate the world mostly on my own, but that didn't mean I didn't still have to see her, all the time. Our fighting at home became volatile, but I was gaining the courage of a girl who realized that she wasn't going to be legally bound to this house for much longer.

23.

"What's the highest math you've taken?" After class one day in freshman year, my chemistry teacher called me aside to ask me this question.

"Business math," I replied.

He looked at me, slightly open-mouthed, and raised his chin. I might as well have said, "Big Bird Counts his Little Piggies! 101."

"Calculus 1 is a prerequisite of chemistry," he said. "So, it's probably why you're struggling with some of the formulas." The gentlest way he could have put it. I nodded, and promptly dropped out of the class.

With very little guidance from a parent figure, or anyone else for that matter, when faced with what classes to sign up for in high school, I had picked the ones I thought looked interesting, or easy. Business math (literally adding three-digit numbers together and things like how to balance a cheque book, which was about two years from being a defunct societal skill) and floral design. I also signed up for chemistry, because I had a whimsical interest in science (watching Discovery Channel documentaries about dark matter and black holes while eating goldfish crackers and Top Ramen). And drama, of course (because at this point I was dead set on becoming an actor).

I'd dabbled in acting in middle school, both before and after the fire – which consisted of things like me hand-writing a scene from *The Breakfast Club* and photocopying it at school, casting myself as the Molly Ringwald character and taking pleasure in casting who I deemed fit to do the other roles. We'd perform the scene only for the rest of the drama class, but I looked forward to these days more than anything else in my life. I still missed a lot of school, but I made sure to come in on scene-performance days.

Then, there were the high-school plays and musicals. Auditioning for roles in real, actual high-school plays seemed like the Big Time. I worked tirelessly on my audition scenes, monologues, songs – and it was obvious to me that most of the other kids auditioning had read the script for the first time literally the second they were on stage, so my competition wasn't exactly stacked.

I landed lead roles in plays straight away, even the ones that were technically for older kids. I played Cherie in *Bus Stop* as a freshman (14 years old, grade nine), even though it was the senior class play which should have involved only 17- and 18-year-olds. But none of those older kids could act, or do a southern accent, so the role was mine. I also played the teacher in *Up the Down Staircase* as a sophomore (15 years old, grade ten), the leading role again, in the senior class play. You would have thought this would give me a lot of clout and popularity, but no one at my high school cared about the school plays. Sequim was more of a sports and farming town, and plays were for the rejects and losers.

There was a boy named Corey in the year below me, who I met in drama. He asked me to a school dance when we were 14 and 15 respectively. Corey was the same height as me, blond, very skinny. He wore thick black-framed glasses and did coding in his spare time. He loved gaming and indulged in being intellectually superior to the other "morons" at our school. He wasn't traditionally masculine, maybe even a little camp, and was completely non-apologetic about it. When he'd get made fun of, usually the taller jock guys calling him "flamer" or "faggot", he'd snap back with smart comebacks that included big words they couldn't understand. When we started dating, we were inseparable.

Mom hated him immediately. You would have thought, compared to John (the smoking boyfriend with the bleeding busty-gal tattoos), she would have been relieved that I was seeing a sweet, non-threatening computer nerd. But apparently, it didn't matter who I dated. Anyone was a threat.

Corey also lived with his mom, a single mother with two boys. She was a nurse. She had very long, blonde hair and wore no makeup and clear-framed glasses. I never, once, saw her smile. She always seemed infuriated about something. Corey and I were over at each other's houses constantly, and when I was at his, his mother obviously had complete disdain for me. I found this odd, because parents always loved me. The way she spoke to Corey was always as follows:

"Will you hang your fucking coat up?"
"Stop acting like a fucking idiot."

"You didn't eat lunch today? Well, that was pretty stupid."

"Stop acting like a dumbass. Get your homework done now."

This kind of chat coming from a mother was shocking to me. My mom had mega problems, sure, but all of her fucked-up behaviour was under the guise of love and nurture and caring, and her being the victim. She would never call me stupid, or a fucking idiot, certainly not with other people around. I wondered how Corey's mom would speak to him when they were alone. While I was there, he would just laugh at her, letting her words roll off him. He never addressed this with me, either. As with my situation, he seemed to be completely oblivious to the fact that this behaviour from a mother wasn't typical.

Corey and I would waste minutes, hours, entire afternoons making out. Every moment alone we got was filled with us sucking each other's faces off. The only issue was finding safe places to do it. Behind the school, in the woods, in the dressing room above the auditorium where the school plays were held, because sometimes it would be left empty but open, so that was great while it lasted, until a teacher clocked on to this and started locking it up.

Corey came home with a hickey one day, from me of course, and his mom absolutely flipped. She called my house and told me directly that it was a "pretty stupid thing to do" and we weren't to be around each other any more without supervision. She also spoke to Mom, and although I didn't hear Corey's mom's side of the conversation, I could see in my mom's eyes that she was getting told off. Mom taking the back seat with crazy people yelling at her wasn't her usual role.

*

Shortly after this incident, Corey told me that someone kept phoning their house late at night. Because his mom was a nurse, she worked late, and his grandmother, who lived with them, would answer the phone, always to silence on the other end. It started out being once or twice a week, then it became nightly, then multiple times per night, and sometimes through the day. The other end would always be dead silence. It was driving them crazy. Finally, the calls started coming in the middle of the night, and they were getting scared. Corey asked if I thought it could be Mom.

"Of course not, why the hell would she do that?" We were on the phone, and I was caught off guard by this accusation. She was nuts in many ways, sure, but calling someone repeatedly for no reason? She wouldn't do this. I'd never heard of her doing this. What purpose would that serve?

Corey called me around 8.30pm one night and told me that they had had the calls traced because it was becoming harassment, and that the calls were coming from our number. An unexpected rage rose in my throat.

"It's your mom," Corey said. "She's been calling my house late at night for months on end," he said. "I mean it's definitely her, we have a long list of calls with your number on it."

My chest burned at this. It wasn't her. It couldn't be. Corey's mom must have made it up to make her look insane. "She hasn't been fucking calling you! I know she hasn't! YOUR mom is the one who's nuts! She's made it all up because she hates us!" I screamed down the phone. I was so sick of Mom being the one everyone was mad at. Surely not *everything* was her fault.

"But think about it, who else could it be, Krystal?! You're just being purposely stupid if you don't look at the facts and the evidence. Your mom does tons of crazy shit, my mom works late at night and her and my grandma are being woken up so much they can't sleep! It's fucking insane..."

"Fuck off," I said, and slammed down the receiver.

Mom had been pacing back and forth in front of my bedroom door listening in on the conversation. I knew this; my dramatic defence of her had been partially for her benefit, I admit.

"Are you okay, sweety?" She leaned into my bedroom, hesitant.

"Yeah," I said. "They think it's you that's been calling them."

She didn't answer me, just tightened her lips and squinted her eyes into a sympathetic half-smile.

The calls stopped after that, and me and Corey made up. The months that followed saw Mom and me drift further and further apart, and I finally relented to Corey, that the calls must have been coming from her. The evidence was too overwhelming; I apologized to him. I just had no idea why she would do it.

A lot of troubled people do bad things for very clear reasons. A man kills his wife for insurance money; a woman keeps running from partner to partner and changing her name because she can't face her past; an online scammer sends fake emails to get elderly people to send them cheques; a man steals from his sister's purse so he can feed his drug addiction; on and on.

Mom's motivation for the things she does has never been totally clear to me, which is the most maddening thing.

The closest explanation I can land on is attention – it all seems to stem from a deep yearning for people to pity her – but even that doesn't completely cover it, because why would she phone my high-school boyfriend's house hundreds of times late at night, not speaking, only to totally deny it and then stop when she was too close to getting caught? It's mental illness, sure, but everyone must have a reason for doing the things they do. Or is that also bullshit? Do some people live moment to moment, doing whatever the random neurons firing in their brain tell them?

Call Corey's house again, Mom's brain might say. *Wake up the grandmother.* She'd do it.

Do it again, her head would tell her. She'd obey. And on and on and on, again, again, again.

Did she ever ask herself, *Why am I doing this?* Did she ever challenge the mental-illness demon inside her head and say, *No. Fuck this. I choose another path*? After all, we've surely all had inappropriate thoughts. Thoughts of screaming at someone in the checkout line or driving our car off a cliff. Thoughts of telling someone exactly what we think of them, or flipping the table in the restaurant over, food flying everywhere, making a scene. *What would happen if I just started screaming, right here right now?* we think while in a crowded elevator. I remember looking at Mom and thinking, *Does she have these thoughts and just indulge in some of them? Has that demon poltergeist taken over to the point where she's only that now?* I could (and have) analyse/d this, endlessly.

I used to wonder, if a team of the best health professionals in the world were made to study Mom, what would her diagnosis be? And what did it stem from? Nature or nurture? Or some weird combination of both?

Historically, we've rolled our eyes at women's problems (especially mothers), and they hardly ever get the help they need. Be it with childcare, finances, from their partners or for their mental health. Concerned adults would sometimes ask me, when I was a kid, "Krystal, are you okay? How are things at home with your mom?" and I'd always answer, "Fine. Great!" and I didn't think I was lying. I also knew, when I was very young, that I needed to protect Mom. Protect both of us. Mom was always getting accused of things, and she had the worst luck, and most people just didn't understand what we had been through.

I'm not a medical professional, but I believe Mom has a mental illness that she had from childhood and never got treated for, and the longer it remained untreated, the more it grew. Mental illness runs in Mom's family, from Grandma Lora's side. A cousin of Mom's reached out to me on Facebook in 2019, and asked me how Mom was doing, as she hadn't heard from her since they were kids. I didn't exactly know how I should respond to a long-lost cousin who was little more than an acquaintance, but in the end I went with honesty.

Not great, I replied. *She's been struggling with her mental state for many years and at this point I lose touch with her for months, sometimes longer. She will disappear and not keep in touch with me or her sisters. Move, change her number, not tell us where she's gone. We've tried helping her, both financially and in person, but she pretty much has a cycle of sabotaging herself and any connections* she's made with people in her life. Even if they care about her, they eventually get fed up and leave.

The reply came within a couple of hours.

Oh, I'm so sorry to hear that, Krystal, but not surprising. Mental illness unfortunately runs in our family and there's been at least one like her in every generation. It's something we've all had to struggle with, but I'm glad to hear you're doing all right, especially after what you both went through back when you were a teenager. All the best.

I asked my Aunt Kelley what she thought had been meant by this, and she said that their Aunt Judy (Grandma Lora's sister) had basically been a replica of Mom.

Kelley read the message from the cousin and confirmed this. "Aunt Judy was nuts, man. She'd cry and make a scene at every family gathering. She never got married and would sleep with loads of younger men, like guys who were 20 when she was in her forties, who would sometimes steal from her. She always needed to be the centre of attention, and to be rescued."

I'd seen one picture of Aunt Judy in Grandma Lora's photo album. She was the only woman in the group wearing shockingly bright colours, her makeup dramatic and outrageous, with bright red lips and blue eyeshadow up to her brows.

Mental illness isn't something you can grasp. It's not like cancer, or a broken limb. It's slippery, frustrating, a hologram. It's common for the sufferer to gain a little ground and then sabotage themselves. It reminds me of some of the many contradictions in "How Do You Solve a Problem Like Maria?" from *The Sound of Music* – she's a riddle, a child, a headache, an angel. Understanding Mom is like trying to catch a cloud and pin it down.

Mom tried to self-medicate with pain medication, acting out to get care and attention, building temporary connections with sympathetic people, then breaking them, on purpose, and running away. She had been prescribed anti-depressants and anti-psychosis drugs, which had varying effects, that she always gave up on. Nothing worked, and I know at times she felt desperate. Then she got to the point where her ailments took over her capacity to function so completely that she'd put herself and her children in constant danger. I'd be lying if I said I wasn't angry about this, but at the same time, I can't blame Mom entirely, because we are living in a time where whatever it is she has isn't fully understood yet.

Mom's illness makes people hate her, and angry at her.

As I type this now, I haven't spoken to Mom in over a year. It's not from lack of trying. There's a part of me deep down that thinks she somehow knows that I'm writing this book, and maybe that's why she doesn't want to talk to me. Mom always knew things she shouldn't have known. Things she should have had no way of knowing. And there's no explanation except that she's extremely perceptive and smarter than she's ever let on.

Of course, when I was a teen, all I knew was that she was freaky about knowing things. I suppose, considering her patterns, I should have expected what happened next.

24.

Corey and I decided we wanted to have sex. We talked about it loads: how we wanted to lose our virginity to each other, and do it in a totally safe way, not like these dumbasses at our school who had sex without protection, without any skill, and it only lasted like one minute and no one really enjoyed it that much. *We're not like them. We're smarter, and better. We'll do it right.*

We approached sex like academics. We talked about it to our friends who had already done it. We read loads about it online, bought books, listened to *Loveline* with Adam Carolla and Dr Drew (a radio programme offering advice on relationships) as much as possible. This was 2002, and there was an old Canadian woman named Sue Johanson who'd give great advice and lectures about sex on late-night television, in a very sex-positive and open way. She'd talk about how penis size doesn't really matter, how to give blow jobs and cunnilingus, how to masturbate, on and on. Corey and I would watch it together, half giggling, half paying very close attention, making mental notes.

When it came time for me to go to the doctor to ask for birth control, Corey came along with me. "We're making the decision together, so I should come along too," he said. Mom drove us both. She waited in the lobby when I was called in. I sat on the bed and Corey took a seat in the green laminated chair by the wall. The doctor was flabbergasted to see us both. We told her that we had decided we wanted to have sex and wanted to ask about birth-control options. She told us that it's important to always pee after sex, and that most women get a urinary tract infection after their first time. This was news to me, and still is to most people I tell to this day. I have always wondered why sex ed is taught from the guise of warning us about the worst-case scenarios, rather than giving us practical advice that will apply to most people.

When we left, Mom told me that the doctor had said she was impressed with Corey; she had never seen a teenage boy accompany his girlfriend to the clinic.

I was feeling very comfortable about my decision to share with Mom that we'd thought about having sex. I did tell her that we weren't planning on doing it yet, and that we wanted to get all the info first. In reality, I wanted to do it as soon as humanly possible, but telling her this was my own way of keeping part of it between me and Corey. *We're going to do it, at some point; we've let everyone know who we are supposed to let know, we've done everything in a legit way, and as to where and when we'll do it, that's up to us. Like adults!*

I had started birth-control pills, and you're supposed to wait a month for them to kick in. We couldn't wait that long, so Corey spent the night at my house one night, approved by both of our parents. There wasn't any discussion of "Hey, you kids better not try any hanky panky in there" or anything like that. I had told Mom, the last time we spoke about it, that I was going to wait a month until the pills kicked in, in any case. It wasn't a promise and, in my eyes, this was now my business anyway. She had done her part, taking us to the doctors for birth control, and now she should just buzz off.

While Corey was over, we, of course, attempted to have sex. I say "attempted" because it wouldn't really go in. He tried and was gentle and we were both patient, but it just wasn't happening. It was like trying to shove a carrot into a buttonhole. "How far in is it?" I'd say. "I think it feels like it's in now?"

"Um, like just the tip, I think?"

"Oh man, really?" we laughed.

He took the condom off, put it in the bin and we went to bed. Better luck next time.

We went to school together the next day, and after school there was play practice for *Up the Down Staircase*. It was a cast of about 20, but as the teacher I was front and centre, and the rest of the kids played my students. We were all on stage together, and in the auditorium were the director and the assistant director, watching us play out quite a dramatic scene where some kids are back-chatting me (it was a classic "young teacher goes to an inner-city school and somehow gets through to the rough teens" story). Right in the middle of this scene, the auditorium door flung open and Mom came hobbling down the middle aisle (she still had a limp from the car accident). It immediately struck me that her eyes looked a lot like her father's. She was coming towards me at full tilt. Anger and shock and fear surged through me. She knew about us having sex. This had to be what this was about.

But there's no way she would confront me about this in front of all these people, I thought. *Please no please no please no.*

The scene we were rehearsing was on pause. Everyone was silent and stunned as she came closer to the stage.

"Krystal!" she shouted from the aisle as she approached the lip of the stage. Every eye in the room looked at her, then at me. "Get down off that stage right now! And you . . ." she pointed at Corey. "You're not welcome in our house any more." Everyone was still, sat in their fake desk chairs on the stage, eyes still darting between me and Mom.

I was frozen. I felt cold, I started shivering internally, the familiar numbness coursing through me, my natural defence mechanism for these sorts of happenings, because this was way too embarrassing for my body to let me feel fully. I only wished it would work a little faster.

"Get off that stage. And get in the car. NOW-wuh." Her head tilted downwards, and her grey eyes burned up at me, daring me to disobey.

I stood, immobile. *What do I say?* No words immediately came to mind. I couldn't look weak in front of my classmates. And in front of Corey. *Come on, think of a good comeback.* Nope. Mind blank. There were more than enough kids present for this to be spread throughout the entire school within hours.

Though I thought of nothing to say, all I knew was I wasn't getting in the car with her, only for her to scream at me all the way home and tell me that I was never to see Corey again.

That's exactly what she wants. I can't do it this time. I never want to be in her presence again. She's wrong. This is wrong.

Everyone held their breath and looked at me, waiting for what I'd say next.

I could rebel. I could be that teenager. I'd seen kids disobey their parents in movies and TV shows and I could do that, too. What could she do? Call the cops? I wouldn't put it past her. But right now, juvey sounded better than going home. I'll bet in juvey they wouldn't make me clean all day. No one would have breakdowns in doctors' offices and have to leave, crying, while I tried not to make eye contact with the staff because we'd definitely stolen medical supplies from the drawers and toilet roll from the bathroom stalls and making a scene was the best way to distract from all this. No one would knock on my door, demanding to know what exactly had happened when I'd been out with my boyfriend. No one would bring home weirdo after weirdo who would be in and out of our lives so quickly that I barely noticed they were different people every time, like episodes of *The Twilight Zone*. I wouldn't have to watch Mom being carted off to the hospital because she'd stepped on a drain or started hallucinating. I could just sit, in a cell, presumably, and take care of me. Eat meals, read, watch TV maybe. In peace. It sounded like Heaven. Yeah. Kid Jail is a better option, I decided. As long as I don't have to live with her any more.

"No," I said, probably a little too quietly.

"What did you say to me?" She pounded her fist on the stage from the auditorium floor. It was clear she was thrown by my answer. I'd never disobeyed her like this.

"No. I'm not going anywhere with you," I said. My brows were slightly furrowed, but my face was neutral. I was scared, but also felt like a slight badass directly disobeying my scary mom in front of everyone. The director stood with a clipboard in the third row of the theatre. She was a middle-aged woman with sleek, dark-red hair and classy makeup. She had been an actor herself in

New York in the 1970s and '80s, had retired here in Sequim and brought a level of sophistication to the high-school plays. She looked concerned, grasping her clipboard tightly and looking back and forth between Mom and me, but said nothing. There's not much you can add when the 16-year-old star of your play is about to be chased out of the auditorium by an intimidating, limping, burned woman who is angry for reasons unknown.

I marched through the cast of students, went backstage, got my stuff quickly and walked out the back door of the theatre. I didn't even run. I walked, outwardly, very calmly. No one said anything. I didn't have to hurry because I knew exactly how fast Mom could limp.

"Krystal, you get back here now!" I heard her shout after me, just as the heavy backstage door of the auditorium closed, hard.

Corey caught up with me a few steps out of the theatre and we walked across the grass outside the back of the school, no plan of where to go. I cried silently, and he put his arm around me.

"God, she is so insane," he said. "I can't believe she did that!" Historically, it used to make me mad for other people to call Mom this off-limits word, but now it felt liberating, like solidarity. Plus, there was no argument against it.

"So fucking insane. What the fuck?" As I spoke, the tears choked my voice and the sobbing came out harder. "We told her we were gonna have sex! Like she came to the doctor with us and everything!" I sniffed and wailed.

We went to Corey's house, a 20-minute walk away. I used his phone to call my friend Brian, who had a car, and he came and picked me up. Corey's mom was at work that afternoon, but I knew I couldn't stay at Corey's because this would be one of the first places Mom would look.

I called a few of my friends to tell them what had happened, and it came out that Mom had also been calling all my friends' houses to ask where they thought I might be. One friend told me that she had indeed called the police, and they were on the lookout for me. To this day, I don't know if this was the truth or a lie she'd made up to scare me.

I wondered what she had told them. "My 16-year-old daughter had sex safely at our house and used a condom and I screamed at her for it in front of like 25 people and now she's not been home in four hours." They must have been, like, "Yeah, ma'am, we'll get right on this shocking case. Top priority."

The same night, while Brian was driving me around, a cop car drove by, and Brian told me to duck down until they'd passed. For a 16-year-old who had never broken the rules before, this was very exciting stuff.

I went to a house party that night, something that I'd never been allowed to do. The guys were playing a game called Edward 40 Hands where they'd take two 40-ounce bottles of beer and duct-tape them to someone's hands, so that they couldn't do anything until they finished both bottles. Very high-class party. I looked down and saw two bottles duct-taped to my hands, but it wasn't necessary. I finished my two in quick succession, even though I'd never liked beer. Being drunk felt excellent. Why wasn't everyone drunk all the time?

The parents were present at this party, and one of them came through and told me that I needed to call my dad. I figured out later that a parent at this party had phoned Mom and told her where I was and that I was safe, so she had then phoned Dad and told him what had happened and, probably feeling at a loss of what to do, had also told Dad that he needed to call me and check on me.

Dad still lived in Mountlake Terrace, the suburb of Seattle where he'd taken care of me after the fire. It was a three-hour drive away from Sequim.

"Hey, Krystal, are you okay?" The concern in his voice was surely sort of real, but also seemed played up a little, because Dad had seldom taken this role in my life.

"Yeah, I'm fine."

I told Dad what Mom had done in the auditorium, and how we were fighting all the time, and how she was crazy, and I felt like I couldn't live with her any more.

He gave a big, knowing sigh. "Man, I can't believe she did that. Um . . . well, are you in a safe place?"

"Yeah I'm at my friend Ben's, his parents are here," I said. I didn't mention that we were playing Edward 40 Hands.

"Okay, well, maybe you can go back home tomorrow when things have calmed down a little? She's really upset." Dad was trying to reason with me, for my own safety but also probably in the hopes that Mom would stop calling him. "Also, y'know, we were talking and I thought maybe you could come and stay with me this summer. Like, the whole summer break? I mean I do have to work, but I go to work really early and the way you sleep in these days you'd only be alone for a couple hours a day."

"That would be great!" I said, filled with gratitude. Dad's house. Why didn't I think of that? I'd been convincing myself all day that my only other option beside Mom's house was Kid Jail. Dad's house. Of course!

Only three more months until summer break. I could stay drunk until then.

25.

After the auditorium incident, things were changed permanently. I had broken the rules, and the consequences weren't that huge. I couldn't trust Mom any more with big things. She had lost a massive amount of power, and she knew it. The dynamic had shifted. I did whatever I wanted now. And what I wanted wasn't anything earth-shattering. I wanted to go out whenever I wanted to and hang out with Corey. I went over to friends' houses freely. I stayed out late and came home when I pleased. She had to accept this. But it didn't come easily.

Having moved from the nice, big house we were renting out in the woods that we couldn't really afford to a smaller, very crappy brown apartment building behind the Safeway in town, my life here consisted of me hearing the *BEEEP, BEEEP, BEEEP* of the huge delivery trucks backing up into the cargo bay of the supermarket. The apartment was very small, and ugly on the outside, but the fact that it was in town and walking distance from everything made my life much easier. Although I could see Corey whenever I wanted, it came to the point where we didn't go to each other's houses any more because our mothers both hated each other, and us, and the fact that we were still dating.

Because of her injuries from the fire and the car accident, Mom was able to get any pain medication or sleeping pills she wanted, which only made her go into greater states of swinging between mania and comatose. She'd mostly sleep, almost all day every day, then wake up and order pizza, watch TV, yell at me for something, then go back to bed. Mom still gathered more lost souls during this time, all in and out of our lives even more fleetingly than before, because she didn't have the energy to keep up a charade of normality for as long as she could in the past.

I started complaining of back pain from carrying such a heavy bag full of school books, or leg cramps from growing pains. She'd sometimes give me half of an OxyContin at first, telling me that undiagnosed and untreated pain is one of the biggest problems in our society, and they would never give strong pain medication to a teenager, citing the many times over the years when I'd gone to the doctor complaining of extreme headaches that came with nausea (we later found out these were migraines). As time went on, Mom became freer with it, sharing her OxyContin and her Ambien whenever I'd ask.

For those unaware, OxyContin is the brand name of Oxycodone, a semi-synthetic opioid, which has been considered the catalyst drug in causing America's Great Opioid Addiction issue, as depicted in popular TV shows such as *Dopesick*.

"Women are never taken seriously, either," Mom would say. "You have to really overblow how much pain you're in to get anywhere with these idiots."

I had a lot of trouble sleeping. I'd stay up until well past midnight, watching TV or talking on the phone to Corey, and then in the mornings, trying to get up for school, my eyes felt like they were made of concrete. My throat felt like it had a brick lodged inside of it. I'd have nightmares, too. Sometimes obvious ones, about Katie, or about the house being on fire and me needing to get out but being unable to move, or just replaying what happened again and again. But sometimes they'd seemingly have nothing to do with anything. Being stuck in an elevator that plummeted, endlessly downwards. Stepping off of a cliff edge. And my eyes would open suddenly, I'd be gasping, my body waking itself up to protect me.

There was one dream that recurred, over and over. The location changed, but it always involved the same ingredients.

I'm on a beach, or a dock. Usually somewhere near the water, and somewhere dark and silent. There's an imperfect, solid cube of concrete, with a single metal loop attached to the top. A woman ties a single strand of hair to it, tries to lift the cube up with it and it snaps. I know, watching her, that you can't lift a concrete block with a single strand of hair. Everyone else around also knows that. Yet she tries again and again, with each strand of hair until she has almost none left. It's heartbreaking to watch, and I wonder, *Why doesn't she just put all her hairs on at once and try to lift it that way, like the circus ladies with long braids? Or at least get a rope or someone else to help her?* This woman would sometimes be Mom, sometimes me, sometimes just an unknown woman. Sometimes the dream would involve me looking into a mirror and the single strand of hair growing out of my face. Out of my upper lip, my eyebrow, the centre of my eyeball. I'd be horrified and try to rip it out, only for it to keep growing longer, forever. Sometimes the hair would be able to hold the concrete block for a little while, and I'd try to protect it. I'd try to lift the block to take some of the pressure off it, but it always broke in the end, the hair destroyed and the block plummeting to the ground.

The dream about a strand of hair might have had something to do with the fact that I started a habit around this time of pulling hairs out of my body. I'd seen someone on TV do it, in a sort of funny sitcom, and I wondered what it would feel like. I started with my eyebrows, and I loved the feeling of the thick, black hair and accompanying white root that sometimes came out with it. I'd sometimes play with the hair, tickling my skin with it, before discarding it and getting another. I then moved on to my eyelashes, which were even thicker and had even bigger roots on them. It felt satisfying to pull them out. The pain lasted only a moment, and after it subsided, an extreme calm would come over me. It started to take up a lot of my time. When I realized I was running out of eyelashes and eyebrows, I moved on to the hair on my head. I started with the crown, which I realized immediately was a bad idea, because it would be too noticeable. I decided to stick to pulling out hairs in the back of my head, near the nape of my neck, as when my hair was down this would be the least noticeable. Once in PE, where all girls were required to put their hair up, another girl asked me, innocently, "Krystal, why do you have bald spots on the back of your head?"

Oh shit. I didn't know it looked that bad.

"Oh – I have this thing where I pull it out sometimes." I laughed. She just looked at me, with blank confusion. Honesty was a big fail. I then started colouring in the back of my scalp with eyeshadow and eyeliner whenever I had to wear my hair up, which I thought was ingenious.

I found out later that this is a real disorder many people have; it's called trichotillomania. I sometimes wonder if we all watched the same episode of *Seinfeld* where Kramer and Newman pull out their eyelashes to make wishes on, and this caused some sort of hair-pulling epidemic. I've read that it's rare, but I've met countless girls in my life who also do it, so in my view it's one of those things that most people never seek help for.

The sleeping problems persisted, so Mom suggested I take Tylenol PMs so that I'd feel like going to bed earlier, and they'd knock me out like a light. Sometimes they weren't strong enough, and Mom would give me an Ambien the next night instead.

One night in the brown apartment, age 17, I had taken two Tylenol PMs out of habit, forgotten about it and asked Mom for an Ambien too. She didn't know I'd taken the Tylenol PMs, so gave me a whole one. I proceeded to lie in my bed talking to Corey on the phone for hours, fighting sleep when the urge came. Then, the next thing I remember is a flash of seeing my white ceiling turn blue and purple and sparkly, swirling and shimmery everywhere, like the inside of a sensory bottle filled with shaving foam.

"Wow, it's so beautiful," I said.

Next thing, Mom was standing over me, pressing a warm washcloth on my forehead and trying to force me to eat toast and drink water.

"What happened?" I said, my head swimming and white flashes bursting before my eyes.

"You started screaming while you were talking to Corey," Mom said, with concern but also slight annoyance. I didn't remember any of this. I reached for the phone and started to call Corey back.

"Krystal, please," Mom said, "just rest for now okay, you can call him back tomorrow."

I ignored her.

"Oh my God, are you okay?" Corey asked. "You screamed and started saying a lion was crawling up your leg and then your mom came in and hung up on me, I didn't know what the fuck was going on." He sounded genuinely scared. I felt embarrassed, for myself and also for Mom. I didn't want to tell him I'd taken three sleeping pills and they'd caused a bad reaction. It would make us both sound stupid.

"I think it was because I was really tired, but was forcing myself to stay awake," I said. "I nodded off and started talking in my sleep."

Mom got me settled and back to bed and we never spoke about it again. She stopped sharing her Ambien.

*

For a few months after the auditorium incident, because of our new understanding that I did whatever I wanted, Mom and I got along pretty well. We'd play the guitar together and sing, watch *Seinfeld* and *Roseanne* and *Conan*. We'd still fight sometimes – some of them were normal teenage fights, others they'd come to us slamming things. I'd slam a door; she'd slam a cupboard. That kind of thing.

Mom invited me to visit Katie's grave with her multiple times in these high-school years. I never went with her. The thought of it was too much to bear. Not seeing Katie's grave, but having to be Mom's support at the same time as feeling whatever it was I would feel was too much to face.

"I don't really believe that she's there anyway," I'd say to Mom, and anyone else who asked if I ever went to her grave. "I'm not religious or anything, so to me it's just a stone in the ground."

When I was 16, after my junior year of high school, I stayed with Dad for the entire summer, as we'd discussed. We all agreed it would be best; Mom and I needed a long break from one another.

Other than just after the fire when he cared for me, I'd never stayed with Dad for more than a week or two. I'd certainly never stayed at his place for this long under normal circumstances. It was illuminating. Dad is an electrician, and he'd go to work very early in the day but was always home by 1 or 2pm. In the afternoon we gardened, played tennis, he even put me to work building a retaining wall with huge concrete bricks in the back yard. My arms felt like Jello afterwards. We'd barbecue most days, and Dad taught me the delicacy of making a beer-can chicken.

Sometimes he would peek out the front window at the lady who lived across the street.

"Oh, Krystal, look, there she is. My neighbour, Cheryl. She's really pretty, eh?" I agreed. A recent divorcee with two teenage boys. She would often be out front gardening, and I encouraged Dad to go and speak to her.

"No, no, I can't. What would I say?!" Dad sighed.

One day, I looked out the front window and saw her struggling with her garage door.

"Dad! Dad!" I yelled. "She can't get her garage door shut! Here's your opening! Go and help her!"

Dad ran out. I heard them both laughing together, and when he came back in, Dad said he'd invited her and her two boys over for dinner. They started dating; it was very that they lived across the street from each other, and me and the boys would get banished to one house while they hung out, alone, in the other. Ah, young love.

26.

The swing of Mom's states of being was getting more dramatic – medication-induced mania, or comatose zombie, screaming at me or criticizing me in between her episodes. This fact was emphasized by the fun summer I'd just had with Dad. The brown apartment in Sequim was an absolute pigsty, dirty dishes piling up again and paths on the floor for walking; and it became clear to me that I could not stay here much longer. The contrast between Dad's house and Mom's was too strong to ignore. One house was normal, calm, well adjusted, the biggest problems being things like a clogged bathtub or a rat living in Dad's barbecue, or the nice lady across the street needing help with cleaning out her gutters. The other house was *One Flew Over the Cuckoo's Nest* with more pizza boxes.

I'd call Dad, sobbing, telling him that Mom and I had had a bad fight and I couldn't live with her any more.

"I know, Krystal," he'd sigh. "You've gotta just finish your last year of high school. It's literally just eight more months. Hang in there."

There was a sum of money, a settlement, that I'd been granted after the fire, from an institution called Child Victim Compensation. It was a $16,000 one-off payment that I was to receive in full when I turned 18. The money was put into Mom's bank account as I didn't have my own yet, and when it came time for her to give me the money when I was moving out, she said, "I've had to take some expenses off of it."

"What? Expenses for what?!"

She gave a sharp exhale and rolled her eyes sarcastically. "Like . . . your laptop? And your car."

I couldn't believe what I was hearing. She had given me my laptop as a Christmas present. And my car was an '89 Honda Prelude that was so rusted on the outside that the original colour wasn't discernible. It had cost her $500 and it had been my birthday present.

I contained my rage. There was no point. "How much is left?" I asked, soberly.

"There's $2,000 left," she answered.

"Fine," I said. I didn't want to waste a fight on this. Having no money wasn't a change for me. It would have just helped me to get away from her faster, but $2,000 I could still work with. I had no choice but to let it roll off me.

I called Dad, livid, and told him what she'd done. "Yep, well," he said. "You'd better just have her transfer it to me before she spends any more of it. I'll keep it safe till your birthday when you open your own account. There's not much you can do about it."

Corey's mom sent him to live with his dad in California for the last two years of his high school life, to get him away from evil me. We were heartbroken, but if anything it only brought us closer together and made us more determined to show these adults that our love was real and miles couldn't keep us apart, blah blah blah. I borrowed Brian's car when I was 18 and took a road trip, by myself, to California to visit him. A 23-hour journey, and I learned to drive a stick shift just for this. Hills were hard and I backed into a tree at one point.

California was incredible. I had to spend $800 of my $2,000 getting the back panel of Brian's car fixed before I returned it to him (dear reader, please don't tell him about this, because I never did). Corey's high school was gorgeous, and his friends were all creative and hot, and had money and pools in their backyards. I was determined to move there as soon as I graduated.

When I got back home, the fights with Mom came to a tipping point.

"Get off the phone, now," Mom leaned into my room and demanded.

"No, I'm talking to Corey."

"Now," she threatened, even though at this point threats were laughable. I hung up. "You're to stay in your room," she said.

"You can't fucking tell me what to do any more!" I screamed, leaning out of my doorway. Mom shoved me back into my room, then pushed her hand against my arm and threw me onto the mattress that lay on my floor. She was unbelievably strong. One slight push was all it took. It was the most violent thing she'd ever done to me. I lay there on the mattress, ready to kill with my words.

"You're a psycho, you're out of your fucking mind and everyone knows it!" That did it. She picked up my guitar, held it over her head and threatened to smash it against the wall.

I flashed back to a story Mom had told me about her own dad, Grandpa Woody, doing this same thing to her guitar when she was a teenager, except he had really smashed it, and she'd cried and cried for days afterwards, grieving over her beloved instrument that she adored playing so much.

"Wow. Okay, Woody," I said. *Take that.*

She realized what she was doing and put the guitar down. She went into her room and slammed the door.

Fuck this. Fuck this forever, I thought. I started packing my things. I called Brian, who was now 20 and, out of all my friends, looked the most like a bouncer at a nightclub. He came over to my house the next day and stood there, arms crossed, while I took all my shit out of the house. Mom didn't argue because Brian was scary. She stayed in her room while I packed everything up. At the last second, I turned back and looked at a photo on the wall of me and Katie, sitting together in one of those cheap Sears studios in the mid-'90s (Sears is a chain of mid-level department stores that used to have photo studios – responsible for those cheesy old American family photos you've undoubtedly seen with dramatic nature backgrounds). Me with dyed purply red hair and Katie with a mullet and glasses, beaming with her two front teeth missing. I grabbed it off the wall and shoved it into my backpack.

I bounced around from house to house while I finished high school. I stayed at a few places with parents, and a few with absolutely no supervision. I even stayed in one friend's walk-in closet for a week. As soon as I left home, Mom and I started getting along great. I'd come over sometimes and we'd talk, and I'd leave. A great arrangement.

Coming to the end of high school, I spoke with my high-school advisor and, as it turned out, I didn't have nearly enough credits to graduate. No one had told me this, or else I just hadn't paid enough attention, but apparently you have to take certain amounts of certain types of classes to graduate high school. Like, you can't just take floral design and drama and having sex with Corey in the costume room above the auditorium.

You have to graduate with 12 credits of math, 16 of English lit., etc., etc. I had just taken whatever the hell I wanted. I always made sure there was a math in there, a science, sure. Sometimes I'd fail them, drop out and join a different class. No one was keeping an eye on any of this, and six months before graduation, I was pretty much screwed. I told Mom and Dad, and Mom told me she'd take me to get my GED at the local college after the school year ended.

A GED (it stands for General Educational Development) is a high-school equivalency test – to prove you're not a total dumbass, basically. Dad had one too, and he was doing fine, so it was like a family tradition. I passed it first try, every score in the 98th percentile or higher.

I didn't feel too bad about it, except to think that I could theoretically have skipped high school entirely and just gotten this bad boy and moved away somewhere way sooner.

I had my mind set on going to a two-year musical theatre school in California called AMDA (The American Musical and Dramatic Academy). They had sent a bunch of pamphlets to my school, and acting and singing were the only things I'd ever done that I'd really connected with. I knew I was good at acting because I'd always be cast as the lead in things, and I loved musicals. My singing voice was okay at best, but that didn't matter so much. Getting into this school would mean that I'd get to leave Sequim.

Dad agreed to apply for student loans for me to pay for the school, and I know it took him over a decade to pay them off because over the course of the next ten years, I'd get letters in the mail periodically that showed the amount owed going down slowly.

I have thanked him for this by never pursuing acting, let alone musical theatre, in any way whatsoever. He has very graciously never brought it up.

27.

"But what are you gonna do when you get down there? For money and things?" Cheryl, Dad's old neighbour and now long-term live-in girlfriend, said with an air of incredulous concern. The move from across the street couldn't have been easier, for both of them. Cheryl was at this time a very pretty woman in her late forties – six years older than Dad – with a warm, kind face and long, thick, sandy-coloured hair. She always had a dark tan and freckles from working in the garden. She was the first woman I'd seen Dad date who he actually had a lot in common with – they both loved cooking, the outdoors and live music. She wore very little makeup and her hair simply, and wasn't controlling of how Dad chose to dress or what he did with his hair, or his spare time, all of which was in complete opposition to previous girlfriends. Cheryl's two teenage sons also got along great with Dad. Dad was clearly in love, and I also liked Cheryl immediately.

"Well, I'll look for a job, I guess. I'm going to be living with Leah," I said. I didn't understand why adults kept saying this type of thing to me. What was the big deal about moving? I'd done it every year since before I gained sentience. Starting a new school, being in a new area, with brand new people? That's just life. And in fact, it would be easier this time because Mom wouldn't be there. We'd always been broke, and now I had $2,000 to my name (minus the cost of getting Brian's car fixed, but in my mind still an endless fortune) that Dad was keeping safe for me until I opened my own bank account. I'd just figure it out as I went along.

"Gosh, you're so brave! I don't know if I could have ever imagined moving that far away at your age," Cheryl said. I just shrugged.

Mom drove me from Sequim to West Hollywood in her car, because my '89 Honda Prelude had broken down permanently. My saviour in LA, Leah, had been in the year above me in high school and had moved to West Hollywood the year before, by herself, to go to another acting school nearby. Her parents had been paying her rent up until now, and she held a job in the costume shop at her school as she was a keen sewer, but a roommate would still lower her costs significantly.

We lived in a set of brown apartments on Sycamore Ave, near La Brea Blvd and Fountain Ave. Almost every other kid in my acting school opted for the student accommodation – huge, open-plan, gorgeous apartments in high rises that were a bus ride away from our school. The student accommodation cost $1,200 a month, per student, and you didn't get your own room. Leah's apartment cost me $400 a month ($800 split between the two of us) and I was within walking distance of school. I wondered if the other students and their parents even bothered to look for alternative housing, or just went with what the school said. *Must be nice*, I thought.

West Hollywood itself reminded me of a movie set. Not just in how it looked, with its constant seemingly fake blue skies and happy sunshine and palm trees, but also there were famous people everywhere, all the time. Billy Crudup in Starbucks. Ben Stiller and Christine Taylor in Target, casually buying things for their new baby. Carmen Electra being helped out of a limousine and led into a restaurant, security all around her. Flyerers desperately trying to give away free tickets to the (then brand new) *Jimmy Kimmel Show* (the traditional late-night talk show in the style of David Letterman or Johnny Carson). Having to shove my way past yet another movie premiere on the red carpet outside of Grauman's Chinese Theatre on the way to school.

I became jaded by all this immediately. I always imagined that, if I saw a famous person in real life, something magical would occur, but they were just people, and either not wanting to be bothered, or the complete opposite, relishing the attention. Combine this with my overwhelming desire not to draw attention to myself or to demand attention from strangers, and the result, from age 18, was a totally indifferent vibe to famous people. People who freaked out over celebs were, in my eyes, incredibly lame.

My school was one block north of the famous crossroads Hollywood & Vine. It struck me that, in 2004, three out of four establishments that resided at one of the most famous crossroads in the world were empty. Defunct. Paint splattered the inside of the dusty walls and posters for local gigs were half-ripped, blowing in the wind on the dirty glass. I'd pass the Capitol Records building that looked like 20 spaceships piled on top of one another, always hitting an uphill at that point and feeling as though I was about to pass out, being unaccustomed to the southern California heat.

My $2,000 evaporated within a couple of months. I'd never considered wealth, or lack thereof, as a factor for categorizing myself in any way (a staunch difference between growing up American vs growing up British), but the fact that I was literally the only student I knew wearing a hairnet and blue plastic gloves while scooping broccoli cheese soup into hollowed-out bread bowls for my fellow students every lunchtime was hard to ignore.

Like back home, I excelled in acting. I could act the pants off any scene, usually on the first go. When it came to singing, I slid back from being one of the better singers at Sequim High School to being mediocre at best. I could hit all the notes and hear harmonies, but there was no denying that my singing was weak, quiet and the opposite of the belting Broadway voice that most musical theatre songs required. My vocal coach told me I should do more core exercises. I didn't know what that meant, but I agreed that I would.

One of our classes was called "on-camera acting" and one day the teacher was going through with us how to make ourselves cry on cue. We were all seated in a circle on the floor, and he pointed at me, his finger very close to my face. He asked if I'd been through anything traumatic in my past that I could draw on to make myself cry. *I wonder if he asked me that because I have burns*, I thought. Or maybe I just have the vibe of someone who has been through some shit. I said yes. He asked me to describe it. There were no coddled feelings in on-camera acting. The goal here was to cry, on cue. So fucking get to it. The sooner the better.

"Well... my house burned down when I was 14 and my sister died in the fire," I said. A few gasps around the room.

"Wow," he said. "You've got quite a well to draw from." He was a black man, and always wore a baseball cap and puffy black jacket, like a director. His energy was intense, and he almost always found a way to get what he was wanting out of us. He picked up a big, professional camera off the floor and leaned it against his shoulder while he pointed it directly into my face and said, "Action."

I felt tears welling up in my throat already. Not from sadness, but from embarrassment. Didn't matter, though. I performed the monologue while crying. Assignment completed.

And then, there was dancing. I had never taken a dance class in my life. Every day, I walked into the dance studio knowing that my body was about to go through the trauma of feeling like it wasn't connected to my brain. I'd experience a total shut-down at some point every class – a point when I was so far behind, so lost as to the steps I was supposed to be doing, that I'd just stand there, let out a single, short laugh and watch, letting the other students dance around me, the ones who had obvious training leaving me miles behind.

It became apparent that the very thing I was training to do, musical theatre, wasn't the thing that came the most naturally to me. Privilege was also becoming something of a poltergeist that floated around me, moving things here and there, and me becoming ever increasingly aware of its presence, but never wanting to look straight at it. The students who could afford the school accommodation and didn't have to work outside of school hours were also the ones who had afforded singing and dancing lessons since they could remember.

"I've been doing ballet since I was two!"

"I was the leader of my hip-hop group at school and we went to New York when I was 16 and got runner-up in the national finals."

"My best friends and I sang the entire score to *Rent* out the roof of our limo on the way to prom!"

I wasn't jealous of all of them, though. There were the students who had very obviously bought their way in and had no talent to back it up. No acting, dancing or singing ability, but the school gladly took their parents' money anyway, promising to make their precious little babies' dreams come true. I felt the sorriest for them. Think of having every advantage imaginable, yearning to be creative, but not becoming Mark Ronson. Just Mark, from accounts. Maybe the "funny guy" in the office. Shudder.

"Babe, I don't give a shit if you can't hit the note," our musical theatre teacher, an ageing, spindly, gay New Yorker, snarled to me as I stood on stage. He made sure to thoroughly humiliate each hopeful bright-eyed darling at least once in the course, and today was my turn.

He was sitting in the second row of the small theatre where class was held. He had a flowy, silk, palm-tree-print shirt, perfectly tailored slacks, sunken cheekbones and bright popping blue eyes surrounded by wrinkles, and was glaring at me over the top of his perfectly circular John Lennon glasses.

"Not my problem. Talk about it with your vocal coach. And Bella," he pointed at the girl I was duetting with, "When you're on stage with someone who's obviously a far more talented actor than you, you have to make up for it in other areas. Make your movements bigger, be more attractive and match her energy." Bella looked devastated.

We all spoke outside of class about what a dickhead he was, but something about a no-nonsense adult figure taking the wheel and telling us exactly how to fix ourselves so we could succeed in this extremely competitive industry made me feel secure. Also, saying out loud what everyone was surely thinking about someone, right to their face, gave me an evil giddiness. I liked it so much, I didn't even mind when it was about me. Being more self-aware than the others, and having a sense of humour about myself, felt like a superpower.

There was something else. I began to see that people around me found me funny. I'd sometimes make people laugh and literally have no idea why. Like when Harry Potter accidentally makes the glass disappear at the zoo in book one because Dudley made him so angry. I didn't know how I did it, and it was difficult to recreate on purpose.

"Bella?"

"Here!"

Our dance instructor was racing through a quick roll call before starting class.

"Monroe?"

"Heeerree."

"Jason?"

"Heeere!"

"Rebecca?"

Rebecca did it full vocal-warm-up style: "He-ee-ee-EE-EE-ee-ee-ee-re."

Barf. They're all so irritating, I thought.

"Krystal?"

"Here."

A small pause, then an eruption of laughter from all the students, sitting down on the floor in their leotards, echoed around the dance studio. My friend Isaac fell over and his grey tights-covered legs flew straight up in the air.

I looked around at what they found so funny, and they all started imitating the way I'd said, "Here." At least an octave below everyone else, monotone, unlike the sing-songy voices of the other students, and with my West Coast inflection, glottal fry on the end. I guess it *was* funny. I didn't mean for it to be, though. It's just my voice.

Being the least funny person in my family, taking a role as class clown was one that I was surprised by, but appreciated.

As my first year of AMDA drew to a close, I got the offer from the school to do my second year at their other campus, in NYC. I'd always dreamed of living in New York, and now my boyfriend Corey, who lived a 20-minute drive from me in West Hollywood, had graduated from high school, we made a plan to move there together in July 2005.

I'd saved a small amount of money from scooping soup at the school cafeteria in LA and used it to move to NYC with little more than two suitcases. Leaving LA behind felt like the most natural thing in the world. Another fresh start! La dee dah.

However, once we arrived, the sight of the New York City skyline from the back of a taxi imposed a small fear inside me, like reverence. *Fuck. I'm actually here.*

28.

"I don't think people here hold hands in public," Corey leaned in and whispered to me as we rode the subway uptown for the first time in our lives. We had looked around at everyone else and both simultaneously thought the same thing. We dropped hands.

"Totally, I think you're right, it probably like shows weakness or something," I said.

We both nodded at each other, proud that we'd figured this obvious truth out so quickly. New York wouldn't get the better of us.

We were desperate to fit in and not fuck up in what were surely the judgemental eyes of every New Yorker, looking at these two dumbasses from the rural West Coast. Corey bought our MetroCards quickly, first try (he'd researched online how to do this), play-acting a bored local, zooming through the touch-screen system and then spinning around to coolly hand me my card.

Our first night in the hot New York City hostel, I had trouble sleeping. It was $29 a night, no air-conditioning, one bed, sharing a bathroom with six other rooms full of creepy, unidentified humans.

The heat was suffocating. When I finally dozed off, I dreamed I was running through a hallway of fire, but it never ended. I twisted and turned around corners, crying out for help. Everywhere I turned there were just more flames. They were crackling, but also roaring, and I heard voices all around me. Scared, angry voices. Someone was calling for me, but I couldn't find them. Corey was there too, just beyond the wall in front of me. He was telling me to calm down, which sent me into a rage. "No, I can't! We have to get out!" I shouted, but he wouldn't open the door. *He wouldn't believe me.* "Please, please get out of there, we have to get out now!" I pounded on the door as hard as I could. The flames started to burn my clothes and my back. I screamed out again in desperation.

"Krystal, shhh, calm down, it's okay. It's okay. Wake up," Corey said, sitting up in bed, looking concerned, but also annoyed. I remembered where I was. Not in a burning house. In New York City. In the sweltering heat of July, in the middle of the night, cars honking and people yelling outside. The sound of an obviously very tall man peeing standing up from the bathroom next door, probably not thinking a thing of the unhinged screaming from a woman in the room next to him.

"Sorry," I sighed, turning over and pretending to go back to sleep.

We found a private room for rent in a flat in Queens for $900 a month – a little pricey for just one bedroom outside of Manhattan, but the voices rang in my ears of all my West Coast family telling me, "It's impossible to find a place to live in New York City" and "It's the highest priced place to live in the country," so I figured that this was probably standard, and the best we were going to find. It was owned by a 60-year-old woman named Debra, who we initially thought was kooky, but nice.

A week into living there, I turned and looked up at our window from the street.

"Hey! Hey, if you're gonna leave, then just fucking go! Get the fuck out of here! Just fucking leave, like everyone else does!" Debra was shouting at me as loud as she could, when I was only on my way to do laundry. *Oh, shit. She's not kooky. She's unhinged.*

I texted Corey, "We have to get the fuck out of here, now."

We were only there four days, so we lost the month's rent and deposit, so that was $1,800 down the drain.

After another couple more days in the horrible hostel, we found an apartment in Woodside, Queens, that only cost $700 a month, an upstairs bedroom and living room above a very nice, quiet Mexican family. I got a job at a call centre in Queens, walking distance from our flat, and I worked the 3pm–11pm shift, going to work directly after classes, which lasted from 8am to 2pm in Manhattan.

Getting a job, going to school and supporting myself were all fine and dandy, but a few snags appeared in the lining of my life in NYC.

One, I started smoking weed. Like, a lot. At first, it was something fun to do on weekends. Weed made everything funny, more interesting, and I started looking forward to it more than anything else in my life. It was superior to drinking, which mainly made me feel nauseous or tired. I also found, when I smoked weed, I had fewer dreams about the fire. My dreams would be either completely wacky, or I simply wouldn't remember dreaming at all. This was a great relief, and a win-win solution, I thought. But my memory started to go to shit. I'd make mistakes at work, and forget my house keys constantly, inconveniencing my flatmates on a regular basis. Damn. Why must everything good have a downside?

Two, Corey was depressed. Every time I came home from work and school, he'd be in the same position he was in when I'd left him: perched at his laptop, playing StarCraft. We got into fights. I had little patience for someone being "depressed". It reminded me of someone I'd had to take care of for years, and I wasn't about to do it again. Out of ideas for work and fed up with staying home while I worked and went to school, Corey eventually took a job at the call centre too.

We moved to Harlem, 114th Street, into a large-ish flat with three bedrooms, shared with two other students from AMDA. By the time we got there, Corey and I had come to a distant place, and we had stopped having sex completely. I tried to talk to him about it, tell him I wasn't in love with him any more, but he wouldn't accept it.

One day before he went to work, I wrote him a letter, handed it to him when he was on his way out the door. In the letter, I couldn't have made it clearer that I was breaking up with him, and he proceeded to write me a scathing one back telling me what an inconsiderate bitch I was, and how I'd abandoned him in a city where he knew no one. He later apologized for some things he said in the letter, telling me he was just angry and that we should try to remain friends, but that was essentially it for us.

I had also begun to fall out of love with musical theatre, generally clashing with the vibe of the other kids I'd gone to school with, their dramatic personas and ability to float through life not working. I convinced myself that the fact that I had to work and couldn't rely on my parents for money meant that I couldn't possibly focus on auditions, the way the other AMDA graduates had.

Besides, the shameful truth is, I didn't actually graduate AMDA. I'd blown off classes and not taken it seriously in the same way that I'd treated high school and, by the time it came to graduation, I did my final performance at the showcase and then simply never came back. I ignored letters sent, and just never followed it up.

Elaine Stritch (legendary Broadway performer) apparently gave our graduation speech, but I didn't attend, because I was too ashamed to show my face, knowing that everyone knew I wasn't graduating.

It's all bullshit anyway, I told myself on graduation day, walking through Central Park smoking a joint, sunglasses on, my stringy, shoulder-length brown hair around my face, a female Bill Hicks, literally too cool for school. *Those kids don't know what real life is even like. They'll all graduate and more than half of them will fuck off back to Michigan or whatever. Besides, I'm not like them at all. I have to work for a living. I don't know what I'm supposed to do, but I know I'm not a musical theatre actor.*

I wasn't treading water in the ocean any more. I had found a boat to sit in. But I felt myself drifting, the oars of the paddleboat swinging back and forth beside me as the tide took me where it wanted me to go. *I'll grab the oars and paddle myself where I'm meant to be*, I thought. *First thing tomorrow.*

I'd then smoke and drink the whole night, knowing in

my bones that I should be pursuing *something*. But, reliably, as soon as sobriety hit the next day, utter terror would drown my aspirations. I'd smoke weed again to dull that sensation. *Tomorrow*, I thought. *When I've sobered up again.*

After I'd left home, Mom had taken the opportunity as a now child-free woman to move to Nashville, Tennessee, to fulfil her lifelong dream of becoming a singer/songwriter. I've never got on with Mom better than I did in this era, circa 2005/2006. She'd phone me and we'd speak for hours. She'd give me advice on writing my resumé so that it would get noticed, and I'd tell her about dates I went on and we'd both watch the same episodes of late-night talk shows and discuss them at length.

One afternoon, we had talked for ages, and I had spoken only about myself, her indulging in letting me tell her about every aspect of my life. I never asked Mom how she was. If I'm honest, I didn't really want to hear the answer. Aunt Kelley phoned me the next day to say that Mom's landlord had done an inspection, and her apartment was so disgustingly dirty that they were about to kick her out.

"Mom, why didn't you tell me this was happening when we talked yesterday?" I said.

"Oh, honey, I just wanted to hear about how things were with you!" she replied. A nice gesture, I suppose, but now Mom's thoughtful listening might mean she was homeless.

I called a cleaning company in Nashville and paid for them to clean her place so she wouldn't get evicted, and she phoned me crying to thank me. Also adding that Kelley was being dramatic, and that she wasn't going to be kicked out. *Of course not*, I thought.

Mom was still on benefits and went through different odd friends as quickly as she had back home, but now it was carers as well. Private ones, and then ones provided by the state. "This idiot woman stole all my pain medication," she would say about the latest person assigned to help her out around the house.

One month after I moved to NYC, she didn't answer her home phone for a few days, her cell was going straight to voicemail and I started to worry. My aunts hadn't heard from her either. I was about to try again when I got a call from a weird Tennessee number. I answered, and a woman with a Southern accent said, "Hi, darlin', is this Krystal? This is nurse Janey. I'm just calling to let you know your mom is in the hospital. Her back went out and then she got an infection; poor thing's had some bad luck, and she wanted me to let you know." I thanked her and put the phone down, wondering why Mom couldn't phone me herself. She was released a week later, and we resumed our phone calls, never speaking about her hospital visit.

An alternative version of this phone call would come through, approximately three or four times per year from the time I moved to New York. Mom is in the hospital, and there's no action to be taken except to know about it and feel bad for her. Cause of hospital admission? Varying from back pain to an infection, to a mental breakdown, to numb limbs, to cause unknown. Little did I know, this was to become another lifelong pattern for Mom.

After Corey and I broke up, I started secretly going to stand-up comedy shows, alone. I'd go to Caroline's, Gotham and, most often, the now shut-down Rififi in the East Village. Rififi was standing room only, the stage almost completely enveloped by the cool, trendy crowd that ate up the onstage comedian's every word. I drank up every second of these shows, standing by myself but surrounded by (in my mind) intellectuals drinking craft beer and laughing, sometimes too enthusiastically, at anything the person on stage would say. Night after night I'd watch Chelsea Peretti, Eugene Mirman, Nick Kroll, David Cross, Kristen Schaal and countless other comedians spin their jokes in an oh-so-cool, I-don't-give-a-fuck-what-you-think-of-me style. It wasn't needy. It was almost never high-energy. It was the opposite of the desperate, polished-vibe comedians brought up at places like The Comedy Store. These guys never said it out loud, but it was as though we were all revelling in being different from those goofy assholes who tried too hard and faked it – we really truly believed that they were just having a conversation with us, and we loved that they couldn't care less if we liked it or not. We were in on a very well-kept secret.

One very late Thursday evening, John Oliver was on stage at Rififi. I stood there with a vodka cranberry (18 years old, underage in the States, but no one checked ID at Rififi). He addressed a heckler in the room, and everyone laughed, then he started narrating the voice in his own head, neck bent and face pointed towards the floor, eyes closed. The voice in his head was self-conscious about the fact that he'd addressed a heckler when he now felt that he shouldn't have, and that he was now wasting all of his new material time doing a stupid voice in his own head, and how the bit was now becoming way too meta, but there was no going back now. He went on and on narrating this voice, lips pressed firmly against the mic, and the audience could not get enough.

Watching him on stage – feet away from me, exploring this idea, producing so many laughs, so deftly, so artfully – fascinated me, very deeply. I felt a lump in my throat, and my eyes stung. I was being moved to tears by an improvised stand-up bit, the way some people are moved to tears by beautiful music. I started laughing even harder at this. *Oh my God, get an actual grip, Krystal,* I thought.

I went home floating, fantasizing about trying it out myself. But more than that, imagining being *friends with comedians.*

You can't ever do this, though, my brain told me. *People will just think you want attention. People will think you're a drama queen. People will think . . .*

I couldn't tell anyone I went to these shows. It would be an admission that I was a little chicken, a scared piece of shit. Months had now gone by since I'd graduated (see: not graduated) AMDA, and I had convinced myself that I had no time to pursue a career in the arts, but if I admitted I went to these shows regularly, that would prove I did have time. I was just terrified.

29.

I felt bad for Mom's obvious declining mental state, and even flew to Tennessee a few times to see if I could help her. Her problems would range from vague and flimsy to wildly dramatic and unbelievable. The more anyone questioned her claims, the wilder they would become. This is a list, off the top of my head, of things

Mom has maintained happened to her, dozens of times over and again, from the past 20 years or so:

> "I had a scan that showed an abnormal growth."
> "I have an infection in my back/throat/lungs/blood."
> "My back went out while I was walking down the street."
> "A doctor left a pair of scissors in my abdomen and I'm suing him because I'll now have chronic pain from it."
> "I've been hit by a bike."
> "I've been hit by a car."
> "I've been hit by a truck."
> "I have pneumonia."
> "I have double pneumonia."
> "I have triple pneumonia and kidney stones."
> "I'm paraplegic."
> "I'm quadriplegic (but it comes and goes)."
> "I have brain cancer and six months to live."
> "I was in a coma for two weeks and now have permanent brain damage."
> "They gave me electric shock therapy and now I have brain damage."
> "They refuse to feed me, so I haven't eaten anything in three weeks."

The list goes on. These episodes of Mom being in the hospital and falling apart would also come with her being severely depressed, tearful, manic and would sometimes get to the point where the things she was saying to me on the phone didn't make much sense.

I theorized that she'd usually pop a pain pill at the start of a phone call with me and, about 20 to 30 minutes into our conversations, they'd take effect, making her less and less comprehensible.

Her moods on the phone would swing from being fun, happy, manic Mom to miserable, angry and despondent Mom every few weeks or so. I knew a hospital visit was imminent when she'd start to drop the phone a lot during our conversations or tell me she couldn't talk because she had to go back to sleep.

At first, these hospital episodes would last a week or two, and then she would get discharged and be at home for most of the time. I could speak to my "real Mom" at these times – the Mom who was creative and gave good advice and was a good listener. The Mom who was funny and easy to talk to; the Mom I could talk to for hours. My teen years had been so tumultuous; in one sense, I hadn't felt this close to Mom since I was a very young child, and it was a relief.

But the episodes kept happening; the hospital visits got longer and more frequent. They'd now be interspersed with her moving or changing her phone number and not telling anyone. I'd have no idea where she was or how to find her. When I did get a hold of medical professionals, they'd have obvious contempt for her because she was so demanding, which made getting any information very difficult.

Eventually, in 2012, Mom had run out of money, and Aunt Kelley had to come to Tennessee to help her move back to Washington state, where her pattern of disappearing and reappearing, in and out of hospitals, continued. Now months would go by with no word from her, until she needed something.

She had no cell phone because she couldn't afford one, so Aunt Kelley paid for one for her.

The more attention Mom demanded, warranted or not, the more my feelings towards her blurred and became numb. What I was experiencing was something I'd later learn was called "empathy fatigue". It was the oddest thing – I oscillated between worrying about her safety to completely losing all interest in listening to her, because I knew that most of it was lies. Any action I took to help her I had to navigate completely on my own, because the things she'd ask me for would inevitably be some twisted manipulation, and the things my aunts and I did to help her would be sabotaged, then she'd disappear again. How do you keep a wave upon the sand?

And though I was coming to terms with the fact that the way I grew up wasn't exactly healthy, I still didn't grasp how uncommon it was. I thought that being away from home and living on my own meant that I'd find way more people who had similar pasts to me, and that the problem the whole time was the rinky-dink place I'd grown up.

Of course no one in Sequim has gone through stuff like I have, I'd think. *Only a few thousand people live here! When I move to a big city, surely, I'll meet loads of people with trauma in their past like me. I won't have to hide it.*

I went through a few years of telling people very bluntly what had happened to me as a teenager, if they asked any of the key questions.

At a job interview to be a nanny to two young kids in New York City:

THE MOTHER:	So, do you have any siblings?
ME:	Oh, I had a sister but she died when she was six years old, in a house fire.
THE MOTHER:	(*face drops completely*) Oh my gosh. I'm so sorry.
ME:	Oh, thanks, I mean I'm, like, totally fine about it, though! Really nice meeting you!

And I'd beam and leave, unaware that I'd not only ruined this woman's day, but also any chance I had of getting this job.

In the tradition of Other Baggage I Carried Around From Childhood, in addition to having absolutely no qualms about moving from place to place, I also had the ability to change entire friend groups with swift precision. *Fuck this place, and these roommates*, I'd think. Someone would do something to piss me off, and that would be it. *I guess they're not such a great friend after all*, I'd think. I never gave it a second thought. I was positive this was how everyone lived. That was, until Stuart came along.

30.

"There's so many hot Irish guys at this bar," my friend Katelyn said as we pulled the heavy metal door open to a bar called McCann's in Astoria, Queens. We'd hung out in Manhattan every night for over a year and she suggested we try a suburb. *Ugh, over the river?*

What are we, heathens? But she was right. Woo nelly. This place was flooded with Irish men (never mind the fact that pretty much every bar in New York City contains at least one Irish person, by law).

The fact that the guy I was talking to was Scottish didn't really matter. Details. His name was Stuart (of course) and he was about 5 foot 8, almost emaciated, with dark circles under his eyes. He wore head-to-toe camo, even his shoes, and had an accent I couldn't understand (hot). A Scottish radge.*

But we don't have those in America, so to me he just looked like a poor, suffering artist, which I could relate to. He was a chef and told me he worked for Gordon Ramsay at his two-Michelin-star restaurant in Manhattan.

"Who?" I said. This was 2007, before Gordon Ramsay became the stratospheric reality star he is today, so the name-dropping was entirely lost on me.

Stuart took me back to his apartment which he shared with two other chefs, and we hooked up on the couch while Katelyn did whatever with one of the others behind a curtain (his makeshift bedroom door) – and the poor chef who hadn't hooked up with anyone took the only room with an actual door.

I'd spent the previous summer hooking up with many, many

---

* radge

INFORMAL • SCOTTISH

noun

   1. a wild, crazy, or violent person.

adjective

   2. wild, crazy, or violent.

(about six) other guys, and for some reason every guy I ever had any sort of physical encounter with wanted me to be girlfriend status, immediately. I rejected them all, knowing that it was too soon after my breakup with Corey (and after that, an eight-month relationship with a rebound guy who was so shitty I don't even want to give him the satisfaction of being written about).

But Stuart I liked, a lot. He'd come over nightly after his shift, around 1am, and we'd spend his one day off a week in bed together, cooking and watching TV, then he'd go back into work and I wouldn't see him for 14 hours. We clicked immediately, having similarly poor childhoods and fucked-up backgrounds, but not letting that define us.

Up until meeting Stuart, I'd cook most of my food on a Pizza Pizzazz: a metal, circular plate that had a black triangle-shaped arm sticking over the top of it, like a record player on a platform, but instead of records, you'd put on frozen pizza. I had found this miracle contraption at a thrift store for ten dollars, and I used it for everything. Even toast. It spun deathly slow, and the arm would emit the heat of the sun upon your frozen food of choice, the hot hand of God blessing your sustenance.

"It's a fire hazard," Stuart told me. "You need to put it in the bin."

As would become a recurring dynamic in our lives, I couldn't argue with the chef. Into the bin it went. That night, he made me prawn risotto, and I never thought about the Pizza Pizzazz again.

Six weeks after our first "date" (drunken fumblings on a bedbug-infested couch), Stuart was set to leave New York City and take up one of two job offers at three-Michelin-star restaurants in either Spain or France. He extended his time at Ramsay's so we could stay together a bit longer and decide on what we were going to do.

"Well, there's no way I'm moving out of New York," I told him. "I have a life here. So, that's a deal breaker." I stood firm on this, despite the lack of any supporting evidence that I actually did have a life in New York other than drinking and smoking and ducking out to late-night comedy clubs in secret. The truth was, of course, even though it had now been nearly two years since I left AMDA, I still thought nightly that I was two seconds away from signing up to an open-mic night and starting my comedy-career destiny. But I couldn't admit this to myself, let alone someone else, even Stuart.

I took a three-week vacation with Stuart to Scotland in January 2008 and learned the phrase "I'm freezing my tits off", a beautiful expression used equally by men and women of the UK. I also learned that Scotland is part of the UK. Like most Americans, I thought it was its own thing, and that "the United Kingdom" was just another word for England. You live and learn.

Stuart's mum and stepdad lived in a cottage halfway between Penicuik and Peebles, just south of Edinburgh. It was quite literally the middle of nowhere, the closest house being a mile away. It was well below zero outside, and the only gas heating in the house reached the "newer" portion of the cottage – the bit that was over 300 years old could only be heated by the fireplace, which was only lit part of the day. Not to mention, they didn't keep the heat on at night, ever. The bloods of these British people were obviously acclimatized to different temperatures from me, and I was now the weak, scrawny American who might not make it through the Scottish winter. I stammered and coughed in bed at night, the cold boreing deep into my soul. I was a medieval princess in a fortress of ice, pressing myself up against my Scottish boyfriend not for pleasure, but for survival. *We will make it out of this*, I thought. *Yes, my love, you and me, together, the steam of my breath sighing out my last incantation, casting a spell over both of us until morning, yes, O lover, my partner, my companion in this barren wasteland, take my hand and we shall go forth into the desolate atmosphere where...*

"Stuart, Krystal, that's your breakfast on the table, shall I pour your coffee?" Sharon, Stuart's mum, yelled from downstairs.

"Yeah, Mum, thanks! Down in a mo," Stuart called back. "Krystal, let go. LET GO! Here, you can wear my jumper."

I squealed with delight and we hopped downstairs, following the clouds of our own breath. I fell utterly in love with Stuart, and with Scotland. We went to Loch Ness, had prawn-flavoured Walkers crisps for dinner because nothing in the little highland village was open after 6pm. We went and got drunk in Edinburgh and they took me to The Stand Comedy Club, where the on-stage host made fun of us all for being "a family of chefs and the immigrant girlfriend". *God damn it. I could have thought of that,* I internally moaned.

Of course, Stuart came back to New York with me and, of course, we got married within three months of meeting for visa purposes – the classic NYC love story. We didn't tell my parents. *We'll get married for real in a few years and they'll never know the difference*, I thought. *It's foolproof.* Stuart told his family, and they were very supportive and, if they had doubts, they kept them all inside. Thanks, Great Britain.

So, after paying $5,000 between us for lawyers and immigration fees, Stuart stayed with me, giving up the very good opportunities he had to work at prestigious European restaurants all because I refused to move from New York City so that I could secretly pursue my non-existent stand-up comedy career. He met me at City Hall on his split shift, around 4pm, we got married and he went back to work. It was utilitarian, nothing but a necessary transaction. In my eyes, the perfect wedding. Every marriage I'd ever witnessed had failed, so what did this matter as long as we could stay together?

"I mean, I can see why you're scared to do it, that would scare the shit out of me," Stuart laughed in bed with me one day. "But you're really funny, I think you'd be great at it. Why do you think you haven't done it yet?"

Because I would suck at it, I thought. *And I can't ask people to listen to me. They'd just think I'm full of shit.*

"I guess . . . I just don't want people to think I want attention, maybe? Which is stupid, like I know obviously if you're on stage you do want some attention, it's just like . . . really scary to think of asking people to listen to what I have to say. Like, I just don't think anyone would care, I guess. I don't know. I'm gonna go to sleep." I buried my head in my pillow.

"Okay, try not to yell like a maniac tonight," he smiled and shoved my arm. I shoved him back. "Like I know your house burned down, but maybe get over it?"

"OH MY GOD, WOW." I pushed him half off the bed with my feet.

The next three years saw me working in restaurants, becoming a highly paid secretary for a year, then finally landing a job waitressing and bartending at a private club where Stuart was the chef. We saved money and, after five years of NYC beating us both down, it became abundantly clear that I wasn't pursuing comedy and that we were both ready for a big change. We moved to exotic locations for Stuart's chef career, first to Cheltenham, England (maybe not exotic to some, but very exotic to me), and then to Barbados, with me always taking bartending jobs wherever we went. We saved enough money to open a restaurant together, and finally decided to settle in Edinburgh, Scotland, his home country and the most beautiful place I'd ever seen. It was 2014, and I was 28.

"They've got the Fringe Festival in Edinburgh," Stuart would say before we went. "There's no better place for you to do your stand-up stuff." He always believed that someday I would do it, and at times I loved him for it, other times I would be mad that he kept pointing towards something I didn't want to look at. Facing this unlived life was not only embarrassing; it opened a very deep wound from childhood. The last time I'd had loads of attention on me, it was after the fire.

If I were honest with myself, one of the main deep-dark fears I had of trying stand-up was not wanting to be like my mother. She craved attention, and I wanted to prove to the world that I didn't. In the act of calling any sort of attention to myself, I felt a piercing glare of everyone around me and heard their thoughts out loud, which would consist of them thinking I was lying or exaggerating. *Drama queen, attention seeker, liar.*

And it all led back to a dark, brooding, subconscious fear.

I can't do it. People will think I'm a freak. I won't be good enough. I'm too old. I'm American and people hate Americans. I could never be on TV, anyway. I have scars on my forehead. And on my arm, and on my back. Women on TV have to be perfect-looking and beautiful. I can't ask for attention. I can't ask people to listen to me.

I can't be like her.

31.

Stuart and I opened our restaurant in an old Chinese takeaway. It was hard labour. Painting, knocking down walls, moving huge kitchen equipment in and out. Realizing the stove Stuart had bought wouldn't fit through the kitchen doorway, so using sledgehammers to make the doorway bigger, and not fixing the gaping hole it left for more than a year because we couldn't afford to. We worked seven days a week for months getting the place ready for opening. We ran out of money before finishing everything we wanted to finish and had to put everything that was left into hiring staff and buying produce. When we opened, people loved it, and the only negative comments we'd get were on the "shabby decor".

Before service one day, a skinny, sallow-looking man came in and asked in a thick Scottish accent if he could use our toilets. I said of course, and the next thing I knew he was running out the door and down the street with something tucked under his jumper. When I went into the toilets, he had stolen all our cloth hand towels. I would roll them up and make a pyramid out of them every night, and my cloth pyramid was gone.

"Don't let junkies use our toilets any more," Stuart said.

"I think that's an offensive term," I replied.

"Maybe, aye, but now we have no fucking hand towels." Stuart stormed back into the kitchen.

We took it in turns to clean the toilets, even having to clean vomit off the floor more than once.

Two months after the restaurant opened, Stuart and I were alone in it, on Father's Day 2014. "Happy Father's Day," I said, smiling.

"Oh, yeah, thanks loads," he said sarcastically. "Did you call your dad yet?"

"No, but I will soon, it's still early over there. But hey, you know what's weird? This is your first official Father's Day as a dad."

His face squinted like he didn't understand what exactly I was talking about.

"I'm pregnant," I said.

"What? WHAT! No waaaay . . ." He picked me up and hugged me. "Wait, really? No, like really?"

We told Stuart's family straight away, even though etiquette says to wait until the 12-week mark, and everyone was over the moon for us. I stopped drinking caffeine and went to prenatal yoga. *Gotta care for this precious sperm*, I thought.

Two weeks after telling all our friends and family, I was working at the restaurant and went to the toilet, and the toilet paper was covered in bright red blood. It was coming out a lot heavier than even a regular period would. It was 8pm, right in the middle of the busiest part of dinner service. I phoned NHS 24, and they informed me that it was probably a miscarriage, which I knew was a possibility, but having it happen just didn't compute.

"It's nothing you've done wrong," the nurse on the line said, softly. "It's your body's way of rejecting a pregnancy that probably wasn't viable. The fact that you and your husband got pregnant at all is surely a good sign." I thanked her, went into the kitchen and told Stuart quietly so the other chefs couldn't hear me, holding back tears.

"Yeah, I think it's, um . . ." I made a slitting motion across my throat, unable to say what I was talking about out loud as we were surrounded by staff. He looked devastated, gave me a hug, and at that moment someone called away the next order. We both straightened up and pulled ourselves back together. He went back to cooking and I went back to serve the next wine pairing to the guests. It was hours before we could speak about it alone.

After the miscarriage, we fought, and I cried. We had rarely fought in our relationship up to this point, so it felt like a huge deal. I thought he wasn't being sensitive enough towards what I'd been through. He just got on with everything like normal. Stuart was so focused on the day-to-day running of the restaurant, I felt he wasn't feeling anything towards me losing the pregnancy.

He was quiet and standoffish, and I took that as a personal insult. I've come to learn that this is how quite a lot of British people deal with big feelings. Carry on.

I hadn't yet told my family about this pregnancy, but I told Mom that I'd had a miscarriage. I braced myself for what her reaction could possibly be, as this would depend on what state of mind I'd caught her in, but she seemed genuinely sad for me.

"Mom, I . . . I've had a miscarriage."

"Oh, I'm . . . I'm so sorry, honey. Oh, that's awful."

I didn't cry, although I wanted to. Crying to Mom still felt like too much of a vulnerability, but I was very grateful she was in the right frame of mind to offer me some support, because this was becoming a rarity.

As women, most of us spend our whole adult lives trying not to get pregnant, and then, for me, I went through a small phase when I had a strong desire to have a baby, got pregnant, but still on the inside wasn't sure if it was the right decision. I lost the baby, and then my brain suddenly wanted it more than anything. What if this was a sign of things to come? What if I could never have a baby?

The pity from the people around us was the worst. "Really sorry for your loss," blah blah blah. I knew they were trying to be nice, but I didn't want anyone's pity. I hated this sad-eyed attention being directed towards me. It was like the fire all over again. Now I knew why people don't tell anyone till the 12-week mark. Those pitiful eyes are the absolute worst. Just fuck off.

Two months later, I got pregnant again. I couldn't wait to tell Stuart. He stared at me blankly, in the hallway of our flat, and said, "Wow. That scares me." He then walked past me and started talking about something else to do with service that day.

I'd never heard myself yell louder than I yelled that night. The rage that pulsed through my veins at Stuart not making this moment as special as the one when I told him on Father's Day killed me. How could he be so insensitive? This pregnancy might become our actual kid. And his reaction is, "Wow. That scares me"? Fuck everyone. More tears.

Hours later, when we'd calmed down, we talked again.

"I was just scared. I'm really sorry," he told me later. "Of course I'm excited. I just feel like I'm so overwhelmed with the restaurant stuff right now, it's like I have no capacity for anything else. I love you so much. I can't wait to tell Mum. She'll freak out, again. And hey, I'll make sure to move the tables farther apart, so you'll fit between them." I punched his arm.

The restaurant was busy, and we had a baby on the way. I was excited, of course, and so proud of what the restaurant was achieving and the cute little home we'd built together in a rented flat in Edinburgh.

I was feeling something more than pride, though. I had a panicky feeling, like I'd forgotten something huge. The panic grew the more tables I waited, the more wine I poured, the more cocktails I shook; even more as my stomach grew bigger and bigger.

The thing that I secretly carried with me, heavier than the baby inside me, the thing I wasn't telling anyone, was this: pregnancy was a big relief, but not only because I was afraid I'd have another miscarriage. In my eyes, I'd soon not have to work in the restaurant any more. I was proud of the restaurant, sure, and I was decent at what I did (decent – not great – sort of like my singing ability back at AMDA), but it was hard labour, long hours and I just wasn't passionate enough about it to get me through the turmoil of it all.

I won't have to do it any more. I'll just be home taking care of a baby, I thought. *That'll be so much easier.*

32.

There's a secret document in the drafts folder in my Gmail account, a draft that contained something so shameful I never dared open it if there was even a slight chance of anyone nearby reading it behind my back. I kept its existence quiet, hidden. *You'll come out when the time is right, my precious*, I truly believed, internally. *Not now, no, not now. But someday.*

This document contained *JOKE IDEAS*. I'd started adding notes to this document in (I'm embarrassed to type this) the Year of Our Lord 2006. Just a note: I thought, just now as I started typing this chapter, that I'd go ahead and put those original joke ideas into this book. But I had a look at them, and HA, no. You're never, ever going to see them. Seriously. They're that bad. Maybe that's why I never started comedy in my early twenties. The universe wouldn't let me, because this is all I had to say:

THE HOTTEST GIRL AT BURN CAMP

One of my worst pet peeves is people who . . . use the term "pet peeves". Also, there aren't enough super-hero movies.

Please, please don't ask me to share more. I don't know what this meant. It was a painstaking process for me to choose which sentence I would include here. I mean, why would I type an ellipsis? Was I telling myself that's where I should pause? If so, that's not even the right place to pause, 24-year-old Krystal.

This document, added to now and then over the course of a decade, was gathering electronic dust. It was a visual, clickable representation of my procrastination, of my fear. Nearing 30, and very pregnant, I dusted off the old document and started making edits.

There's nothing like giving birth to your first child to make you wake up to the reality of the world, and your place in it. I stared down at this perfect little infant, completely reliant on me, who would only get bigger and have more and more complex feelings and thoughts as the years rolled on, and I thought, *Oh, shit. I cannot let this child grow up to have a husk of a mother who never even tried to go after what it was she always wanted to do in life.* Also, he'd be looking up at a mother who only supports her husband's career and ambitions and has none of her own. I saw my whole life before me: a part-time stay-at-home mom, and a part-time sommelier and bartender at my husband's restaurants. I'd cook a lot, and garden and do yoga and become all homey, and sometimes make snidey jokes and perhaps have a casual interest in comedy and as the years drew on I'd grow bitter and never, ever want to watch stand-up comedy again. I'd avoid anything to do with that world, and I'd start to hate my children, and my life, and myself. And in my obituary it would say, "RIP Krystal, she had a great sense of humour." Ick. That life looked awful.

The other life, however, comprised me trying stand-up comedy. But I couldn't see past that. The trajectory was empty. The path it charted was dark, unknown.

"Going after your dreams" sounds so cheesy and lame and doe-eyed and American, but here we are. *I need to do it, and I need to do it now. No more excuses (oh sure, "I have a baby now", how convenient). No more stalling. It's now or never.*

I typed "open mic comedy nights edinburgh" into Google, and hit enter.

The Stand Comedy Club in Edinburgh, starting place for many Scottish comedians, had a policy in 2016 of only opening applications for new acts in October and April. I signed up in October, and they offered me a five-minute spot the following March. A five-month wait. *I've waited this long,* I thought, *so what's a few more months?* Not to mention, I was looking after an infant, which took up a bit of my time.

Baby Sonny, although the light of our lives, was a terrible sleeper. I admit, now, that it may not have been his fault. When we left the hospital, the midwives told me to "feed on demand". They didn't mention when I should stop feeding on demand, so I thought they just meant forever. Breastfeeding came relatively easily to me, so that was no problem at all. At first. Breastfeeding was what put the baby to sleep. It's what calmed him down. It's how he'd settle. Every nap, every bedtime, he needed to be nursed.

If that boob wasn't present, sleep would not come, for anyone. This wasn't a problem, until it was very much a problem.

It resulted in a baby who needed to be nursed approximately 10 to 12 times per night if he was to fall back asleep, as babies' sleep cycles are about 45 minutes long in the first months of their lives. Nursing a dozen times a night turned into habit and, before I knew it, Sonny was still waking up 10 to 12 times per night at a year old, way after this should have stopped. Stuart helped as much as he could, but he worked at the restaurant until about 1am most nights and, of course, even when he was home, he couldn't breastfeed.

When Sonny was eight months old, I woke at about 11.30 one night to the sound of his cries. When I sat up in bed, I was surrounded by thick black smoke. The baby was in trouble. *He's screaming because he can't breathe. Oh my God.* I needed to get us both out. I saw flames coming from the kitchen on the way to get him. "Sonny!" I screamed and I picked him up, breathing heavily, and ran out the heavy front door of our flat and into the cold, echoey hallway. When the stony concrete hit the bottom of my feet, I froze. *Wait a second.* I turned around. There was no sound of fire. No smoke. The flat was dark, but just as it always was. The baby was crying louder than ever, squirming in my arms. He was cold. Probably wondering why the hell I had brought him into the freezing, echoey hallway. I breathed in, silent tears rolling down my cheeks, and went back inside to nurse Sonny back to sleep for the sixth time so far that night.

These hallucinations continued for a month or so, mostly during the night and fuelled by lack of sleep, and almost always involved me smelling smoke. I'd also startle, screaming, during the day because I thought I'd seen someone out of the corner of my eye who was in the house about to attack us. A man, who always turned out to be the clothes horse or a coat hanging on an open door.

And, I thought about Katie. I thought about her more often than I had since her death. Looking at this perfect little baby of mine brought a new layer of grief to what I'd lost, and at times it was too much to bear.

I started post-natal therapy, provided free by the NHS, which included childcare. (Thank you, thank you, thank you.) It helped, but I wasn't ready to talk about the fire and Katie stuff in depth yet, and the therapist didn't prod much. When I told her about my childhood, and the fire, she seemed shocked, like she was a bit out of her depth. Instead, we'd mostly talk about the general difficulties of looking after a baby and she seemed more comfortable with that.

What helped me more than anything, though, was when a no-nonsense mum friend of mine told me straight up to stop nursing the baby so much at night. "He'll be getting used to being fed at night and expecting those calories. He's probably getting hungry. Plus, he can't fall asleep without the boob. He needs to learn how to do that." This all made a lot of sense. Once he was free of the boob crutch at night (at 14 months – far too long), we all slept a lot better, and my hallucinations stopped.

On 27 March 2017, I floated, dazed, into the backstage area of The Stand. I needed the toilet and had full-on diarrhoea immediately. *God damn it.* As if doing my first-ever gig wasn't bad enough, now I'd stunk up the backstage toilet. I ran hot water and squirted tons of soap into the sink to get the steam to waft soap smell around the room. Not much more I could do. I shudder to think of the stories the backstage toilet at The Stand would have, if it were sentient.

I sat among the other comedians, many of whom seemed to know each other already, still and silent, not saying a word. *Maybe if I stay still enough, I'll melt right into the chair*, I thought. I looked at the lineup. Fourth in the first section. I had no idea if this was good or not.

A Canadian gal, wide-eyed and upbeat, was draped across the couch and making generally positive North American-accented comments about the gig and the other comedians in the room. I wasn't fully listening as in my head I was going over the set I had memorized for the last five months. Boots, Sushi, Trump, Lizard, Grandma, Muslims. Boots, Sushi, Trump, Lizard, Grandma, Muslims.

I heard, from the corner of my mind, the Canadian gal say to a young man in the room, "Oh, it's your first gig? Don't worry, this is a really nice room!"

Well, this was my opening, if I wanted to make any sort of chat. "It's my first gig, too," I said.

"Oh my God, really?! You seem so calm!" the bubbly Canadian laughed.

This surprised me. I had just shit my guts out in the toilet and I felt as though I might hyperventilate. Surely, they were all avoiding me because of my unstable nature.

"Oh, no way, I'm so nervous," I said. Everyone in the room laughed at this, and I realized it was for the same reason the kids back at AMDA had laughed when I'd said, "Here." My flatline voice made it seem like I was being sarcastic. "I'm just good at hiding it," I said, smiling.

"I'm Heather," the Canadian gal said. Heather is about five foot seven, medium, wavy brown hair, angled features, high-set cheekbones and the style of a tomboyish, late-twenties millennial. Checked flannel shirt, baseball cap, very little makeup, drinking a pint.

"Krystal," I said, extending my hand. "Where you from?"

"I'm from Canada, Prince Edward Island. You know *Anne of Green Gables*? Yeah, that's where I'm from! You?" she said.

"American, Washington state," I answered. We chatted a bit more about Vancouver, where Heather had lived for a few years, right above where I was from. She seemed nice, but I secretly wanted this conversation to end so that I could go back to saying my set list over and over instead of being social.

I was on next. The oxygen in my body seemed to have been replaced with some sort of chloroform-type gas. I was dizzy. My eyes were swimming. I stared at the back of the stage door, listening to the host hype the audience up saying, "Two more acts in this section, are you ready? I SAID ARE YOU READY?!" Gigantic whoops and hollers from drunk audience members.

I started coughing right before he said my name to clear my throat of the nausea I could feel rising in it. The smell of old, musty wood, alcohol and spray cleaner that I'd later become so accustomed to now only made me more queasy. I felt like a small child who shouldn't be allowed to be in this grownup place. *Why did they let me in?*

"Please put your hands together for Krystal Evans!"

I somehow made it on to the stage and was glad to see that the stage lights were so incredibly bright I could only make out the first row of people, who all seemed smiley and non-threatening. I couldn't see Stuart's face, or my friend Sally and her boyfriend Pav, the only people I'd invited. I wished now, more than ever, that I had invited no one.

"Hi, I'm Krystal," I said. I had literally written this line down in my notebook. Had I not written it, I was sure I would have forgotten my own name.

"So, yesterday I saw a man buying sushi . . . at Boots. First of all, I didn't know until yesterday that you could buy sushi at Boots. Secondly, how hungry do you have to be to buy raw fish from a chain chemist 10 feet away from where they sell a cream that stops your butt itching?"

The laughter was immediate, rippling across the room. My first joke ever said on stage, sort of making fun of British culture too – a risk, surely – had landed. I smiled, and relaxed. Slightly.

I went on in the rest of my five minutes to talk about how Donald Trump was a secret lizard alien and how Americans are made mostly of Kraft cheese, then ended by saying that lizard aliens now have to stay on a strict diet of Canadians, because they're healthier than Americans. I realized this would probably endear me to my new acquaintance, and first-ever comedian friend, Heather. I finished the set to uproarious applause.

I stepped backstage and was absolutely buzzing, a literal ringing sang in my ears. I then laughed to myself, leaning against the stage door, taking some deep breaths before heading back into the green room. *This is what you should have been doing the entire time. You're a comedian. You always have been*, I thought. *You absolute dumbass.*

Heather had been in the crowd watching; she came back into the green room and walked straight up to me. "That was your first time on stage?" she said.

"Yeah," I replied.

"That was, like, really good. You should definitely keep doing it," Heather said, earnestly. Now I *knew* I liked her. At the end of the gig, she gave me her number and we met for coffee, where she encouraged me yet again to keep doing comedy.

"I always want to make sure female comedians who are funny keep going, because so many of us quit, and mediocre men keep going!" she told me, laughing. I was grateful.

That panicked feeling, the giant heavy weight I'd been carrying around – the one that I'd forgotten something huge – lifted. I had finally remembered the thing. The big, huge thing that I'd forgotten. This was it. All these years I had been ignoring who I really was. And what to do about it? I couldn't go back and change my past, so I just said sorry to myself and moved on. I'm a comedian now, no matter what.

33.

"I'm trying to get power of attorney over your mom," Kelley told me in 2017. "She's just not in the right state of mind to make her own decisions any more." I couldn't have agreed more. *Thank God, finally, someone will be able to take care of her and she won't be able to run.*

Mom was up for the arrangement, but when it came time to sign the papers, she refused. This happened three times over in the course of a year.

Her pattern of being checked into the hospital increased, as did her months of disappearing and non-contact with any of us. The only consistent people left in her life were me, Aunt Kelley and Aunt Tina. She was now in hospital more than half of the time, the reasons ranging as far and wide as you'd like.

I kept in contact with her as best I could, but the years of me being devoted to seeking her out and figuring out how best to help her in any given situation had worn me thin, and now I had a baby of my own to look after, not to mention a new career that I was very excited about. When I told Mom about starting stand-up comedy, she'd sometimes be excited for me, but then in the next conversation she wouldn't remember anything I'd told her about my gigs, or about my son. It hurt that she couldn't retain any information, and even though I was a full adult woman, it still hurt the same way as for a five-year-old trying to show a drawing to a parent who is too busy to care.

I stopped trying so hard, because it felt fruitless, but also to protect myself.

Now that I was in Scotland, it became harder for Mom to get hold of me, in the rare case that she wanted to. Calls and texts would come in from my aunts, telling me that Mom needed more money, or that she had been phoning them in the middle of the night demanding they go shopping for her; or they'd come from someone else who Mom had convinced to make calls for her. She would put her sisters' names and addresses down at hospitals instead of her own, so they'd get charged for her medical bills (which is fraud – a felony – but Mom knows her sisters would never press charges). Both of my aunts went through long phases of not speaking to Mom, then coming back around to helping her again because their poor sister had obviously not been in her right mind and had no money or resources to her name.

"I told her I'm done with her," Kelley said to me over the phone one day, getting slightly choked up. "I told her she keeps sabotaging herself and I just can't spend any more mental energy on this. I can't help her any more." She sighed. "It's such a sad situation, it really is. Your mom has been through so much, but she's brought so much of it on herself and I just can't be at her beck and call any more. I'm sorry, Krystal."

"Oh my God, no, Kelley, I can't believe you've stuck it out this long," I said.

"Yeah, and now she's escaped this hospital she was at and has been transferred somewhere else. They freaked out because they thought she couldn't walk," Kelley said, anger rising in her voice.

"I guess she's not paraplegic this week," I smiled, hoping Kelley could hear this over the phone, and we both laughed, slightly relieving the pressure.

I spoke to doctors about her; tried to gently but firmly tell them that Mom went from hospital to hospital, care home to adult family home. This was a pattern.

The issue was, almost everywhere she went, there would be a brand-new team of medical staff who had never met her before – and most of them wanted to get to the bottom of her issues, and many felt very bad for her – especially after she told them the story of the fire (reliably the first thing she tells everybody she meets). Other doctors and nurses might be suspicious of her condition and symptoms, but I've now learned they can't, legally, let on that they feel this way.

I started to do personal research on Mom's situation and found a condition I'd heard little about previously. It's called Munchausen's, a more advanced version of another condition called factitious disorder, or malingering (not to be confused with Munchausen syndrome by proxy, where people bring illness upon their children for similar reasons of seeking sympathy).

There are very few academic books on the subject (though countless memoirs), but I eventually found one called *Playing Sick?* by Dr Marc D Feldman, which proved to be illuminating. I devoured this book within a few days, as I'd never come across anything that described my mother with more clarity.

In the book, Dr Feldman explains that people with Munchausen's and factitious disorder/malingering (which I believe Mom has, with a sprinkling of borderline personality disorder – and this book confirmed that the two commonly go hand in hand) are extremely hard to treat, the greatest irony being that the patient will say they have every ailment under the sun except the one they actually have. There aren't many courses of treatment for people who have this disease, and there are even fewer for people who don't admit they have it.

Dr Feldman spoke of patients who fake cancer to get sympathy from coworkers, who weave complicated tales of trauma and suffering, some real and some imagined, but the sympathy they get is never enough. The patient must always go further and further, upping the ante and then travelling from medical facility to medical facility whenever someone clocks on to their falsehoods. It's a pattern of thousands of known patients, apparently, and many medical professionals are well aware of their existence.

Here's a quote from the book, which, after I read it, I highlighted the shit out of:

> It isn't as hard to fool medical professionals as one might expect . . . As in any business, doctors want to please their customers. If a patient says, "You're missing something. I'm still in pain," doctors are likely to make every effort to please the patient, and so they conduct more tests. In other situations, a physician may say, "Everything looks normal, but since you're so sure of the ailment let's just go ahead and treat it." Having no cause to doubt their patients, physicians are motivated by a sincere desire to relieve the patient's suffering. Add to this benign intent the fear of malpractice litigation

in an increasingly scrutinized profession and the result is a treatment approach that leaves no stone unturned. As a result, patients end up exposed to unnecessary medications, medical procedures, and even surgeries.

This paragraph floored me. Never had someone described Mom's life so accurately. She has had countless surgeries, procedures, treatments. And because of her prolonged time staying lateral and sedentary in beds, she then gets real infections and makes herself very authentically sick, which only complicates the matter more.

I don't know what the path forwards for Mom would have been back then, or if there is one now, but I can only hope writing it all down gets us closer to some sort of solution. Not just for Mom, but for other people who are surely going through the same thing. She's the most frustrating person on earth, but I try to remember that she was once a young child who needed help, like I did, and my sister did, and no one gave her the help she truly needed, because no one knew what was wrong.

In 2017, Mom was in a recovery ward for patients who needed special care and rehabilitation in Seattle, the first place where she had claimed that she had become quadriplegic (all four limbs paralysed). Up to then, there'd only been claims of paraplegia (only two of the four paralysed – usually the legs).

When I came in, unbeknown to her, I saw her reaching for her phone on her side table, and I said, "Oh – you can move your hand? I thought you couldn't move anything."

Mom jerked her head to the side to look at me.

"Oh, I can do this, just this one movement, but that's literally it," she said, sighing.

While I was visiting her, a psychiatrist came in. I spoke to her alone outside Mom's room, while Stuart took two-year-old Sonny off to walk around outside.

"What's her official diagnosis?" I said.

"So, because of confidentiality I can't tell you anything like that," she said, an upswing at the end of the sentence. "But . . ." she looked down and to the side, "you can tell me things. That would be helpful."

"Well, this is her pattern. She gets checked into places and then moves on to another hospital or adult family home until she gets discharged or kicked out."

"Mmmhmm. And . . . has this . . . paralysis thing," she narrowed her eyes and looked slightly upwards, ". . . happened before?"

"Oh, yeah. That's been going on for years. It keeps getting more and more extreme."

"Mmm," she said knowingly. "Well, all we can do, really, is treat your mom in the ways that we're trained to."

"But where does someone like my mom fit in, in the medical system? She just floats from place to place, no one knows her history of lying at the next hospital or doctor's office. I mean, this is her whole life. When does it end? I'm at a loss of what to do for her," I asked this woman, desperate to cling on to this one medical professional who seemed to actually know what was going on.

She just shrugged, and kept her mouth shut. Fucking brilliant.

*

As the years went on, I stopped trying so hard. Mom seemed beyond any sort of help and, whenever I did speak to her, it was draining. I didn't feel like there was a way to help her or to get through, so what was the point?

I had tried everything else, so thought I'd go the direct confrontation route one day when she was being particularly difficult on the phone. At the end of *Playing Sick?*, Dr Feldman said that sometimes direct confrontation works but, in his defence, I definitely didn't go about it in the way he'd recommended.

"You have fucking Munchausen's syndrome," I told her one day, straight up. She cried, but she was already crying about something else. She took this "everyone thinks I'm lying" thing as another way to play the victim, and it pissed me off even more. Nothing changed.

34.

At the end of 2019, I had been doing stand-up for nearly three years, had broken into doing weekends at the major comedy clubs in Scotland and won a few gong shows in England that got me some decently paid gigs down south. My profile still wasn't huge, but I was having a great time. I'd found what I was meant to do and, along with that, a group of friends that I liked. Comedians are misfits, weirdos, extroverts who make everything into a joke. Normal people don't understand this. Normal people take serious things seriously, and repeat jokes they've heard on TV. Comedians understand how lame this is. These were my people.

I got pregnant again in April 2019 and I just have to tell you – doing jokes on stage while pregnant is something I hope more people can experience. It's magical. People don't expect a pregnant woman to say crass, sexual things (ironic considering the deed required to get pregnant).

Most gigs when I was pregnant went very well, but I did one in the outskirts of Manchester, eight months gone with a huge belly, where a drunk woman in the audience started accusing me of not really being pregnant, spouting about how she'd "seen this act before" (very possible – I milked these pregnancy jokes for as long as I could for the four or so months they were relevant, up and down the UK. But crucially, I was indeed pregnant). "You SHOULDN'T BE saying that when you're NOT really pregnant!" she screamed. "That's a fake stomach! I've seen this before! You should be ashamed of yourself," she spat. There was a man and woman on either side of her, the woman was grabbing her arm telling her to be quiet, along with the rest of the audience, and after I started speaking back to her, the man on her right stood up and left the auditorium.

"Uh oh, your boyfriend left," I said. I couldn't think of anything cleverer than that. The rest of the audience turned against her, which was nice, but didn't make it any easier to finish my set.

If it had been me now, I'd have offered to show her my swollen vagina or told her to come up and lick my haemorrhoid-covered asshole or something, but in that moment, no cutting comebacks came into my brain. The only thing I could think was, *What if this woman has lost a baby?* or some other annoying empathetic thought, so I just moved on, and then felt really awful after I got off stage. A real comedian would have *ripped her a new one.* The host came back on stage and had her kicked out. I got about ten private messages on Instagram afterwards from audience members apologizing for this woman giving their small town a bad name and saying how great they thought I was, but I still felt like shit about the whole thing.

"You are allowed to not know what to say when someone verbally abuses you. I mean you're eight months pregnant and you were ambushed." Heather was giving me friendly comedy advice. "It shouldn't be your job as a comedian to handle outright cruelty. You are a mother, and you know what it's like to lose a pregnancy, and the empathy part of your brain took over. It's understandable."

She was right, but I still felt like the comedian part of me and the mother part of me hadn't merged in the way I'd have liked them to. I put that on my mental to-do list.

Part Four

35.

I pushed Jesse out on my living-room floor on 21 January 2020. We'd planned a home birth and hired a huge inflatable bath for a water birth, the whole works. The two midwives who helped me out were wonderful. Just as with having Sonny, I could not believe my luck that this was all free. The water bath ended up relaxing me too much, though, and the midwives eventually had to get me out of it to move the birth along. It was all relatively smooth (except pushing the head out – fuck me, I don't believe any amount of hypnobirthing could hippy me out of that sensation), and he was healthy and gorgeous.

Shortly after having Jesse, I felt panicky again, similarly to how I'd felt after Sonny was born. Jesse was a way better sleeper, though, because I kept the boobs under wraps at nighttime after age three months, and also mastered the art of pumping milk so that Stuart could do some night feeds. They recommend the baby go into their own room after six months, but Jesse slept in the box room from five. Also, sometimes we'd use formula if there wasn't enough breastmilk to go around. I was *not* going to let what happened with Sonny happen again. And it worked. Jesse was a great sleeper right from the start. My panic this time came for different reasons.

One overwhelming thought was, *I need to get back into*

stand-up as quickly as possible. I couldn't let a little thing like giving birth let me fall behind. If I did, I'd be back where I started. Back to being that terrified person who couldn't remember what it was she'd forgotten to do because her brain was now filled with kids' needs. Back to being fearful of becoming like Mom and letting that stop me from doing things. No way.

Three weeks after Jesse was born, I started gigging again. I was still heavily bleeding (a normal occurrence for about five or six weeks after giving birth), but my local gigs, at The Stand and Monkey Barrel, were nice and comforting and felt like home. I'd bring the baby with me and make someone look after him for the 15–20 minutes I was on stage. But then I started doing road trips again, further south, leaving the baby at home, and while I was at those gigs I had a desperate feeling that I shouldn't be there. Swathes of drunk audiences, comedians I didn't know bombing on stage and then coming off to pats on the back from their pals. And me needing to sneak off to my car to pump breast milk. I didn't feel funny. *What even is a joke?* I couldn't remember. I'd have intense intrusive thoughts about something horrible happening to my kids. Ha, ha. Ha.

Four weeks after baby Jesse was born, I flew down to London with him and Stuart to compete in a new act competition. In my eyes, this was an unmissable opportunity. I pumped loads of milk for days leading up to it, which took hours and hours of my time, so that I could leave Jesse in the hotel with Stuart for three or four hours during the competition and the baby would have plenty of food.

Then I accidentally left the case of pumped breastmilk at

airport security and had to go back for it. A nice, stressful way to start the trip.

The night of the competition, I left Stuart and Jesse at our hotel as planned while I went to compete in what turned out to be a very casual gig with very amateur comedians performing to about 40 people in a hired room of a major hotel. Before the competition, the woman running it actually gave us all a lesson in how to use a microphone. *Maybe this competition wasn't as prestigious as I'd built it up to be*, I pondered.

The two comedians who got the biggest laughs were me and an Irish gal.

Okay, so it's between the two of us, I thought.

Neither of us placed. Three men took first, second and third. I left the competition weeping, breasts hard as boulders from not nursing in three hours, walking back to my hotel in the pouring rain.

What the actual fuck am I doing? I thought. *Making my husband and newborn come to London so I can stand on stage in front of a bunch of freaks who I'll never see again.*

When I walked in, Stuart told me Jesse had slept the entire time and none of the milk I'd pumped had been needed. I nodded and cried some more.

"I think you maybe should chill on the gigs a little bit?" Stuart said, lovingly rubbing my leg. "It's all gonna be there for you when you get back. And hey, isn't this supposed to be fun?"

I sneered at him. *How dare he say something so ridiculous?* I thought. *Comedy? Fun? Grow up.*

36.

I planned on doing my debut hour at Edinburgh Fringe 2020 – a very big deal for UK-based comedians – and was going to name it "Fresh Out the Oven", centring around Jesse's homebirth.

We all know what happened in March 2020, so I'll skip all the details there, but suffice to say my debut did not happen. I was relieved at first – *Thank God the pressure to gig is gone, right at the time I have a newborn baby. Now I can just concentrate on him, no questions asked.* But having a newborn baby in the pandemic was not the prance through the flowery meadow I thought it might be. Instead, it was that boat ride from Willy Wonka: a beautiful pristine paddleboat leading towards a freak show in a dark tunnel, complete with crying parents and screaming children.

Intrusive thoughts started pouring in. I was incapacitated by the fear that I would accidentally spill the hot kettle on the baby or drop him out the window. I cried, all the time. Sometimes the crying felt like it would never end. I had to turn away from five-year-old Sonny while making him breakfast to hide the tears streaming down my face. A hard knot formed in my stomach and neck, the kind that signals you are about to cry, but crying never released it. Taking my daily walk didn't release it. Walking and crying at the same time didn't release it. The knot was always there, a warning from my body that something awful was right around the corner.

To top it off, I'd get an intense wave of depression every time I breastfed. I'd have to bury my head in my hands while nursing Jesse to get through it. I eventually found out that this is called dysphoric milk ejection reflex, or D-MER, and it's something that many women experience. There are support groups online for breastfeeding parents who go through it, but, as with many of these disorders that historically affect only women, little research has been done on it. I felt completely debilitated, and like a failure. How could I ever go back to comedy or even be funny again? What would I talk about on stage now? "When I breastfeed, I wanna die!" Ha, ha, ha.

I started therapy over Zoom with a psychiatrist recommended by a friend, who specialized in extreme trauma. He was about 70, with a posh English accent and a very gentle manner. I was hesitant at first to open up to someone so different from myself, especially over Zoom. But he told me stories of other patients he'd helped, shocking things they'd been through, and knowing that he knew what he was doing when it came to trauma, had helped people who had gone through even more extreme things than me, made me relax and put trust in him. He unquestionably knew what he was doing.

We did a version of exposure therapy, which involved me telling him everything that happened the night of the fire, and then going away and writing letters that contained my deepest, darkest thoughts. Thoughts about what had happened to Katie. Thoughts about what Mom might have done. Everything, the worst of it, all exposed on paper.

I smashed the printer into the window, and shards of glass fell all around my feet. I could feel my shoulder getting hot and the heat of the flames was too much to look towards. I hurled myself out of the window and landed on the grass... I wondered where Mom was and if she'd gotten Katie out...

On and on I'd write. Every thought. Every feeling. I'd start to shiver, while writing. I'd realize that I had stopped breathing completely, then take a desperate gasping inhale, and exhale slowly. I felt so cold, I half expected to see my breath in front of my face. I'd have to stop writing and go put on a jumper. Extreme fear would flood my body, as if the fire was happening all over again.

"Yes, that's what it's meant to do," my therapist told me. "Did you ever hear that expression 'It gave me the chills'? Scary things literally do that to you."

He had me write a letter to myself at age 14. "How about when you saw yourself in the mirror in the neighbour's bathroom?" he suggested. "From your perspective now, stop her, and talk to her."

Hi. Are you okay? Listen. You're amazing. You're incredible. What you've just done is unbelievable and beyond what most adults are capable of. I can tell you right now that this is the worst thing that will ever happen in your life. You're going to be okay. Your burns will heal.

Life with Mom has been so hard, I know. But in a few years, things start to change for you. You move in with Dad when you're 16. Spending months with him will make you realize that life with Mom was never normal or safe. After you graduate high school, you immediately move to LA at age 18. You live there for a year and then move to NYC. You spend five amazing years there where you make loads of friends from all over the country and the world. You meet your husband there. He's a chef. You become very passionate about food and learn cocktail bartending. You work at a private club and meet and serve tons of celebrities. You move to England, then Barbados (a great two years – you go back on many holidays with your kids in the years to come), then Edinburgh with him. In Edinburgh, you give birth to two beautiful boys. Your kids are gorgeous and funny and fulfil you so much. You live in a beautiful flat. You love living in Scotland.

You finally start doing stand-up comedy in Edinburgh, at age 30. You love it. You realize immediately that this is what you're meant to do. You have your own shows at the biggest comedy festival in the world. You find a deep confidence that you've never known before.

You don't know this yet, but what you've gone through in your life up to this point is not normal. Not at all. I know it's hard to hear, but Mom hasn't protected you and kept you safe in the way that she should have. A parent's job is to keep their kids protected. And to be a strong, capable, stable figure in their kids' lives. There are good things about her, but she's very mentally ill. For most kids, her behaviour would have been very damaging; but somehow, you've managed to see through all that and become a well-adjusted, capable person. I know it's hard to understand, but you've been the sober, logical, strong one in almost every stressful situation. You are insanely smart beyond your years. You're funny. You're down to earth. It's completely understandable why you'd react the way you've reacted to what has just happened.

The vast majority of people don't go through anything close to this traumatic in their entire lives. You'll meet very few people who can understand what this is like, but you make great lifelong friends, who you love and who love you. Hang in there. Your life is going to be amazing.

Love, Krystal

Hours and hours of sessions with me sobbing, telling my therapist things that I'd never told anyone. Fears and dark thoughts I'd had, about the fire, about Katie, about Mom. I didn't want to go there, but he assured me it was necessary. So, we went there. Deep down, to the dark depths and back again.

"Write it all out," he instructed. "All of it. Even the worst bits. The bits you thought you'd never bring into the light."

What happened between Mom running out of her bedroom, the room I was in, towards the kids' rooms?

What happened in that space while I was escaping out the back of the house?

What actions do people take when they're being eaten alive by fire? What actions do mentally ill people take when faced with the same scenario?

The therapy was rough, draining. But it was like weight training. I was getting stronger.

"So, Krystal, when we look at the damage from all you went through, a really important part is of course the fire, and the fact that you now have the intrusive upsetting thoughts. If you were to pick two of the biggest fears you have right now, what would you say they are?"

"That something bad is going to happen to my kids," I said. "And... that I'll lose my identity to motherhood, or that if I do pursue the things I want to pursue in comedy, I'll end up being mediocre or bad. Also, that people won't accept me any more."

"Mmm. And just to steer in another direction for a moment – what do you think 14-year-old you needed?" he asked.

"Someone I could trust," I said. "And maybe some guidance... I'm not sure what else."

"Yes, I think you're right. I think she needed an older person who was there for her, who was reliable, responsive, loving, capable... who could have allowed and encouraged her to 'just be a 14-year-old', rather than having to take on all that responsibility and having to cope with so little support or help," he said.

"Yeah, definitely. For sure."

"How would you now, at 34, have spoken to your mother back then, in front of the 14-year-old you?" he asked.

God, that's a hard one, I thought. I imagined me, an adult woman, standing in front of myself as a 14-year-old and protecting her with my body, putting a protective hand out in front of her, pointing a finger at Mom and telling her that she wasn't giving Krystal what she needed.

"Stop expecting her to take care of everything. She's still a child. She needs a parent," I'd say. "She needs to rest."

37.

When Jesse was six months old I finally told a visiting midwife about how it felt like a dementor attack every time I breastfed, and her face went immediately sympathetic. "You can stop breastfeeding," she said. *Thank fuck*, I thought. *No need to tell me twice.* We went immediately to formula.

Coming out the other side of therapy and rising from the deep dark depression of post-natal hell, I knew something deep down: I wanted to write about the fire, and my childhood, and Mom, and Katie. I needed to tell my story of the fire, on stage. I'd hidden it from people for years; not on purpose, but just because telling other people about it became a burden on me. But how to do it? I still wanted it to be a comedy. But on paper it just wasn't funny.

"The Edinburgh Fringe loves this sort of sob story," many a cynical comedian would tell me. "These are the kinds of shows that win all the awards."

"Really?" I'd say. Of course, I'd heard the stereotype of the "Dead Dad Show" (a saying quipped by comedians and reviewers to express how many hour-long shows have cropped up at the Edinburgh Fringe that are about someone's tumultuous relationship with their father, and then the father dying, and them realizing their relationship was nuanced, coming to terms with it. Because of the sheer number of these, some feel it's a desperate and shameless grab for awards).

I knew emotional, personal comedy shows existed, of course, but I always thought they were sort of "lesser than" the ones that were purely jokes. *We've all been through tough shit. Get over it*, was what I thought was the general attitude of both comedians and most audiences. *Besides, despite all the work I've done in therapy, I still think if people know these things about me, they won't accept me. They won't laugh. They'll just nod and back away slowly. I have to keep my I-don't-give-a-fuck persona up on stage.*

"But this story is so fascinating," Heather said to me one night, sitting on my couch while we munched popcorn together.

"Really? Is it? It's just depressing, right?" I said.

Heather laughed. "Oh my God, Krystal." She smacked her own forehead. "No one has a story like this."

I went through the rest of 2020 and 2021 in a daze, doing gigs over Zoom which were mostly awful, sometimes when regulations loosened doing gigs in person which were slightly less awful, and keeping my kids alive and safe. The therapy helped, but my mental health felt like it was still teetering on the edge at all times. If I didn't keep to my strict regimen of eating healthily, exercising and sleeping enough, all hell would break loose. It's so annoying that those three things make so much of a difference.

"Heather, I have no idea how to make this funny," I told her on the phone, walking through the city on a cold, dry, crispy day in February 2022.

Heather came over one rainy Edinburgh night to help me

with my writing. "Okay. Tell me the story, all the way through," she said. "No jokes, just tell it straight."

"Well, it was the night of 18 March 2000. I remember waking up and seeing flames coming in through the bedroom door, and hearing screaming . . ." I went on, and on. "If I hadn't been a barely 100-pound 14-year-old girl, there's no way I could have fit out this window . . ."

"Skinny legend."

"Skinny legend?" I said.

"Yeah. Trust me. Saying 'skinny legend' is very funny. Gen Z will love it," Heather assured me.

"So Dad came to visit me every day in the hospital, because . . ."

"Because it was on his way to work?" Heather smiled. I burst out laughing.

Heather continued, "If I'd been on the East Coast, who knows? I would have just gotten flowers and a card that said, 'Sorry about What's-Her-Name'."

I perished with laughter at this. "Oh my God, Heather, what the fuck . . ." Tears streamed down my face. This was the funniest shit I'd ever heard. "I've always found people with normal parents complain about them a lot. Like in high school I'd be like, 'God, my mom is such a psycho' and a friend would be like, 'Omg I know what you mean. Like yesterday, when I wasn't home, my mom went into my room and cleaned it.'"

Heather chimed in, "Oh my God, exactly, like when I was seven my mom used to make me hold the steering wheel while she lit her cigarettes."

By the end of this night, my stomach ached from laughing so hard. Speaking to Heather unlocked some door in my brain that connected the tragic shit I'd been through with the comedic joke-writer part. It felt electric.

38.

In 2022, a neurosurgeon called me, a very sweet woman with a kind and tender voice, who told me that Mom was in a coma and "probably doesn't have much time left". I asked the doctor specific questions about her condition, which she answered with much empathy. I knew there was no point trying to convince this woman that my mom might be faking this coma – *also, was that even possible? Could you fake a coma?* If there was one person in this world who could manage it, I knew it would be Mom.

Okay. So, she might die now, I thought. I made plans to go home, even though in the back of my mind I didn't truly believe she could be at death's door. The doctor had said she was on life support and had an infection. "If we were to detach her from life support, it wouldn't be long," she said, "She has been through so much. Your mom is one tough cookie." The tone in her voice telling me that if I were a good daughter, I'd come there immediately. I thought to myself that the only way that a member of medical personnel would feel this kindly towards Mom would be if she were in a coma.

We'll see how bad you feel for her once she wakes up, I thought. *If she wakes up.*

Two days later, Mom awoke from her "coma".

"She's being demanding towards the hospital staff," Kelley said. "They told me she's pushing the nurse call button more than 80 times per day. They want me to come pick her up, but she has nowhere to go and there's no way she's staying with me."

"Back to her old self, then," I said. I didn't hear from the neurosurgeon again. Thank God I'd held off on buying the plane ticket. I tried to call her that evening, and she didn't pick up. Her outgoing message (the one where most people would just say, "Leave a message after the beep") was along the following lines – she had put on a very high-pitched, scratchy, squeaky babyish voice, as though she were a toddler who had just got done crying:

> Hi, you've reached Tracy Truth. If this is anything urgent you can leave a message, but I'm in Harborview Hospital right now... the same hospital I was in in the year 2000 when my house burned down and 80 per cent of my body was covered in burns. My daughter Krystal was also in the fire and 40 per cent of her body was burned. And... (*she starts crying here*) my other daughter Katie... died in the fire! (*She wails.*) Please don't leave a message unless it's very important because I'm trying to focus on healing... BEEEEEEP...

I put the phone down without leaving a message.

*

It's extremely difficult to feel sorry for someone who continually breaks your trust, crosses your boundaries and demands oceans and mountains from you, only to have it never be enough, and after you give everything, to find out they were lying.

In February 2023, Mom went through an episode of sending me emails (voice to text, I think – although I'm unsure this is even possible coming from someone who's supposed to be quadriplegic). They became frequent, obsessive and ultimately upsetting, addressing my kids and other aspects of my life that she'd gathered from looking online.

Sometimes they would be her begging for help; other times, like a message she sent through the contact form on my website, she'd be angry at me, accusing me of lying about her in my stand-up, and then making a joke about it all in the same message.

Some emails would be blank, and only come through with a subject line. One stated that there are "worse things in this world than losing your sister or a child, like being quadriplegic", and how I could never understand this.

I tried to feel bad for her, but my body would only let me feel numbness and indifference. *If I let myself feel how sad this is, I won't be able to function and properly take care of myself and my children* was what I told myself as I struggled to get to sleep at night. It's the most painful thing, but I can't help her when she refuses to help herself.

39.

I had an overwhelming desire to write. I knew now that I wanted to tell the story of the fire from my perspective, and I wanted to tell it my way: on stage, with jokes. I was positive about this. I felt, in my bones, that this was the right thing to do. Jesse was two, in nursery, and Sonny was in school, so I had a few days free per week. I committed myself to writing about my childhood and the fire every single day, and the story flowed out of me. Some of it in joke form, some of it just facts. But I kept writing no matter what. I'd sit down for at least an hour every day and unload everything I could think of about that time period.

I started dipping my toes into doing material on stage about my fucked-up childhood, how I grew up very poor, Mom's mental health or the fact that my house burned down and I suffered major injuries in the fire.

"So, mental illness runs in Mom's side of the family. So does being hilarious. And they tend to go hand in hand, so sometimes I'm like oof, I might be in trouble. Some of you are like, 'Nope, you're fine.'"

I came to realize that this material wasn't normally suitable for a 20-minute set for a club weekend – it should be kept for the alternative nights, or new material nights, or any gig where woke-as-hell young people hang out. For me, though, that wasn't good enough. I wanted the material to be screamingly funny, to as many people as possible. I never spoke of my sister dying in these shorter sets – I knew that if I was to deal with that at all it would have to be in the hour-long version.

I have to try out the whole thing. I need to tell the whole story on stage and see if it's all too much, both for them and for me.

I bit the bullet and scheduled my first hour-long work-in-progress of this show, whatever it was, at Monkey Barrel Comedy Club in Edinburgh for May 2022.

Finally, the date arrived. 27 May 2022. Fifty people turned up: a really good crowd for that room, which made my nerves soar. *How dare people actually turn up for something I told everyone to come to? Rude.*

As I stood in the wings waiting to go on stage, I felt as panicked as I had for my first-ever gig. My heart was beating out of my chest, my head swam and I kept purposely coughing, sharply, to try to clear my urge to vomit.

No one will want to hear this, the voice in my head said. *What the fuck do you think you're doing saying these things on stage? This isn't comedy. People will think you want pity, or attention. People will think you're a drama queen. They'll see right through all of it and no comedians will want to hang out with you any more. They'll think you're just trying to win awards. You're not even a real comedian. A real comedian doesn't talk about this kind of shit. You're a freak. You're just like HER . . .*

"Please put your hands together and welcome to the stage, Krystal Evaaaans!"

I stepped on stage into the spotlight.

The audience's eyes were eager and welcoming.

Oh my God. So many comedians had come out to see this

show – which was simultaneously humbling and maddening. As a comedian, you never value anyone's opinion higher than that of other comedians. Other scattered friends were here too.

I stared out at all the supportive, listening faces. I recognized at least ten of them.

"Wow, so nice of you guys to all come out tonight. But I think I've actually changed my mind – can everyone I know personally just get out, please?" Light, timid laughter. *Oh God.*

"So, this show that you're about to see is very personal. A lot of things I talk about in this show are things that, if I were to just tell you in a normal conversation, might make you very uncomfortable. You'd be like, 'Oh no, she's one of those oversharers.' And you'd make an excuse and leave. Which is why, for my show, we lock the doors."

They laughed, harder this time. I relaxed.

I told my story.

They listened.

I said the darkest stuff my heart contained, and made fun of it. I got off stage and waited for the awkward "Great job", but also expected to see fear in people's eyes, the tentative judgement I'd seen so much in the past, and then the inevitable not wanting to be friends with me any more, just like people had done my whole life whenever I'd dared to share who I really was and what I'd really gone through.

But, you know, the opposite happened. I don't know if it was because of my commitment, or the way it was presented, or the rawness of it all, but sharing what I'd been through had brought everyone in the room closer together. My peers, my friends and the audience. And every time I performed my "fucked-up childhood" show, as I lovingly called it before it had a title, I'd get people coming up to me in tears, private messages on Instagram, emails after the show from people telling me how much it resonated with them, that my mother reminded them of their mother or father, or their sibling, or of themselves. And so many of them said, "Thank you for sharing your story." I really didn't know why at first, but although I'd performed the show for, ultimately, very selfish reasons, I could see that people were taking away something that they themselves found useful. Dark thoughts have less power when we bring them out into the light.

I had thought, up until I had the breakdown that required therapy after the birth of my second child, that I would never talk about my fucked-up past on stage. It was something hard I'd gone through, moved past and recovered from, fully. It wasn't a part of my comedic persona. I was a comedian *despite* it happening to me. I had risen above it. I had successfully buried it. Bye bye.

But now, I'd excavated it and shown it to people, and they hadn't run away.

I knew that snidey whispers might come from other comedians, saying things like, "Fuck sake, how is making people cry considered comedy?", "It's not real comedy" or "Oh great, are you gonna pull a Hannah Gadsby?"

A few other comedians who cast a cynical eye towards people talking about this sort of stuff told me that they saw my show and thought, *What the hell. I'm going to be a little more vulnerable on stage.* And I thought, *Yesssss. Fuck what people think.* Our life experiences are all we have, ultimately. And the fact that I had inspired some other people was the greatest compliment I could have ever received.

40.

I got the show recorded and sent an early version of it to Dad. Honestly, I sent it to him so that he could see the jokes I make about him being a fiend for Bud Light Clamato and being great at drunk driving – just some light-hearted ribbing.

I waited for his reaction over the course of a couple days, and nothing. I sent him a text on a Thursday in September.

KRYSTAL:	Dad, have you watched my show yet and have you disowned me as a daughter? Ha.
DAD:	No disowning. We watched it Monday night, and it was pretty heavy stuff. I'm kinda blown away a little. Stuff I hadn't heard or known about. I was going to watch it again before feedback. Work is just crazy sideways busy. Stress level is riding high.
KRYSTAL:	Ahhh okay, cool. Yeah, I know. If you want to talk about it/have a call, let me know!

Another three weeks went by, and we finally had a phone call.

After five or ten minutes of small talk about work and great sandwiches he'd had lately, I jumped in.

"So, you watched the show?"

He sharply exhaled. His tone, normally calm and even, changed to slight annoyance, which for Dad is a lot of emotion. "Yeah, I did, y'know, it's just – I never knew a lot of that stuff."

"Yeah, like what?"

"I don't know, I just... I know things were bad, like I knew your mom had problems. I guess I just never knew... things were *that* bad."

"Right," I said. The silence between us grew. We were waiting for the other one to talk, both of us wanting to just stay silent.

"Look. When you were a kid, Krystal, I was just told to never, *EVER*, bring it up. I was told that by you, by Grandma, by Cheryl." He was on a frustrated rant now. Emotions from the past were coming to the surface. "Everyone told me to just shut up about it and not bring up your mom. So I did! I just stopped talking about it altogether. I was worried about you, but I thought that was the best thing to do."

"Right, well, I mean, do you see there's a difference between bringing up something tactfully and telling me Mom is a crazy psycho bitch or whatever?" I was in full hurt teenage mode. I felt like I was 15 again, defending myself and my actions to Dad, who was angry for reasons I had no control over. "I *had* to live with her. She's my mom, and I was a kid. I had no choice, y'know?" I took a breath and let the 36-year-old Krystal step in and talk for me. "Can you see how maybe that wasn't helpful?" There was silence for a moment, at the other end of the phone. I could just picture my dad standing in one place in his garage, then pacing every time he started speaking again.

"I just didn't know how bad things were, I guess. And like," he sighed. "I'm just in shock, a little bit, I guess."

I felt rage pulse through me. I wanted to scream at him. I wanted him to say he was proud of me, and I wanted the same reaction from him that audience members and other comedians had given me.

One of the most frustrating facts about growing up is that you realize that, no matter how old you get, you always want approval from your parents. Their opinion matters more than anyone's. It's so utterly annoying.

"I guess . . . I don't understand why you're mad at me right now," I said. The tears came up then. I couldn't help it. "Like, what have I done wrong? Most people are really liking the show, and have been supportive . . . and I'm just telling the story the way I remember it. I thought you'd hopefully look at this from the perspective that, like, you're my good, sane parent."

"I'm not mad! I'm just . . ." Dad intentionally lowered his frustration, and his tone, ". . . a little shocked, that's all. I'm glad if people are liking this show and you're getting a good response from it, but like . . . I'm not a normal audience member. I was there. I lived it, with you. I saw you in the hospital and took care of you afterwards. I remember what you said to me in the hospital about how you escaped out the window, by the skin of your teeth, and I realized that you'd almost died. What you said to me that day in the hospital is burned into my brain forever."

I was taken aback by this. I hadn't considered, when I sent Dad the show, that this would bring up some very intense bad memories for him, too. I hadn't considered Dad's feelings because, to be frank, I'd forgotten he had them.

I thought the bits Dad would care about were the things I said about him and his drinking habits, but as it turned out he couldn't give less of a shit about any of that. I'd forgotten that the fire wasn't something that just involved me. It was probably the hardest thing Dad ever went through, too. Of course it fucking was. He just showed it differently.

"Okay, I get that, I guess." I went silent. Blank, no idea what to say. Me, a 36-year-old surly teenager wanting Dad to just go away and leave me alone.

41.

Finally, I felt ready to do a proper full one-hour version of the show. I had been reaching in the dark for this for two years, but now I could see how to do it, and I felt strong enough (I thought). But because it was the third iteration of the show (and the final one, surely), it needed a proper title, something with humour and truth all wrapped up into one.

Not easy.

But help came to hand in the shape of Heather.

She and I sat in a café on the Royal Mile in Edinburgh in

THE HOTTEST GIRL AT BURN CAMP

September 2022, and I happened to be telling her about the summer camp Mom had taken me to in the months following the fire. She stared at me, gawping, though I didn't fully understand why.

"It was a Burn Camp. Y'know, a camp for kids who have been burned. But the weirdest thing was, like, I wasn't nearly as burned as most of the other kids there."

Heather looked at me, wide-eyed. "Wait a second, Krystal. Are you telling me you were – the hottest girl at Burn Camp?"

"Oh, totally." I sipped my coffee.

"That's the title."

"What's the title?"

"The Hottest Girl at Burn Camp."

"How has your upbringing affected your own mothering?"

"Oh . . . I'm a good mother." I smiled.

"Well done," my therapist said. "Write yourself a letter about what mothering means to you."

Ugh, I thought. *Fine. If I have to.*

I already know what's important. My issues have always been internal, but I don't let them affect what needs to get done for the kids to feel safe and to thrive. I want to prove to everyone that what I went through isn't a life sentence of fucked-up behaviour from me. She had a rough childhood, so did her parents, and it affected them. It won't affect you. I won't let it. I can handle anything. I will be on time. I am a good, safe driver.

You will have clean clothes. You will eat freshly cooked food. And I'll work on myself on my own time.

When I tell myself I'm lazy, or not good enough, or I'm failing, or I look like shit, or nothing will ever happen the way I envisioned, I will step in and protect myself. "You are doing great," I'll tell myself. "You will make it through this. You are amazing and smart and talented, and you have all the tools you need to succeed," I'll say. I'll imagine giving myself a big hug. "You deserve love," I'll say. I won't embarrass you. I'll support you. I'll make sure you go to bed on time and have time to yourself and say kind, encouraging words to you. I'll call you out when you need a kick up the ass. "Get out of bed and get going. You'll feel better," I'll say. Because I'm your mother, a good mother, and that's my job.

You also deserve to have motherhood not be your entire identity. You deserve support from the people around you. When a stand-up comedian talks about how kids should still be hit like the good old days, or some influencer talks about the only way to be truly happy is to be childless, and forgets that the point of feminism is that women should be able to have any life we want and not be judged for it, I'll remember that being independent and strong doesn't have to only look one way.

I started comedy after I had my first kid. I found myself after having kids. I realize how incredibly lucky I am to have this privilege.

We also hate kids. We hate them because we've forgotten that we used to be them. We are them, still. They're in there, wanting to play. And I can't deny the kid version of me. I love her so much. She also deserves a good mother and I'm that now for her.

When I wake up early with my kids and feed them breakfast, make sure they have everything they need for school and get them out the door, I'm patching up a tear from my childhood. When I drive them safely long distances with no accidents. When I pick them up and drop them off with a relative with no drama. When I get along with the other adults in their lives. Their teachers, their friends' parents, their relatives. And if there ever is a conflict, I don't involve them. They are able to focus on growing up and learning, not taking care of my feelings. And I'm experiencing their childhoods too. Little Krystal is safe now.

I can handle anything you want to throw at me. I am safety. I am here for you, always. And I don't want anything in return. That's what being a mother is.

42.

I took a trip, with my husband and two boys, back to Washington state in November 2022, to visit Dad for Thanksgiving.

While I was there, I could tell Dad wanted to say something to me. I'd gotten all geared up, with fuel from my therapist, to speak to him frankly about the phone call we'd had. I wanted to apologize to him for sending him the show without pre-warning him what it contained.

But I lost my nerve once I saw him.

Luckily, he was more keen to speak to me about it than I'd been to speak to him. We were staying in an Airbnb in Corvallis, Oregon, near my Aunt Janet's house as she wanted to host Thanksgiving at hers, and I'd forgotten Jesse's bottle back at her house. It was about a seven-minute walk back to hers.

"I'll come with you," Dad said.

Oh, here we go, I thought.

We stepped outside into the crisp November air.

"Hey, so, I heard you're going back to Sequim," Dad's eyes blinked and he walked way faster than me, so I struggled to keep up.

"Yeah, we're gonna go on Monday," I said, flatline. "Just to see the place where the fire happened and Katie's grave and stuff. I haven't been back for so long."

"And Stuart said you're gonna try and talk to the firefighters? Are you gonna ask how they think the fire started?" Dad's eyebrows were raised, and he looked too eager to know my answer.

This line of questioning was making me slightly queasy.

"I don't think I'll ask that question, no. I really just want to thank them and ask what they remember about that night. I want to clarify some stuff for myself. I mean, you know Mom, she pisses everybody off at the best of times, so if they remember us at all they probably won't want anything to do with me," I said.

"Yeah. Yeah, because you know – after we talked – I thought about it, and your mom's thing has always been attention.

And like, losing one daughter and having the other one horribly burned, that's definitely something you'd get sympathy for for the rest of your life, y'know?"

I nodded. Then I sighed. I couldn't think of anything to say back that would convey the relief, sadness, anger, fear and disgust that I felt at him saying this, so I just whispered, "Yeah."

"Well, I've emailed them," I said. "The firefighters. This week. They haven't answered me, so I don't know if it'll happen. But I'm going next week either way."

"Yeah. Yeah, because, you know – after we talked – I thought about it, and what you said in the show made a lot of sense," Dad said sharply; he is getting to the age where he always repeats himself, and I'm at the age where I've stopped pointing it out. He seemed slightly manic. "It was hard for me too, back then."

"I know. And hey, I'm really sorry I didn't pre-warn you about what was in the show when I sent it to you." Then, "I have to give this bottle to Jesse," I said and I turned to go back into the house.

"And hey, one more thing." Dad stepped in front of me before I could reach the door. "I realize now that the things I said to you about your mom when you were growing up were definitely not helpful. You were just a kid, y'know? And you couldn't help your situation, and I shouldn't have unloaded that on you." Dad put one hand on my shoulder.

"Thanks, Dad, I really appreciate that." It was all very sweet and nice, but the saccharine levels in the air were reaching a saturation point, so I turned and went indoors.

I told Stuart what Dad had said outside. "Yeah, that's great,"

Stuart said. "He asked me about us going to Sequim too. Think he was pre-gaming talking to you. He does really care."

43.

"But where are Grandpa Woody's ashes?" I asked Kelley during that same visit. We had been discussing the location of Katie's grave, so that we could go and find it the next day, and she had told me that Grandma Lora was also there, but that Grandpa Woody had been cremated. After that, his remains had been given to Tina, the oldest of his four kids, and she had contacted her two sisters, Kelley and Mom, to find out if either of them wanted the ashes, because she didn't have room for them.

"They were in a huge leather-bound box with his name on the front on an embossed golden plaque," Tina later told me. "When the lady from the funeral home lifted the box into my trunk, she literally said, 'Wow, he was a big boy!' and I was like, 'I don't know, he looks like he's lost weight to me.'" Razor-sharp wit from Tina, even while picking up her father's ashes.

Kelley told Tina she didn't want Grandpa Woody's remains either, and so Mom volunteered to take them. When Tina went round to drop them off, Mom didn't answer her door, so she left the box of ashes on her doormat.

"Then next thing I know your mom is calling me, very pissed off," Kelley said. "She said that Tina had written 'DAD' with an arrow pointing down, taped to the box, on the back of a Taco Bell receipt."

"Oh my God. It was not a Taco Bell receipt," Tina said later, indignant. "Such a drama queen. It was a coupon for a *free taco from Taco Bell.*"

Years later, after Mom had moved many times, she had a load of stuff in storage and, because she hadn't paid her bill in years, the storage unit was auctioned off, the way that you see on those American reality shows like *Storage Wars*. Whoever bought the unit contacted Kelley to tell her that they had someone named Woody's ashes, and asked if she wanted them back. So Kelley now has the ashes in her possession again.

She shook her head at me incredulously.

"Unbelievable."

I knew I wanted to go to Sequim, but I wasn't exactly sure what I planned to do when I got there. I'd been writing and talking about this very specific place in such great detail for the past year that I felt sort of like I was talking about someone behind their back, and it was only fair to go and see these places in person to get a sense of something. Of what, though? Unsure.

I had a vision of Harry Potter going back to Godric's Hollow in book seven and being tricked by that old lady who turned out to be a snake. I also have scars on my forehead, and had a fucked-up childhood, and read the books in my teen years, so Harry Potter has always resonated with me.

We drove together, me and Stuart, with our two boys in the back seat of our rental car. Kelley and her best friend wanted to join us, so they were in a separate car behind us. Over the three-hour drive, we took the Edmonds/Kingston ferry across Puget Sound, something I hadn't done in over a decade. The smells of the passenger deck brought me back to my teen days when I'd take the ferry on my own to visit Dad. When we reached the Hood Canal bridge, I eagerly looked out into the sound for seals. I always used to see seals from the bridge. I saw no seals today. *Did I ever see seals? Were they always just ripples I'd convinced myself were seals? Or did an adult tell me they were seals, and I wanted to believe it so much I just went with it?*

I had no address to type into Google Maps to get us to the locations I needed to see. I had to do it all on memory. I was sure I could. First, we went to see Katie's grave. We found the graveyard easily enough, but finding the grave itself was another thing.

I recalled the funeral and standing at Katie's grave when I was 14, with my grandparents and Mom weeping beside me. That was 22 years ago. There were more graves now, and I realized my recollection of where we stood that day may have warped.

As we approached the graveyard, a crunchy gravel drive led our rental car to the top of a flat hill. In my memory, the graveyard was small, surrounded by trees on all sides, and contained maybe 50 or so headstones. This place had hundreds upon hundreds of graves, stretched out in endless rows and columns, some hidden behind little hills and tiny valleys. Memories of childhood usually convey things as bigger than they are in reality, but this one had been flipped on its head.

The ground and the air were saturated in damp. Brown and

yellow leaves were sprinkled across the neatly cut grass; someone obviously raked the grass regularly, but in November the falling leaves are constant and relentless.

We pulled the car up to the edge of the drive, the pointy little gravel rocks making a grinding sound to announce our arrival. I sat in the running car for a moment, just searching with my eyes out of the front windscreen. *Why am I scared to get out of the car?*

The kids were both asleep. "Do you want me to come with you, or do you want to have a look by yourself?" Stuart asked, his face clearly up for either option.

"I'll go by myself," I said. "You just wait with the kids." I was overcome with a deep, internal need to be quiet, invisible, reverent. Why oh why had I invited so many people along with me to this place?

Kelley and her friend had parked on the far opposite side of the graveyard, Kelley being certain Katie's grave was somewhere over there. I knew she was wrong, but I let her look anyway, happy to search alone.

My feet squished into the saturated grass, a small puddle of brown water squelching around my boots with each step.

Where are you? I can't find you. Where are you?

The familiar feeling of having forgotten something planted itself in my throat and stomach, again.

Headstone after headstone, I wandered past, snidely checking the ages of the people who had passed away. 89 . . . 91 . . . 69 . . . 79 . . . *Yeah, so sad*, I thought superciliously.

Then, a name I recognized. Not Katie. *Lora Dunn Wixom. 1926–2004.*

"Hey," I croaked. My voice was more constricted than I'd been aware of. I tried again, louder. "Hey! I found Grandma!" I shouted across to Kelley. They walked across to join me.

"Where's Grandpa Woody?" Kelley's friend asked.

Kelley cleared her throat. "He wanted to be cremated," she said. She shot a glance at me, and our gazes both fell back to the ground.

I searched the stones just around us. I knew Katie was nearby. A flat, dark grey stone with a big pink star in the middle lay adjacent to Grandma's.

"Here she is," I said to myself, in a near whisper.

Katie Marie Truth, 1994–2000. Missed by Mom, Sister, Family and Friends. I just stared. I was frozen. Grandma and Grandpa had bought this headstone and sorted out all the funeral arrangements because Mom was still in the hospital. The stone itself is very basic; now, it stood out to me as one of the smallest in the graveyard. It was all we could afford.

Twenty-two years. I'd never once revisited her grave in all that time. Had anyone? I'd thought about Katie, sure, but her grave? I hadn't considered it important. In my teens and early twenties, I'd say things like, "Graves aren't really important to me because I don't believe in God, so I don't believe that Katie is there at her grave. I grieve in my own way." Then, as time went on, the gravestone's existence faded from memory almost completely.

Now, I felt as though my six-year-old sister had been here, cold and alone, up on this hill for 22 years; I imagined her being sad that no one had visited her. I felt deeply ashamed. I also wished, more than ever, that I was alone. I didn't want to have to cater for other people's emotions right now. I didn't want them to try to cater for mine, or do that game where people try to say the right thing. I just wanted everyone to fuck off.

I got back into the driver's seat of the car, the kids still sleeping soundly. "God, her grave is so small. It's like the cheapest grave out there," I said to Stuart.

"We could sort out a new one, if you wanted?" he said.

When I started the engine, Sonny, my seven-year-old, stirred and yawned, "Hey, where are we?"

"Sequim," I said. "I was just visiting my sister's grave and now we're going to my old house." I said it in a "Mom voice" – that tone where you feign being upbeat, but it just comes across sarcastic, especially if you're me.

"Hey, I want to see it!" he sounded slightly hurt, like I should have known this would be important to him.

"Oh, I'm sorry, sweety, of course." I turned the engine off again and left Stuart and Jesse in the car while I led Sonny to Katie's headstone.

When we walked up to the grave, he read the whole thing in its entirety. "Katie Marie Truth. 1994–2000. Missed by Mom, Sister – hey, that's you, Mommy! – Family and Friends. I like the star," he said.

"Yep, she loved stars. Whenever I see a star, I think of her. Her favourite colour was purple too, so if I see a purple star, it's like a double whammy." I breathed in the cold fall air and took in the smell of the wet forest.

We both just stood, silently, for about 20 seconds, taking in the sight of Katie's gravestone. Sonny reached out and tightened his arms around my hips, squishing his face into me. This little boy, who I'd given birth to, raised and kept safe, was comforting me because I'd lost my sister. "I'm sorry she died," he said. I marvelled at him and felt a flood of gratitude. *How does this sweet little boy know the perfect thing to say in this moment?* I put my arm around him and felt a calm fall over me.

I couldn't remember our address, but I knew instinctively how to get there.

The sign at the entrance to the housing estate stood exactly where it always had, in stone. "Dungeness Meadows," it read. Behind the sign were thick vines, bushes, tree trunks.

"I used to hide my bike behind that sign," I said. I slowed the car and peeked behind it as we drove past. Just imagine . . . nah. Nothing there.

The long, pointlessly curvy road led us down through close-cut, bright-green grass, the road purposely winding to give a sense of countryside and luxury. Our car wound through the golf course that spread over every inch of land not crowded with pine trees or mobile homes. We passed the A-frame brown clubhouse, the one designed to look like a Swiss chalet but that, among the evergreens and manicured, plastic homes, looked more like a giant cartoon doghouse.

The road split, and I took the one on the left. It was only a few houses down. I saw the place where our mailbox sat. In a tiny island in the middle of the road, along with about 20 other mailboxes.

Although most of the surrounding homes had changed, they were still in the same positions, so spotting ours was easy. A tiny white wooden spike stuck up from out of the ground, with the numbers running top to bottom:

9
6
8

968 Dungeness Meadows. Of course. How could I have ever forgotten that? 968 Dungeness Meadows. That's where it happened. The house that stood here now wasn't even a whisper of the one that burned down. It was white with grey trim, and a huge wicker heart had been hung on the front. It was in a different position from ours; sideways rather than longways. The driveway had been repaved with a different colour gravel. The plants were all changed. Still leaning out from the window of the parked, idling car, I scanned the skyscraper-high trees around the house – a small part of me wanting to see burn marks, or scars on the trees. I looked at the fence in the back. I felt a deep need to see any evidence at all of the fire taking place. The pavement? The ground? Nothing. Erased completely.

I could smell the fire, though, both the way it smelled that night and the way it smelled when Mom made me come back and we found the photo albums. Burning flesh, melting plastic, then cold, sweet-smelling ash.

I looked across the road, at the old woman's house where she had invited me in and told me to run my hands under the cold water. It had changed too. Unrecognizable except for the position.

I looked at the man's house where I'd called 911 from. It looked similar, but was covered by trees, so I couldn't be sure it was the same home. *So American*, I thought. *To preserve nothing of the past at all, just pave everything completely and start again. Not that anyone would want to preserve what had happened to us. The people who live there now surely know nothing. Should they know? Has it been hidden to preserve market value on the house? That's kinda shitty, right? Or is it? No one would want to live around here if they knew, that's for sure. Or maybe they still would, and that's even worse. Or is it? Does it matter? Am I making everything about me again?*

I pressed lightly on the accelerator again and kept rolling onwards, to the end of the street, not wanting to attract any attention. I drove to the end of the cul de sac, peeked through a few houses at the end of the drive and caught a glimpse of railroad tracks. Were they still there? Had there even been railroad tracks, or am I remembering wrong? There's definitely a river around here too. I turned around and passed the house again.

The railroad tracks. Katie. *The thing I forgot.* What was it?

I was in the hospital. They thought I was asleep, and they were talking about Mom. Hushed, concerned voices.

> I mean, I just went in to see her, she's completely out of it. She started screaming at me, "Katie's not dead! She escaped and she's running around in the woods on the railroad tracks, I know you don't believe me but I swear I saw her out there . . . please go and get her . . ." I was like, Tracy, honey, they found her . . . I don't know, she's just not thinking straight right now . . .

We passed the house again. My biggest fear was that someone would want to know why I was looking at it. My eyes darted all around us, checking we weren't being watched.

"This neighbourhood is actually a lot nicer than I pictured," Stuart said. "Like when you said, 'trailer park' I was picturing something different. Some of these homes aren't too bad."

"Yeah, I guess. Let's go."

I didn't know if I'd achieved what I'd set out to, but I felt like my invisible time limit was up. I got us out of there, confused and slightly unfulfilled. *I'll come back again on my own at some point*, I thought. *The firefighters never answered my emails either. They probably recognize my name and remember what a psycho Mom was, so they almost surely want nothing to do with me.* It felt as though the whole town was glad to be rid of us.

We drove east out of Sequim, Aunt Kelley's car 50 feet or so behind us. Five minutes past the town limits, Kelley's headlights flashed me, again and again. She did this sometimes, so I just thought she was saying hi. I waved. She continued flashing. *What the hell?* I checked my phone, and I had missed calls, and she'd texted me.

We pulled over on a country lane and she got out of the car, out of breath, ran up to my window.

"Hey," she laughed. "Sorry. The lady from the fire department just called me. She wants you to call her back! Maybe you can still see them."

This really threw a spanner. Although logically I really did want to talk to the firefighters, like I had taken all the steps to speak to them, in a sort of zombified mode – in reality, it terrified me. There was a huge part of me that had hoped they wouldn't respond, and then I could again blame Mom and my upbringing for people treating me like a social pariah. But now, someone had reached out. She wanted me to call her. I workshopped a bunch of stuff to say to them, but when the moment came, what would I actually say? *What if I go blank? What if I forget something?*

I dialled the number Kelley gave me.

"Clallam County Fire Department, Cathy speaking, how can I help you?"

"Oh, hi, this is Krystal, I'm returning your call, I emailed last week."

"Krystal! Oh, I'm so glad you called back!" The voice on the phone was warm and reassuring. "You know I saw your email and I immediately knew who you were. I remember when the fire happened. And I think you went to school with my son, Curtis?"

I was jarred. I wasn't expecting to be welcomed like this.

More guilt flowed into my body; these people, this town, had tried to help me and we never said thanks. There was always a thin, plasticine layer of Mom's actions tainting our environment. Things that had been said, done, that no one had told me about. People would be out of our lives suddenly; friends would be cold and distant; situations remained unfinished and unexplained. Hesitation surrounded us. We were the toxic people who needed to be escaped. So I couldn't imagine what Mom had said or done to the firefighters who were there that night. Did she blame them? Mom is capable of saying unimaginable things when she's in a bad state.

"Oh . . . yeah! Yes, I definitely did. Wow," I heard myself

say back to her. I'm a normal person. I'm sane. I'm not asking anything of you. "How are you?"

"Good, good. You know, so I've looked up your file and I have a list here of all the first responders who were there that night of the fire; firefighters and police officers. Some are retired, but I can send them all your email, so that they can contact you, if you'd like?"

Oh my God. This was everything I had asked for. "Oh . . . that would be amazing. Like I said, I'm really just wanting to thank them and sort of ask what their memories are of that night; I'm writing about it, so just want to get all perspectives possible." I tried to put on my best reporter voice.

"Oh, Krystal, I'm sure they'd love to talk to you. And just to say, I'm so sorry about what happened to your family," she said.

"Thank you, thanks so much."

I gave her my email, got back into the car. I gripped the steering wheel and Stuart looked at me, eagerly awaiting the details.

"She's gonna give all the firefighters my email," I told him.

"Wow." Stuart's eyes went wide and he waited for me to say more. I didn't. I started the car and we drove away from Sequim.

44.

Later, I checked my email and Cathy confirmed that she'd sent the firefighters my email as promised. Four of them, and beside all their full names was their working status (retired, semi-retired, active).

Anticlimactically, none of them ever reached out to me, which was of course entirely their right, though I tried many times over the course of a year to follow up. I didn't even know what they looked like, because I had been whisked away in the ambulance before they had arrived.

People encouraged me to keep on the trail, but I was hesitant. It felt like a vulnerable thing to pursue. I didn't want to invade someone's privacy. Their silence was telling, if only to me. Old shame crept up my insides. *Mom has done something*, I thought. *Not now, but back then. She must have accused them of something, scared them off, and they don't want to talk to me now out of fear of being sued or, at the very least, attracting her attention again. Maybe.*

They had entire conversations among themselves that existed only in my head.

> *That woman is crazy, don't ever make contact with her daughter again*, a firefighter would say.
> *Her intentions seemed genuine, but I could be wrong*, Cathy would reply.
> *We can't take any chances. Remember when the mother went back to the scene before we'd finished doing our investigation?*
> *Okay, so should I just tell her you don't want to talk?*
> *No, even that would look suspicious to blood-sucking lawyers. Trust me, just steer clear.*

Their imagined anger and disgust would make me want to crawl into a hole.

Then my head would go in other directions. Maybe they were covering their own asses because the investigation hadn't been done correctly, and they never pursued the matter fully back then. Maybe because they were bribed (*with what money, though?*). Maybe because it's just a small town and they didn't have the resources. Maybe everyone felt so bad for us that pursuing something along these lines felt inescapably wrong; so, they just dropped it. But now the past is coming back to haunt them.

Or maybe all my emails following up on the situation had gone to junk mail.

Of course, this was all completely fabricated in my head. I had no idea if Mom had messed up the scene of the fire, or harassed firefighters, or if someone had been bribed or an investigation covered up or anything of the sort. But why else wouldn't they answer me? I couldn't help but quietly blame her, as I let my curiosity fade into the background.

45.

I once did the Burn Camp show, when I was previewing to random audiences, to a bachelor party in the Lake District, who chatted and heckled throughout the show; presumably because the title had "hottest girl" in it, they thought that it would be more of a sexy hot lady telling jokes about sex and they could all go *WEEYYY!!* and get a chub on.

I noticed them before I went on stage, and (I think because I had recently started on antidepressants) felt absolutely no fear. *I can handle this*, I thought. I was sadly wrong. They were all voluntarily sitting in the front row, for one, which is a major red flag in any show. Any time I got to a part about something emotional, they'd start whispering to each other and laughing in a way that reminded me of teenage bullies.

"Hey, guys, everything okay?" I'd say.

"Yeah, yeah, fine! Sorry, sorry, we'll be quiet."

They were not.

When that didn't work, I moved on to things like, "Hey, can you shut the fuck up?" to applause from the rest of the audience. Even that didn't shut them up for longer than 11 seconds or so. I saw the cringey awkwardness in the eyes of the rest of the crowd and wondered why oh why I hadn't got these assholes kicked out before the start of the show.

I stood there, lump in my chest, the scent of the musty old museum-turned-theatre mixed with the smell of pints and gin that I now associated with stage fright, pleading with time to go faster.

I somehow got through the show with a combination of ignoring, complete denial, going numb (my speciality) and thinking about how great it was gonna be to get into my car and drive far far away from this place.

After the show, many people came up to me and said they liked it and "Well done handling those dickheads", etc., but in my mind the only way to handle that situation properly would have been to kick them out before the show started. I had failed at dealing with asshole audience members, once more. It was "You're not really pregnant" all over again.

The stags exited the theatre last. I had a bucket that people could chuck some extra money in if they wanted to, which most people graciously had. When the pack leader of the stags approached me, red-eyed and pink-faced, his polo shirt stretched to the maximum over his bulging stomach, hanging onto the waistband of his trousers for dear life, he leaned towards me and said, "Hey, well done, love, great stuff, can I have a photo with you?" He held up his phone while putting his sweaty arm around me. There was a crowd of people watching this scene.

"Eh, I don't know, you gonna give me a tip?" I joked.

"Uh, no. Fuck you, then." He and his mates laughed aggressively, and he let go of me and gave me the flying V as he left the theatre.

I got into my car, started it numbly, and drove out of this town with tears streaming down my face. The whole drive, fantasies of how I wished it had all gone played over and over in my mind.

"Okay, you guys, get the fuck out," I'd say, with my arms crossed, American sass ramped up to 11.

"Applaud if you want these cunts to leave!" I'd shout over them.

Visions of the guy rushing the stage and me smashing my pint glass of water over his head. Me calling him a fat boring fuck, even though I'm super body positive. But he was surely not, and I knew that would rile him.

"This is the one night of fun you have a year and you have

to fuck it up for everyone else because your wife and children will have to watch the life drain from your eyes while you drink yourself to death at your pathetic office job while you fuck your wife in the ass on your birthday while she stares at the wall because she has to give you a present but she can't bear to look at you because you're a fucking mutant."

Yeah. Should have said THAT. That would have been great. I cried harder, breaking the speed limit until I reached the "Welcome to Scotland" sign.

46.

"Aren't you afraid your mom will find out about this?"

"What does your family say about you telling these things on stage?"

Voices from others came, mainly encouraging, but some critical. The previews of my show continued, mostly to supportive crowds. The more I did the material, the more I could feel myself grounding into it. *This is my story, and I can tell it the way I want to tell it.* The shame I used to feel about my past solidified into resolve.

"I could never talk about my family like that."

"I'm surprised you're getting away with this."

I was reminded of things people had said to me back then. These same voices from my teen years came back to me at once.

"Your mom has been through so much."
"Your mom is one tough cookie!"
"You're all she has left."

In not so many words, I was being told how I was supposed to feel towards her, and towards my situation. The guilt I felt for the anger I had towards her, and the shame I felt about her being my mother, and then retroactively feeling more shame and guilt for having those feelings, had forced me to keep any dark thoughts I had about my situation buried deep down. Whatever I was feeling, it was the wrong thing. People had been telling me that my whole life, it seemed.

The subject matter of my show had garnered attention from the press.

"Comedian finds the light side of unimaginable tragedy."
"I lost everything in a housefire, and comedy saved me", the headlines would read.

There were two big emotional reveals in my hour-long show, and they were the two biggest selling points in terms of press latching on to my story. The problem was, I didn't want these details revealed, because they were major spoilers for someone coming to the show. Also, I didn't know if I wanted these details on the internet forever, for anyone who googled my name.

We went ahead with the press opportunities anyhow, because it was decided in the end that ticket sales trumped spoilers.

I had major articles in arts sections of proper, serious, broadsheet newspapers, like *The Times*, *The Guardian*, *The Telegraph* and many more. My inbox was flooded with more and more press requests, opportunities for interviews, writing one-off pieces for commission, charities for kids who have burn injuries and other random things. My socials jumped up by the hundreds (a lot for me) and my ticket sales for the Fringe were flying. I'd sometimes break down in tears at the sheer volume of people who wanted something from me. I ended up ignoring a lot of it.

I still didn't have an agent, which was a good thing in my eyes. I was free to do the show however I wanted, and even more so because it was my debut hour – I didn't have a backlog of shows for this one to be compared to. Clean slate.

The Hive is made of stone and metal, and smells like all the earthly sins of humanity. An underground nightclub, you walk in, cough slightly, move away from one area to clear your nostrils and throat of the sting of centuries-old scents, only to realize that the entire space is enveloped in this wafting, putrid aura of moist decay. This is mainly because The Hive resides underground, and is constructed of centuries-old stone that is resistant to modern cleaning chemicals. The toilets are metal and have no seats on them; small plastic rims bolted down with screws to ensure no one can break them off and bash any of their fellow clubgoers.

But after getting the room set up, I realized the rough nature of the place actually worked well with the vibes of my show. It was like, "Hey, guys, I had kind of a rough time, and now we're all here together and you get to listen to what I went through. Compared to that, this smell is nothing, right?"

Besides... *Undersell and overwhelm*, I thought. That's the idea. There are way worse venues at the Fringe. I was extremely lucky to be with Monkey Barrel comedy, the venue that, to be honest, everyone wanted to be with, because they gave the best deal to comedians in a festival that is increasingly becoming a way for big companies to make vast amounts of money off struggling artists. Even successful shows that sell out their entire runs will make a loss, and comedians just accept it, because it's considered an honour to even be performing at the prestigious Edinburgh Fringe.

Monkey Barrel had accommodated me in every way they could, even attempting to combat the smell with dehumidifiers, candles, scented sprays – but unfortunately the smell at The Hive is sentient. It writhes and screams and becomes stronger the more you try to fight it. I swear I saw the embodiment of it once, backstage, before going on – it looked like Hexxus from *FernGully* and was also voiced by Tim Curry. "You'll never defeat me," it hissed. *Fair*, I thought.

Besides, it gave me a great opening line. "Hi, guys, welcome. My goal is to make this show so traumatic that we all forget about the smell." Gold. And every night, I'd say I did a pretty good job of just that.

Performing *The Hottest Girl at Burn Camp* for 28 days straight gave me a different focus and a clearer viewpoint on what it was I was trying to convey. These crowds knew, for the most part, what it was they were coming to see, having been prompted by the press, so most of them were well up for it.

People's reactions floored me. A story that I thought I was

numb to opened up inside me as though I were seeing it for the first time. It was like I was hearing someone else's story and looking in on myself.

The first time I cried in a performance was when I came to the part where I called Grandpa on the night of the fire and lied to him, telling him we were all out and we were all okay. I looked at a woman, whose eyes already looked red and swollen, and when I said that part, she shut her eyes and two tears silently rolled down her cheeks. It made something stir in me.

Oh. Yeah. That IS really sad, I thought.

When I say, "I cried", what I mean is I felt my throat tighten and my eyes become slightly moist. I'd make a wager that no one in the audience perceived that I felt at all choked up. But seeing other people react to my story forced me to face the gravity of what I'd gone through all over again.

The entire month of August was a whirlwind. I got several £100 tips in my bucket post-show. Agents and producers gave me their cards and told me to get in touch. People wanted to tell me the deepest darkest secrets of their lives, while I was holding a bucket, some bizarrely similar to mine. Hugs, tears, selfies with people. Comedians I'd loved and respected for years but never met personally came to my show.

One night, a couple weeks in, I was counting the cash in my bucket and I came across a Turkish ten-euro note. The man's face on the front had been graffitied with a black marker to make medium-length black hair, like my haircut. And in Sharpie across the face of the bill it read:

THE HOTTEST GIRL AT BURN CAMP

Krystal Evans
Da Hot Girl
Banksy

Yes, I know what you're thinking, but it turns out that this is very, very likely real. Certainly, it is according to the rules set out in my head, so please never burst this bubble.

I went to an industry party and a very young male comedian hit on me. As a 37-year-old mother of two, this was a huge confidence boost. I told my husband about it, and we laughed at first, then I could tell he was slightly perturbed. My life was going a million miles an hour, and it scared us both.

47.

Despite this excitement, I found myself, three weeks into the Fringe, sitting in my car in an alleyway off the Cowgate in Edinburgh, 20 minutes before I was supposed to go in to do a live comedy panel show, bawling my eyes out. I sobbed and sobbed and wailed and let everything out, indulging in my makeup being ruined and taking huge, gasping breaths, knowing that letting tears out is a good thing, but also fearful the sobbing would never end. Every time I slowed down, the high-pitched tightening around my throat and chest travelled up, and came out in more yells, forcing me to reach that point where you feel that you're about to throw up. This was supposed to be a happy time, and I was crying and screaming my guts out.

It's normal, I thought. *Surely these are happy tears?* They didn't feel like happy tears. They felt like my body telling me, *Go move to the woods and don't get wifi and crochet blankets or something for the rest of your life. Raise your boys away from technology and become Amish or something. This life, this fame crap, is not meant for you.*

Hilarious now that I thought that this was "fame". It was nothing. A few DMs, a sold-out show in a basement nightclub and a few positive career opportunities? If I can't handle that, how will I ever handle anything bigger?

I've always wondered what it does to one's body to experience the feelings of stage fright, adrenaline and comedown night after night as a performer, like we do as stand-up comedians. It surely can't be good for us. Has anyone ever done a study on this? And the feelings being ramped up to the maximum during something like the Edinburgh Fringe, where you check your ticket sales and see that awards panel judges are in, or the *Guardian* is in, or a big-name agency – even though these things are good, and exactly what you wanted to happen (even asked for), when they do come to you, they are often too much for one person to handle, unless you're utterly dead inside.

So, I let the tears come, as often as they pleased. Sometimes I even felt I needed a release faster before the show, so I'd put on something like "When She Loved Me" from *Toy Story 3* in my car and let that set me off. Like a porno but for crying, when you just don't have time to search your own brain and need the deed done lickety split.

Towards the end of August, the Edinburgh Awards nominations were announced, and I hadn't been nominated. I had anticipated this and thought it would come as a big blow, but honestly, I surprised myself in that I didn't care that much. I'd had such an incredible month, stellar reviews, the attention of agents and great amounts of money in the bucket day after day. Thinking back on the person I was before I started comedy compared to now, I couldn't have felt luckier.

And before the month ended, Dad came to Edinburgh to visit me, accompanied by stepmom Cheryl and Uncle Chuck, Dad's youngest brother. They came to my show in its second-to-last performance, and sat in the middle, three rows from the front.

The nerves in my body were so lit up waiting to go on stage, my brain decided to just numb me out completely, which I was grateful for. I was aware of Dad's reactions, but tried my best not to let it sway me from telling the story and performing the show like I normally do. I caught a glimpse of him laughing when I told the story of him making me go and watch the Kingdome be demolished, and a wave of relief swept over me.

Afterwards, I met them in the bar area for a chat.

"That was so great, Krystal! We loved it!" Cheryl said as she gave me a hug.

"It *was* great. I can see now, seeing it in person, why people have liked it so much. Really proud of you. Great work."

Dad patted my 37-year-old self on the head like I was a ten-year-old.

"Thanks, Dad," I smiled, also like a ten-year-old.

48.

The academic textbook I quoted earlier, *Playing Sick?*, sits on my bedside table. Sonny, my now nine-year-old, has expressed an endless curiosity about it.

"*Playing Sick?* What's this book about?" he's asked. I've told him the truth, that it's about people who pretend to be sick because they think it's the only way to get love and affection from people.

The other day, before his bedtime, after I'd read him the ending to the third Harry Potter book, for the second time in a few months, we were sitting on the couch and I put my arm around him and called him "my little love". I scrunched up my eyebrows and laughed a little bit.

"Whoa, that's weird," I said. "My mom used to call me 'little love'. It's so weird how things like that come out of my mouth sometimes."

"How come I don't ever see your mom?" Sonny asked.

"Well, you did see her. The last time you saw her was when you were two," I said, matter-of-factly. He just stared at me. He wanted more information. "My mom is very sick, in her brain.

Actually, I guess you're old enough to know this now. You know that book I have in my room? *Playing Sick*?"

"About people who pretend to be ill?"

"Yeah. That's what my mom has. She's been doing it for years, and I bought that book to try and learn more about her condition to see if I can understand her and what she's going through any better."

"That's really sad! I feel bad for her," Sonny said, looking genuinely worried.

"You're right. It's so sad. I've tried to help her over the years; also, her sisters – you know, Aunt Kelley and Aunt Tina – they've tried to help her, but she disappears a lot. She changes her number or moves and doesn't tell anybody. We've gone to her house, and she hasn't answered the door, or called her when she was supposed to meet us, and she just doesn't pick up. So, I have tried." I wanted to convey to this sweet little boy in front of me that I really do still love my mom, and have tried my hardest to help, and I hoped he understood. I didn't want to disappoint him.

I went on, "And the worst part about it really is that she doesn't get to see you and Jesse. You guys are so great and it's so sad that she doesn't have a relationship with you. She's just so lost in her own . . . problems." I attempted to keep it age-appropriate, but honest. "She just really craves this sort of attention, and my best guess is that she thinks this is the only way she can get care and love."

"Well, I love her and I don't even know her!" Sonny said, in his pure, genuine, nine-year-old voice.

I melted. "Oh sweety. I know she loves you too. And you

know..." I held back tears, "... you drew her a picture when you were five that I brought to her room – you couldn't come in because she was in a place kids couldn't come – and it was a picture of her playing the guitar and singing in a café with a heart-shaped pizza beside her. All her favourite things – guitars, singing, pizza, hearts. She loved it so much, and the last time I spoke to her she told me she still had it beside her."

"Oh. That *was* really nice of me! I'm glad she still has it!"

"Yeah, and, you know, I do love my mom and I always try and remember the good things about her too. That's why I have her picture around the house. And Daddy has a picture of his dad, too. Even though he wasn't a great guy a lot of the time. But they were still our parents and they taught us things that were important, too. No one in this world is all good or all bad."

"Yeah! Well, I hope that book will tell you a way you can help your mom."

"Yep. I'll let you know," I smiled. "Gosh, you're such a good listener. Thanks for talking to me about this." Sonny hugged me.

"I love you, Mom."

"I love you too."

49.

My little sister was only a part of my life for six short years, and sometimes the most heartbreaking thing is that I feel like I've forgotten her. Her face, her voice, her personality. So, it was hard when my therapist quietly said, as I had always known he would, "I think now you need to write a letter to Katie."

Any angle I came at, this letter caused me pain. But I'm so glad I wrote it, to make sure that I won't ever let myself forget about her.

Hi Katie,
This letter is very hard for me to write. I feel like I've let you down in a way for not thinking about you or talking about you as much as I could have over the years. It's just been so hard to think about the terrible thing that happened to you.

I remember how you always wanted to play pretend games with me and would try to involve the cats, but they were never interested. I remember how despite being raised by someone who couldn't cook, you loved all kinds of foods. We'd go to a pizza place and you just helped yourself to all the vegetables at the salad bar. One of my favourite memories is when I'd take you with me to the bus stop for school on my bike. I'd put a pillow on the middle bar and you'd balance on it while I rode us there. Sometimes it was pouring down rain and we'd get soaked. I'd say goodbye to you as you got on the little kids' bus.

I'm so sorry your parents were so shitty. It's not fair at all. I know you looked up to me and I tried to be the best sister I could to you. It's not fair that your life ended in the way that it did. I don't know how my life would have turned out differently if you'd lived, but I know I would have always been there for you. If you'd ever needed an escape from Mom, I'd have come to pick you up. Always would have been there to talk to you on the phone. I will always remember you.

    I know you had a lot of hard things happen to you in your young life. I wish I could have protected you more. I was young too. I didn't fully understand the gravity of what was happening to both of us. I have two little boys now. They remind me of you so much. I talk to them about you and show them pictures. I tell them how much I loved you. I know you loved me too.

    I love you so much. You were the best little sister.

Love,
Krystal

Acknowledgements

Firstly, thank you to Stuart, my ex-husband and best friend who has been there since the beginning of my comedy journey and before (and encouraged me to do it for years until I finally relented). Thank you to Heather Kondak Ross for giving me the fucking brilliant title that everyone can't stop going on about, and always having the perfect punchline. Thank you to Chris Weir who has never relented making jokes about the most serious subjects in my life, no matter how dark things get and knowing that I'll always appreciate that. To Aunt Kelley, the funniest person I've ever known and the person who always listens to my gig recordings, especially because I never do. To Aunt Tina who taught me to perfect my sarcasm. To Dad, who has watched my show and now read my book even though it was surely a hard thing to get through, and still told me it was good. To Sonny and Jesse for being the best little boys I could ask for.

This monoray book was crafted and published by Jake Lingwood, Sybella Stephens, Caroline Taggart, Mel Four and Sarah Parry.